239
C 84

D0221367

APOLOGETICS
AN INTRODUCTION

NCML
BT 1
1102
.C66
1984

APOLOGETICS
AN INTRODUCTION

BY

WILLIAM LANE CRAIG

91- 00013805

MOODY PRESS

CHICAGO

© 1984 by
THE MOODY BIBLE INSTITUTE
OF CHICAGO

All rights reserved. No part of this book may be reproduced in any form without permission in writing from the publisher, except in the case of brief quotations embodied in critical articles or reviews.

Except where otherwise indicated, all Scripture quotations in this book are from the *New American Standard Bible*, © 1960, 1962, 1963, 1968, 1971, 1972, 1973, 1975, and 1977 by the Lockman Foundation, and are used by permission.

Library of Congress Cataloging in Publication Data

Craig, William Lane.
  Apologetics: an introduction.

  Bibliography: p.
  Includes index.
  1. Apologetics—20th century. I. Title.
BT1102.C66   1984   239   84-14682
ISBN 0-8024-0405-7

2 3 4 5 6 7 Printing/BC/Year 88 87

Printed in the United States of America

*For my sister
by birth and by new birth*

Contents

Preface

As a Christian philosopher of religion, I have been privileged to teach the subject of apologetics over several years to graduate students. This book is the product of those classes. In fact, this book *is* my lectures in apologetics, with only minor revisions. My intent in preserving the oral style in the work is to involve the reader as much as possible as a member of my class. It is my hope that its informal style will prove to be both more enjoyable to read and more personal than a literary, scholarly style.

A word, too, should be said concerning the number outline that structures the lectures. Though it appears at first complex, it is actually very simple and can be used where the traditional outline using Roman numerals and letters would be unmanageable. Under the system used in this book, one simply adds an additional digit to a numbered step to obtain a subpoint. For example, 2.0 is the main step, 2.1 is the subpoint under it, and 2.11 is the subpoint under 2.1. Subpoints are numbered in order. For example, three subpoints under step 2.0 would be 2.1, 2.2, and 2.3. Further, if there were three subpoints under 2.1, these would be 2.11, 2.12, and 2.13. The Analytic Outline gives the title for each numbered point in the lectures, and the indentation helps the reader to discern at a glance what points are subordinate to others.

This course represents my personal approach to apologetics. I cover neither the history of apologetics nor options in evangelical apologetic systems, but assign reading to the students to cover these two areas. For the history of apologetics, I recommend Avery Dulles, *History of*

Apologetics (Philadelphia: Westminster, 1971), a scholarly masterpiece and an invaluable reference work. As for evangelical systems, I assign Gordon Lewis, *Testing Christianity's Truth Claims* (Chicago: Moody, 1976), which surveys the systems of the most prominent evangelical apologists of our day. In addition, I recommend that the student read my two books, *The Existence of God and the Beginning of the Universe* (San Bernardino, Calif.: Here's Life, 1980) and *The Son Rises* (Chicago: Moody, 1981), as background for the sections on the existence of God and the resurrection of Jesus respectively; both books also contain material pertinent to the absurdity of life without God. Finally, a very helpful pamphlet on the practical application of apologetics in evangelism is published by British Campus Crusade for Christ, entitled "Turning the Tables in Witnessing." In order to gain maximum profit from my book, the reader, like the students in my class, ought to avail himself of this adjunct reading.

The course is designed to provide background and critical discussion pertaining to the basic issues of a positive case for Christianity. I consider the two "hinge" issues to be the existence of God and the resurrection of Jesus. Due to limitations of time, I do not lecture on certain issues crucial to a defensive case for Christianity, such as the intelligibility of God and the problem of evil. Perhaps I shall treat these in another future volume, but for now I omit them, asking merely that the reader understand my limited purpose in this book.

Special thanks are due to Jo Lewis for her production of the typescript of this work.

Introduction

Apologetics is primarily a theoretical discipline, though it has a practical application. That is to say, apologetics is that branch of theology that seeks to provide a rational justification for the truth claims of the Christian faith. It is not training in the art of answering questions, or debating, or evangelism, though all of these draw upon the science of apologetics and apply it practically. This means that a course in apologetics is not for the purpose of teaching you "If he says so-and-so, then you say such-and-such back." Apologetics, to repeat, is a theoretical discipline that tries to answer the question, What rational defense can be given for the Christian faith? Therefore, most of our time must be spent in trying to answer this question.

Now, this is bound to be disappointing to some. They are just not interested in the rational justification of Christianity. They want to know, "If someone says, 'Look at all the hypocrites in the church!' what do I say?" There is nothing wrong with that question; but the fact remains that such practical matters are logically secondary to the theoretical issues and cannot in our limited time occupy the center of our attention. The use of apologetics in practice ought rather to be an integral part of courses and books on evangelism.

We dare not ignore the theoretical issues. We need to grasp a wider picture of Western thought and culture, rather than concentrating exclusively on an immediate evangelistic contact. As Francis Schaeffer reminds us, we are living in a post-Christian era, when the thought-forms of society are fundamentally anti-Christian. If the situation is not to degenerate further, it is imperative that we turn the whole intellectual climate of our culture back to a Christian world view. If we do not, then what lies ahead for us in the United States is already evident in Europe: utter secularism. Throughout Europe, evangelism is immeasurably more difficult because the intellectual climate and culture there are determined by the conviction that the Christian world view is false. Therefore, Christian missionaries often must labor years to get a handful of converts. If we lose the theoretical issues, then in the end our practical application will be fruitless.

That being true, there nonetheless remains the problem of how to apply the theoretical material learned in this course. I have always thought that this problem was best left to each individual to work out according to the type of ministry to which he feels called. After all, I am not interested only in training pastors but also systematic theologians, philosophers of religion, and church historians. But it has become clear to me that some people simply do not know how to translate theory into practice. Therefore, I will make two moves to help resolve this difficulty: First, I recommend the pamphlet "Turning the Tables in Witnessing," published by British Campus Crusade; and second, I shall include a sub-section on practical application after each major section of the course. I *know* the theoretical material is practical because we employ it in evangelism often, and we see God use it. And as for the pamphlet, it is the result of an enormous amount of experience in evangelism and is excellent in its suggestions on how to use apologetics to pinpoint needs in the unbeliever's life.

This book is structured according to the *loci communes* of systematic theology. Let me tell you why. I often used to hear that modern theology had become so irrational and fideistic that apologetics no longer found a place in the course offerings of neo-liberal theological schools. But during a summer of study at the University of Erlangen, West Germany, I discovered that that was not exactly correct. It is true that no courses in apologetics *per se* are offered, but it is also true that German theology itself is very apologetically oriented. Hence, in classes in, say, Christology or soteriology, one will discuss as a matter of course various issues and challenges raised by non-Christian philosophy, science, history, and so forth. (Unfortunately, the result of this interaction is inevitably capitulation on the part of theology and its retreat into non-empirical doctrinal sanctuaries, where it achieves security only at the expense of becoming irrelevant and untestable.) It bothered me that in evangelical seminaries our theology courses spend so little time on such issues. How much time is spent, for example, in an evangelical course on the doctrine of God on arguments for God's existence? Then it occurred to me: maybe the theology professors are expecting *you* to handle those issues in the apologetics class, since apologetics is offered as a separate course. The more I thought about that, the more sense it made. Therefore, I have structured the lectures around various apologetic issues in the *loci communes theologiae*.

Let us look more closely at the Analytical Outline. The *loci communes* were the so-called "common places" or chief themes or topics of post-Reformation Protestant theology. It was Luther's colleague Melanchthon who first employed these "common places" as the framework for writing his systematic theology. Some of the most frequently discussed *loci* included *de Scriptura sacra* (doctrine of Scripture) *de creatio* (doctrine of creation), *de peccato* (doctrine of sin), *de Christo* (Christology), *de gratia* (soteriology), *de ecclesia* (eccesiology), and *de novissimus* (eschatology). In almost all of these *loci* apologetical issues confront us. In our limited space, I have chosen to discuss several important issues in the *loci de fide* (faith), *de homine* (man), *de Deo* (God), *de creatione* (creation), and *de Christo* (Christ). I have taken the liberty to rearrange these *loci* from their normal order in a systematic theology into an order following the logic of apologetics. That is to say, our goal is to build a case for Christianity, and that determines the order in which we shall consider the issues. I am painfully aware of other issues that are also interesting and important, but that I have omitted. Nevertheless, we shall be considering the most crucial issues involved in building a positive case for the Christian faith.

More specifically, we shall be considering under *de fide* the relation between faith and reason, under *de homine* the absurdity of life without God, under *de Deo* the existence of God, under *de creatione* the problem of miracles and the problem of historical knowledge, and finally under *de Christo* the personal claims of Christ and the historicity of the resurrection of Jesus. Our consideration of each question will fall into four sections. First, I will provide bibliographical information on the literature cited in the lectures or books that I recommend for your future reading. Second, we shall take a look at the historical background of the issue in question to see how past thinkers have dealt with it. Third, I shall present and defend my personal views on the topic at hand, seeking to develop a Christian apologetic on the point. And fourth, I shall share some thoughts and personal experiences on applying this material in evangelism.

For many of you much of this course material will be new and difficult. Nevertheless, *all* of it is important, and if you apply yourself diligently to mastering and interacting personally and critically with this material, you will, I am sure, find it as exciting as it is important.

Analytic Outline

1.0 DE FIDE

1.1 FAITH AND REASON: HOW DO I KNOW CHRISTIANITY IS TRUE?

Before presenting a case for Christianity, we must come to grips with some very fundamental questions concerning the nature and relationship of faith and reason. Exactly how is it that we know Christianity to be true? Is it simply by a leap of faith or on the authority of the Word of God, both unrelated to reason? Does religious experience assure us of the truth of the Christian faith, so that no further justification is needed? Or is a rational foundation for faith necessary, without which faith would be unjustified and irrational? We can better answer these questions if we briefly survey some of the most important representative thinkers of the past. But before we do so, let me present some literature on the subject.

1.11 LITERATURE CITED OR RECOMMENDED

1.111 HISTORICAL BACKGROUND

Augustine. *Against the Epistle of Manichaeus called Fundamental.* Translated by Richard Stothert. In *The Nicene and Post-Nicene Fathers.* Vol. 4, *The Writings Against the Manichaeans and Against the Donatists.* Edited by Philip Schaff. Reprint. Grand Rapids: Eerdmans, 1956. Pp. 125-50.

———. *City of God.* 3 vols. Translated by D. B. Zema, et al. Introduction by Etienne Gilson. Fathers of the Church. New York: Fathers of the Church, 1950-4. See particularly 21.61; 22.5.

———. *Confessions.* Translated by V. J. Bourke. Fathers of the Church. New York: Fathers of the Church, 1953.

————. *Letters.* Vol. 1. Translated by Sister Wilfrid Parsons. Fathers of the Church. Washington: Catholic University of America, 1951-56. See particularly letters 22, 28, 82, 147.

————. *On True Religion.* Translated by J. H. Burleigh, introduction by Louis O. Mink. Chicago: H. Regnery, 1959. See particularly 24; 25.

————. *The Teacher; The Free Choice of the Will; Grace and Free Will.* Translated by R. P. Russell. Fathers of the Church. Washington, D.C.: Catholic University of America, 1968.

Barth, Karl. *Dogmatics in Outline.* Translated by G. J. Thomson. New York: Philosophical Library, 1947.

————. *The Knowledge of God and the Service of God According to the Teaching of the Reformation.* Translated by J. L. M. Haire and I. Henderson. New York: Scribner's, 1939.

Bultmann, Rudolf. "The Case for Demythologizing: A Reply." In *Kerygma and Myth.* Edited by H.-W. Bartsch. Translated by R. H. Fuller. London: SPCK, 1953. 2:181-94.

————. "Reply to the Theses of J. Schniewind." In *Kerygma and Myth.* Edited by H.-W. Bartsch. Translated by R. H. Fuller. London: SPCK, 1953. 2:102-33.

————. *Theologie des Neuen Testaments.* 7th ed. Edited by O. Merk. Tübingen: J. C. B. Mohr, 1961.

Cragg, Gerald R. *Reason and Authority in the Eighteenth Century.* Cambridge: Cambridge U., 1964.

Dodwell, Henry. *Christianity Not Founded on Argument.* 3d. ed. London: M. Cooper, 1743.

Gilson, Etienne. *Reason and Revelation in the Middle Ages.* New York: Scribner's, 1938.

Locke, John. *An Essay Concerning Human Understanding.* Edited with an introduction by P. H. Nidditch. Oxford: Clarendon, 1975.

————. *The Works of John Locke.* 11th ed. Vol. 9, *A Discourse on Miracles.* London: W. Olridge & Son, 1812.

————. *The Works of John Locke.* 11th ed. Vol. 7, *The Reasonableness of Christianity.* London: W. Oldridge & Son, 1812.

Pannenberg, Wolfhart. *Jesus—God and Man.* Translated by L. L. Wilkins and D. A. Priebe. London: SCM, 1968.

————. "Redemptive Event and History." In *Basic Questions in Theology.* Translated by G. Kehm. Philadelphia: Fortress, 1970. 1:15-80.

————. "Response to the Discussion." In *New Frontiers in Theology.* Vol. 3, *Theology as History.* Edited by J. M. Robinson and J. B. Cobb, Jr. New York: Harper & Row, 1967.

————, ed. *Revelation as History.* Translated by D. Granskou. London: Macmillan, 1968.

————. "The Revelation of God in Jesus of Nazareth." In *New Frontiers in Theology.* Vol. 3, *Theology as History.* Edited by J. M. Robinson and J. B. Cobb, Jr. New York: Harper & Row, 1967. Pp. 101-33

Plantinga, Alvin. "Intellectual Autobiography." Forthcoming in the Pro-
files series. Dordrecht, Holland: D. Reidel.
———. "Is Belief in God Rational?" In *Rationality and Religious Belief.*
Edited by C. F. Delaney. Notre Dame, Ind: U. of Notre Dame, 1979.
Pp. 7-27.
———. "The Reformed Objection to Natural Theology," *Proceedings of
the Catholic Philosophical Association* 15 (1980): 49-62.
Stephen, Leslie. *History of English Thought in the Eighteenth Century.*
3d ed. 2 vols. New York: Harcourt, Brace, & World; Harbinger, 1962.
Strauss, Gerhard. *Schriftgebrauch, Schriftauslegung, und Schriftbeweis
bei Augustin.* Beiträge zur Geschichte der biblischen Hermeneutik 1.
Tübingen: J. C. B. Mohr, 1959.
Thomas Aquinas. *On the Truth of the Catholic Faith [Summa contra
gentiles].* 4 vols. Translated with Notes by A. C. Pegis et al. Notre
Dame, Ind.: U. of Notre Dame, 1975. See particularly 1.3, 5, 6, 9;
3.99-103, 154.
———. *Summa theologiae.* 60 vols. London: Eyre & Spottiswoode
for Blackfriars, 1964. See particularly 1a.32.1; 1a.105.8; 2a2ae1.4;
3a43.1-4; 3a55.6.

1.112 ASSESSMENT
Green, Michael. *Evangelism in the Early Church.* Grand Rapids: Eerd-
mans, 1970.
Hackett, Stuart. *The Resurrection of Theism.* 2d ed. Grand Rapids:
Baker, 1982.
Hick, John. *Faith and Knowledge.* Ithaca, N.Y.: Cornell U., 1957.

1.12 HISTORICAL BACKGROUND

1.121 MEDIEVAL

In our historical survey, let us look first at two approaches that were determinative for the Middle Ages, that of Augustine (354-430), and that of Thomas Aquinas (1224-74).

1.1211 *Augustine.* Augustine's attitude toward faith and reason is very difficult to interpret, especially because his views apparently evolved over the years. Sometimes he gives the impression of being a strict authoritarian; that is to say, he held that the ground for faith was sheer, unquestionable, divine authority. This authority might be expressed in either the Scriptures or in the church. Thus, Augustine confessed, "I should not believe the gospel except as moved by the authority of the Catholic Church"[1] The authority of Scripture he held in even higher esteem than that of the church. Because they are inspired by God, the Scriptures are completely free from error and are

---

1. Augustine *Against the Epistle of Manichaeus called Fundamental* 5.6.

therefore to be believed absolutely.[2] Such a view of authority would seem to imply that reason has no role to play in the justification of belief, and sometimes Augustine gives that impression. He asserts that one must first believe before he can know.[3] He was fond of quoting Isaiah 7:9 in the Septuagint version: "Unless you believe you shall not understand." The fundamental principle of the Augustinian tradition throughout the Middle Ages was *fides quaerens intellectum:* faith seeking understanding.

But certain statements of Augustine make clear that he was not an unqualified authoritarian. He maintained that authority and reason cooperate in bringing a man to faith. Authority demands belief and prepares man for reason, which in turn leads to understanding and knowledge. But at the same time, reason is not entirely absent from authority, for one has to consider whom to believe, and the highest authority belongs to clearly known truth; that is to say, the truth, when it is clearly known, has the highest claim to authority in that it demands our assent. According to Augustine, it is our duty to consider what men or what books we ought to believe in order to rightly worship God. Gerhard Strauss in his book on Augustine's doctrine of Scripture explains that although Scripture is for Augustine absolutely authoritative and inerrant in itself, it does not carry credibility in itself— that is, men will not automatically accept its authority upon hearing it. Therefore, there must be certain signs *(indicia)* of credibility that make its authority evident. On the basis of these signs, we can believe that the Scripture is the authoritative Word of God, and submit to its authority. The principal signs adduced by Augustine on behalf of the authority of Scripture are miracle and prophecy. Though many religions boast of revelations showing the way of salvation, only the Scriptures have the support of miracle and prophecy, which prove it to be the true authority.

Thus, Augustine's authoritarianism would seem to be drastically qualified. Perhaps this inconsistency is best explained by the medieval understanding of authority. In the early church, authority *(auctoritas)* included not just theological truths, but the whole tradition of past knowledge. The relationship between authority and reason was not the same as that between faith and reason. Rather it was the relationship between all past knowledge and present-day understanding. Knowledge of the past was simply accepted on the basis of authority. This seems to have been Augustine's attitude. He distinguished between what is *seen* to be true and what is *believed* to be true. We see that something is true by either physical perception or rational demonstration. We believe that something is true on the basis of the testimony of others. Hence,

---

2. Augustine *Letters* 82.3; idem *City of God* 21.6.1.
3. Augustine *On Free Will* 2.1.6.

with regard to miracle and prophecy, Augustine said that the trustworthiness of temporal events either past or future must be believed, not known by the intelligence. Elsewhere he declared that one should believe in God because belief in Him is taught in the books of men who have left their testimony in writing that they lived with the Son of God and saw things that could not have happened if there were no God. Then he concludes that one must believe before he can know. Since for Augustine the historical evidence for miracle and prophecy lay in the past, it was in the realm of authority, not reason. Today we would say that such a procedure would be an attempt to provide a rational foundation for authority via historical apologetics.

Now the obvious question at this point is, Why accept the authority of the writers of the past, whether they be the classical writers or the authors of Scripture? Clearly, if Augustine was to avoid circular reasoning, he could not say that we should accept the authority of the evangelists because of the authority of Scripture, for it was the evangelists' testimony to miracle and prophecy that was supposed to make evident the authority of Scripture. So Augustine had to either come up with some reason to accept the evangelists' testimony as reliable, or abandon this approach. Since he lacked the historical method, the first alternative was not open to him. Therefore, he chose the second. He frankly admitted that the books containing the story of Christ belong to an ancient history that anyone may refuse to believe. Therefore, he turned to the present miracle of the church as the basis for accepting the authority of Scripture. The very existence of the mighty and universal church he saw as an overwhelming sign that the Scriptures are true and divine. Now notice that Augustine was not basing the authority of Scripture on the authority of the church, for he held the Scripture's authority to exceed even that of the church. Rather, his appeal was still to the sign of miracle, not indeed the gospel miracles, which are irretrievably removed in the past, but the present and evident miracle of the church. In *The City of God* he stated that even if the unbeliever rejects all biblical miracles, we are still left with one stupendous miracle, which is all one needs, namely, the fact of the whole world believing in Christianity without the benefit of miracles.[4] It is interesting that, by appealing to a present miracle as the sign of the authority of Scripture, Augustine seems to have implicitly denied authoritarianism, since this sign is not in the past, in the realm of authority where it could only be believed, but in the present, where it can be seen and known. Be that as it may, Augustine's emphases on biblical authority and signs of credibility were to set the tone for subsequent medieval theology.

    1.1212 *Thomas Aquinas.* Aquinas's *Summa contra gen-*

---

4. Augustine *City of God* 22.5.

tiles, written to combat Greco-Arabic philosophy, is the greatest apologetic work of the Middle Ages and so merits our attention. Thomas develops a framework for the relationship of faith and reason that includes the Augustinian signs of credibility. He begins by making a distinction within truths about God. On the one hand, there are truths that completely surpass the capability of human reason, for example, the doctrine of the Trinity. On the other hand, many truths lie within the grasp of human reason, such as the existence of God. In the first three volumes of the *Summa contra gentiles,* Thomas attempts to prove these truths of reason, including the existence and nature of God, the orders of creation, the nature and end of man, and so forth. But when he comes to the fourth volume, in which he handles subjects like the Trinity, the incarnation, the sacraments, and the last things, he suddenly changes his method of approach. He states that these things are to be proved by the authority of Holy Scripture, not by natural reason. Because these doctrines surpass reason, they are properly objects of faith.

Now at first blush that would seem to suggest that for Aquinas these truths of faith are mysteries, somehow "above logic." But here we must be very careful. For as I read Aquinas, that is not how he defines his terms. Rather he seems to mean that truths of faith surpass reason in that they are neither empirically evident nor demonstrable with absolute certainty. He makes no suggestion that truths of faith transcend Aristotelian logic. Rather it is just that there are no empirical facts from which these truths may be inferred. For example, although the existence of God can be proved from His effects, there are no empirical facts from which the Trinity may be inferred. Or again, the eschatological resurrection of the dead cannot be proved because there is no empirical evidence for this future event. Elsewhere Thomas makes it clear that truths of faith cannot be demonstrated by reason alone, either. He maintains we must use only arguments that prove their conclusions with absolute certainty; for if we use mere probability arguments, the insufficiency of those arguments will only serve to confirm the non-Christian in his unbelief.[5] Thus, the distinction Thomas makes between truths of reason and truths of faith is rather like Augustine's distinction between seeing and believing. Truths of reason may be "seen"—that is, either proved with rational certainty or accepted as empirically evident—whereas truths of faith must be believed, since they cannot be proved either rationally or empirically. This does not mean that truths of faith are incomprehensible or "above logic."

Now because truths of faith can only be believed, does this imply that Thomas is in the end a fideist or an authoritarian? The answer

---

5. Thomas Aquinas *Summa theologiae* 1a.32.1; cf. idem *Summa contra gentiles* 1.9.

seems clearly no. For like Augustine he proceeds to argue that God provides the signs of miracle and prophecy, which serve to confirm the truths of faith, though not demonstrating them directly. Because of these signs, Aquinas holds that a man can see the truths of faith: "Then they are indeed seen by the one who believes; he would not believe unless he saw that they are worthy of belief on the basis of evident signs or something of this sort."[6] Thomas calls these signs "confirmations," "arguments," and "proofs" for the truths of faith.[7] That seems to make clear that Aquinas believes there are good grounds for accepting the truths of faith as a whole. The proofs of miracle and prophecy are compelling, although they are indirect. Thus, for example, the doctrine of the Trinity is a truth of faith because it cannot be directly proved by any argument; nevertheless it is indirectly proved insofar as the truths of faith taken together as a whole are shown to be credible by the divine signs.

Thomas's procedure, then, may be summarized in three steps: (1) Fulfilled prophecies and miracles make credible that the Scriptures taken together as a whole are a revelation from God. (2) As a revelation from God, Scripture is absolutely authoritative. (3) Therefore, those doctrines taught by Scripture that are neither demonstratively provable nor empirically evident may be accepted by faith on the authority of Scripture. Thus, Aquinas can say that an opponent may be convinced of the truths of faith on the basis of the authority of Scripture as confirmed by God with miracles.[8]

Again the question arises: How do we know that the purported miracles or fulfilled prophecies ever took place? The medieval thinkers, lacking the historical method, could not answer this question. They developed a philosophical framework in which the signs of credibility confirmed the truths of faith, but they had no way of proving the signs themselves. About the only argument was Augustine's indirect proof from the miracle of the church. Thus, Thomas declares,

> Now such a wondrous conversion of the world to the Christian faith is a most indubitable proof that such signs did take place. . . . For it would be the most wondrous sign of all if without any wondrous signs the world were persuaded by simple and lowly men to believe things so arduous, to accomplish things so difficult, and to hope for things so sublime.[9]

A final word might be added. With Aquinas we see the reduction of faith to an epistemological category; that is to say, faith was no longer trust or commitment of the heart, but became a way of knowing,

6. Thomas Aquinas *Summa theologiae* 2a2ae.1.4 ad 2.
7. Thomas Aquinas *Summa contra gentiles* 3.154; 1.6.
8. Ibid. 1.9.
9. Ibid. 1.9.

complementary to reason. Faith was essentially intellectual assent to
doctrines not provable by reason—hence, Aquinas's view that a doctrine cannot be both known and believed: if you know it (by reason),
then you cannot believe it (by faith). Thus, Aquinas lost the view of
faith as trust or commitment. This same intellectualist understanding
of faith characterized the documents of the Council of Trent and of
Vatican I but was adjusted in the documents of Vatican II.

1.122 ENLIGHTENMENT

The fact that the Enlightenment is also known as the Age of Reason
no doubt gives us a good clue as to how thinkers of that period regarded the relationship between faith and reason. Nevertheless, there was
not complete agreement on this issue, and the two figures we shall
survey represent two fundamentally opposed viewpoints.

1.1221 *John Locke.* The thought of John Locke (1632-
1704) was determinative for the eighteenth century. His *Essay Concerning Human Understanding* (1689) laid down the epistemological
principles that were to shape religious thought during that age. Though
he rejected the philosophical rationalism of Descartes, Locke was nevertheless an ardent theological rationalist. That is to say, he maintained
that religious belief must have a rational foundation and that where
such a foundation is absent, religious belief is unwarranted. Locke
himself attempted to provide such a rational foundation.

Locke argues for the existence of God by means of a cosmological
argument—indeed, he maintains that the existence of God is "the most
obvious truth that reason discovers," having an evidence "equal to
mathematical certainty."[10] When one moves beyond such matters of
demonstrative reason into matters of faith, Locke insists that revealed
truths cannot contradict reason. God can reveal to us both truths at-
tainable by reason (though reason gives greater certainty of these than
does revelation) as well as truths unattainable by reason. The revealed
truths unattainable by reason cannot contradict reason, because we will
always be more certain of the truth of reason than we will be of a
purported revelation that contradicts reason. Therefore no proposition
contrary to reason can be accepted as divine revelation, for to do so
would undermine the divine revelation itself. Thus, although we know
that a revelation from God must be true, it still lies within the scope of
reason to determine if a supposed revelation really is from God and to
determine its meaning.[11]

More than that, revelation must not only be in harmony with reason,
but must itself be guaranteed by appropriate rational proofs that it is

10. John Locke *An Essay Concerning Human Understanding* 4.10.1.
11. Ibid. 4.18.5.

indeed divine. Otherwise, one degenerates into irresponsible enthusiasm:

> Revelation is natural reason enlarged by a new set of discoveries communicated by God immediately, which reason vouches the truth of by the testimony and proofs it gives that they come from God. So that he that takes away reason to make way for revelation, puts out the light of both; and does much the same as if he would persuade a man to put out his eyes, the better to receive the remote light of an invisible star by a telescope.[12]

Religious enthusiasm was the form of religious expression most scorned by the intellectualist believers of the Age of Reason, and Locke will have nothing to do with it. Only if reason makes plausible that a purported revelation is genuine can that revelation be believed.

Hence, in his subsequent works *The Reasonableness of Christianity* (1695) and *Discourse on Miracles* (1690), Locke argues that fulfilled prophecy and palpable miracles furnish proof of Christ's divine mission. He lays down three criteria for discerning a genuine revelation: First, it must not be dishonoring to God or inconsistent with natural religion and the natural moral law. Second, it must not inform man of things indifferent, insignificant, or easily discovered by natural ability. Third, it must be confirmed by supernatural signs. For Locke, the chief of these signs was miracle. On the basis of Jesus' miracles, we are justified in regarding Him as the Messiah and His revelation from God as true.

As the fountainhead for both Deist works and orthodox apologetics, Locke's outlook shaped the religious thought of the eighteenth century. Be they Deist or orthodox, most thinkers of the century after Locke agreed that reason was to be given priority even in matters of faith, that revelation could not contradict reason, and that reason provided the essential foundation to religious belief.

   1.1222 *Henry Dodwell.* That is not to say that dissenting voices could not be heard. Henry Dodwell (d. 1784) in his *Christianity Not Founded on Argument* (1742) attacked the prevailing theological rationalism as antithetical to true Christianity. So out of step was Dodwell with his times, he has even been suspected of being an unbeliever who appealed to an a-rational, subjective basis for religious faith as a subterfuge for undermining the rationality of Christianity. It seems to me, however, that Dodwell is to be taken straightforwardly as a spokesman for the anti-rationalistic religious tradition, which was not altogether absent even during the Enlightenment.

He argues that matters of religious faith lie outside the determination of reason. God could not possibly have intended that reason

12. Ibid. 4.19.4.

should be the faculty to lead us to faith, for faith cannot hang indefinitely in suspense while reason cautiously weighs and re-weighs arguments. The Scriptures teach, on the contrary, that the way to God is by means of the heart, not by means of the intellect. Faith is simply a gift of the Holy Spirit. What then is the basis of faith? Dodwell answers, authority—not indeed the arbitrary authority of the church but rather the inner light of a constant and particular revelation imparted separately and supernaturally to every individual. Dodwell's appeal is thus to the inner, faith-producing work of the Holy Spirit in each individual person's heart. His subjectively based apologetic appears to have generated no following among the scholars of his day, but later a similar emphasis on the witness of the Spirit by the Wesleys and Whitefield was to be an earmark of the great revivals that opened fresh springs for the dry souls of the English laity.

1.123 CONTEMPORARY

During the present century, theological discussion of the relationship between faith and reason has replayed many of those same themes.

1.1231 *Karl Barth and Rudolph Bultmann.* Both the dialectical theology championed by Karl Barth (1886-1968) and the existential theology propounded by Rudolf Bultmann (1884-1976) were characterized by a religious epistemology of authoritarianism.

According to Barth, there can be no approach to God whatsoever via human reason. Apart from God's revelation in Christ, human reason comprehends absolutely nothing about God. The fundamental reason for this agnosticism concerning human knowledge of God seems to be Barth's firm commitment to the thesis that God is "wholly other" and therefore transcends all categories of human thought and logic. This belief led Barth to deny the Roman Catholic doctrine of an analogy of being between God and man, that is, the doctrine that creation as the product of its Creator shares in an analogous way certain properties possessed most perfectly by God, for example, being, goodness, truth, and so forth. According to Barth, God is so transcendent that no analogy exists between Him and the creature. Hence, it follows that there can be no natural knowledge about God at all. But God has revealed Himself to man in Jesus Christ; indeed, Christ is the revelation or Word of God. In Him alone there is found an analogy of faith that affords some knowledge of God. But even this seems to be experiential rather than cognitive: it is a personal encounter with the Word of God, who confronts us now and again through different forms, such as the Bible or preaching. Even in His self-disclosure God remains hidden: "He meets us as the One who is hidden, the One about whom we must admit that we do not know what we are saying when we try to say who

He is."[13] God remains incomprehensible and the propositions we assert about Him are true in an incomprehensible way.

This might lead one to think that for Barth fideism is the only route by which a man might come to the knowledge of God. This does not however, seem to be precisely correct. For Barth emphasizes that the personal encounter with the Word of God results entirely from the sovereign divine initiative. Lost in sin, man cannot even begin to move in the direction of faith, so that even a leap of faith would be impossible for him. No, it must be God who breaks into man's indolent sinfulness to confront him with the Word of God. As Barth writes, "Knowledge of God is a knowledge completely effected and determined from the side of its object, from the side of God."[14] Or again, "the fact that he did come to this decision, that he really believed, and that he actually had freedom to enter this new life of obedience and hope—all this was not the work of his spirit, but the work of the Holy Spirit."[15] Barth believes that the Reformation doctrine of justification by grace through faith is incompatible with any human initiative—even fideism. If knowing God depends wholly on God's grace, then even the act of faith would be a sinful work were it not wholly wrought by God. If it be asked how one knows that it is indeed the Word of God that confronts him and not a delusion, Barth would simply respond that such a question is meaningless. When the Word of God confronts a man, he is not free to analyze, weigh, and consider as a disinterested judge or observer—he can only obey. The authority of the Word of God is the foundation fo religious belief.

Like Barth, Bultmann also rejects any human apprehension of the Word of God (which he seems to identify primarily with the call to authentic existence embodied in the gospel) apart from faith. Bultmann construes faith in epistemological categories, opposing it to knowledge based on proof. In the existentialist tradition, he considers it essential to faith that it involve risk and uncertainty. Therefore, rational evi dence is not only irrelevant, but actually contrary to faith. Faith, in order to be faith, must exist in an evidential vacuum. For this reason Bultmann denies any significance for the Christian message to the historical Jesus, apart from His bare existence. Bultmann recognizes that Paul in 1 Corinthians 15 does "think that he can guarantee the resurrection of Christ as an objective fact by listing the witnesses w had seen him risen."[16] But he characterizes such historical argumenta

13. Karl Barth, The Knowledge of God and the Science of God According to the Teach ing of the Reformation, p. 27.
14. Karl Barth, Dogmatics in Outline, p. 24.
15. Barth, Knowledge, p. 109.
16. Rudolf Bultmann, Theologie des Neuen Testament, p. 295.

tion as "fatal" because it tries to adduce proof for the Christian proclamation.[17] Should an attempt at proof succeed, this would mean the destruction of faith. Only a decision to believe wholly apart from evidence will bring one into contact with the existential significance of the gospel. Bultmann emphasizes that this does not mean such a step is made arbitrarily or light-heartedly. No, the existential issues of life and death weigh so heavily that this decision to believe is the most important and awesome step a man can take. But it must be taken in the absence of any rational criteria for choice.

This might lead one to think that Bultmann is a pure fideist; but again this does not seem quite correct. For he insists that the very authority of the Word of God strips away all demands for criteria: "As though God had to justify himself to man! As though every demand for justification (including the one concealed in the demand for criteria) did not have to be dropped as soon as the face of God appears!"[18] As Pannenberg explains, the "basic presupposition underlying German Protestant theology as expressed by Barth or Bultmann is that the basis of theology is the self-authenticating Word of God which demands obedience."[19] Thus, it would seem that in both dialectical and existential theology the final appeal is authoritarian.

1.1232 *Wolfhart Pannenberg.* Pannenberg's rigorously evidential approach to theological questions has been widely acclaimed as ushering in a new phase in European Protestant theology. In 1961 a circle of young theologians for whom Pannenberg served as the principal spokesman asserted in their manifesto *Offenbarung als Geschichte (Revelation as History)* that revelation ought to be understood exclusively in terms of God's acts in history, not as some self-authenticating Word.

Because this "Word," which was understood as God's self-disclosure in a divine-human encounter, needs no external authentication, theology, according to Pannenberg, has depreciated the relevance of history to faith and walled itself off against secular knowledge. On the one hand, Bultmann's existentialist theology has neglected objective historical facticity in favor of finding the conditions for authentic human existence in the apostolic proclamation, to which historical facts are thought to be strictly irrelevant. On the other hand, Barth's understanding of peculiarly Christian events as belonging, not to the course of ordinary, investigable history, but rather to redemptive history, which is closed to historical research, equally devalues real history. Both schools share a common motive in their depreciation of the importance of

17. Rudolf Bultmann, "Reply to the Theses of J. Schniewind," 1:112.
18. Rudolf Bultmann, "The Case for Demythologizing: A Reply," 2:191.
19. Wolfhart Pannenberg, ed. *Revelation as History,* p. 9.

history for faith, namely, the desire to secure for faith an impregnable stronghold against the assaults of modern historical-critical studies. Dialectical theology fled into the habor of supra-history, supposedly safe from the historical-critical floodtide, while existential theology withdrew from the course of objective history to the subjective experience of human authenticity. Theology's attempt at self-isolationism backfired, however, because the secular sciences turned upon it to criticize and contradict it. "For much too long a time faith has been misunderstood to be subjectivity's fortress into which Christianity could retreat from the attacks of scientific knowledge. Such a retreat into pious subjectivity can only lead to destroying any consciousness of the truth of the Christian faith."[20]

Therefore if Christianity is to make any meaningful claim to truth, it must, according to Pannenberg, submit to the same procedures of testing and verification as are employed in the secular sciences. This method of verification will be indirect, for example, by means of historical research. A theological interpretation of history will be tested positively by "its ability to take into account all known historical details," and negatively by "the proof that without its specific assertions the accessible information would not be at all or would be only incompletely explicable."[21] Since the Christian faith is based on a real past event, and since there is no way to know the past other than by historical-critical research, it follows that the object of Christian faith cannot remain untouched by the results of such research. On the one hand, a kerygmatic Christ utterly unrelated to the real, historical Jesus would be "pure myth"; and on the other hand, a Christ known only through dialectical encounter would be impossible to distinguish from "self-delusion."[22] Therefore, the unavoidable conclusion is that the burden of proving that God has revealed himself in Jesus of Nazareth must fall upon the historian.

Pannenberg acknowledges that should the historical foundation for faith be removed, then Christianity should be abandoned. He is, however, confident that given the historical facts that we now have, this eventuality will not occur. Pannenberg realizes that the results of historical investigation always retain a degree of uncertainty, but nevertheless, through this "precarious and provisional" way a knowledge of the truth of Christianity is possible. Without this factual foundation logically prior to faith, faith would be reduced to gullibility, credulity, or superstition. Only this evidential approach, in contrast to the subjectivism of modern theology, can establish Christianity's truth claim. The

20. Wolfhart Pannenberg, "The Revelation of God in Jesus of Nazareth," p. 131.
21. Wolfhart Pannenberg, "Redemptive Event and History," 1:78.
22. Wolfhart Pannenberg, *Jesus—God and Man*, pp. 27-28.

historical facts at the foundation of Christianity are reliable, and therefore we can base our faith, our lives, and our future on them.

1.1233 *Alvin Plantinga.* Appealing to what he (erroneously, I think) calls the Reformed objection to natural theology, Alvin Plantinga has recently attacked theological rationalism with regard to belief in God. Plantinga wants to maintain that belief in God is rational wholly apart from any rational foundations for the belief.

This brings him into conflict with what he calls the evidentialist objection to theistic belief. According to the evidentialist, one is rationally justified in believing a proposition to be true only if that proposition is either foundational to knowledge or is established by evidence that is ultimately based on such a foundation. According to this viewpoint, since the proposition "God exists" is not foundational, it would be irrational to believe this proposition apart from rational evidence for its truth. But, Plantinga asks, why cannot the proposition "God exists" be itself part of the foundation, so that no rational evidence is necessary? The evidentialist replies that only propositions that are properly basic can be part of the foundation of knowledge. What, then, are the criteria that determine whether or not a proposition is properly basic? Typically, the evidentialist asserts that only propositions that are self-evident or incorrigible are properly basic. For example, the proposition "The sum of the squares of the two sides of a right triangle is equal to the square of the hypotenuse" is self-evidently true. Similarly, the proposition "I feel pain" is incorrigibly true, since even if I am only imagining my injury it is still true that I *feel* pain. Since the proposition "God exists" is neither self-evident nor incorrigible, it is not properly basic and therefore requires evidence if it is to be believed. To believe this proposition without evidence is therefore irrational.

Now Plantinga does not deny that self-evident and incorrigible propositions are properly basic, but he does demand, How do we know that these are the *only* properly basic propositions or beliefs? If they were, then we are all irrational, since we commonly accept numerous beliefs that do not have evidence and that are neither self-evident nor incorrigible. For example, take the belief that the world was not created five minutes ago with built-in memory traces, food in our stomachs from the breakfasts we never really ate, and other appearances of age. Surely it is rational to believe that the world has existed longer than five minutes, even though there is no evidence for this. The evidentialist's criteria for properly basicality must be flawed. In fact, what about the status of those criteria? Is the proposition "Only propositions that are self-evident or incorrigible are properly basic" *itself* properly basic? Apparently not, for it is certainly not self-evident nor incorrigible. Therefore, if we are to believe this proposition, we must have evidence that it is true. But there is no such evidence. The proposition appears to be just an arbitrary definition—and not a very plausible one at that. Hence, the evidentialist ·cannot exclude the possibility that belief in God is a properly basic belief.

And in fact, Plantinga maintains, following Calvin, belief in God is properly bası.. Man has an innate, natural capacity to apprehend God's existence even as he has a natural capacity to accept truths of perception (like "I see a tree"). Given the appropriate circumstances—such as moments of guilt, gratitude, or a sense of God's handiwork in nature— man naturally apprehends God's existence. Hence, Plantinga insists that his epistemology is not fideistic; there are circumstances that make the belief in God a properly basic belief. In fact, it may be more correct, he admits, to say that the proposition "God exists" is not itself properly basic but is entailed by other beliefs that are truly basic, such as "God is convicting me of sin" or "God is speaking to me." Hence, one is perfectly rational to believe in God wholly apart from evidence.

One interesting footnote to Plantinga's position emerged in discussion at a philosophical conference: Plantinga admits that there is no connection between a belief's being properly basic and its being true. He has only tried to show that belief in God is rational, not that it is true. One could be rationally justified in accepting a false belief; for example, it is rational to believe the world was not created five minutes ago. But maybe it was! In this case one would be rationally justified in accepting a false belief. Analagously, it needs to be asked whether belief in God might not also be both properly basic and incorrect. In such a case, Plantinga has said nothing to help us know whether our faith is true, but only whether it is rational. On the other hand, the circumstances to which Plantinga appeals to ground belief in God as basic were conceived in the Reformed tradition (in which Plantinga stands) to be unmistakable, and perhaps he thinks the same.[23] In this case, belief in God would not only be rational but correct as well.

1.13 ASSESSMENT

"How do I know Christianity is true?" Probably every Christian has asked himself that question. "I believe God exists, I believe Jesus rose from the dead, and I have experienced His life-changing power in my life, but how do I *know* it is really true?" The problem becomes especially acute when we are faced with someone who either does not believe in God or Jesus or who adheres to some other world religion. They may demand of us how we know Christianity is true and to prove

---

23. At more recent conferences and in his forthcoming intellectual autobiography, Plantinga makes quite clear that because of a divinely implanted "belief forming mechanism," that is to say, a sort of innate tendency and ability leading us to apprehend God, our belief that He exists is not only rational, but true.

it to them. What are we supposed to say? How *do* I know that Christianity is true?

In answering this question, I think we need to distinguish between *knowing* Christianity to be true and *showing* Christianity to be true.

1.131 KNOWING CHRISTIANITY TO BE TRUE

Here I would like to examine two points with you: first, the role of the Holy Spirit, and second, the role of reason.

1.1311 *Role of the Holy Spirit: Self-authenticating Witness.* May I suggest that, fundamentally, the way we know Christianity to be true is by the self-authenticating witness of God's Holy Spirit? Now what do I mean by that? I mean that the witness, or testimony, of the Holy Spirit is its own proof; it is unmistakable; it does not need other proofs to back it up; it is self-evident and attests to its own truth. It is this self-authenticating witness of God's Spirit that assures a person that Christianity is true. And this is the case for believer and unbeliever alike.

1.13111 *For the believer.* First, let us look at the role of the Holy Spirit in the life of the believer. When a person becomes a Christian, he automatically becomes an adopted son of God and is indwelt with the Holy Spirit: "for you are all sons of God through faith in Christ Jesus . . . And because you are sons, God has sent the Spirit of His Son into our hearts, crying, 'Abba! Father!' " (Gal. 3:26; 4:6). Paul emphasizes the point in Romans, chapter 8. Here he explains that it is the witness of the Holy Spirit with our spirit that allows us to know that we are God's children: "for you have not received a spirit of slavery leading to fear again, but you have received a spirit of adoption as sons by which we cry out, "Abba! Father!" The Spirit Himself bears witness with our spirit that we are children of God" (Rom. 8:15-16).

The apostle John also makes quite clear that it is the Holy Spirit within us that gives believers certainty of the truth of Christianity. "You have an anointing from the Holy One, and you all know. . . . the anointing which you received from Him abides in you, and you have no need for anyone to teach you; but as His anointing teaches you about all things, and is true and is not a lie, and just as it has taught you, you abide in Him" (1 John 2:20, 26-27). Here John explains that it is the Holy Spirit Himself who teaches the believer the truth of divine things. John is clearly echoing the teaching of Jesus Himself, when He says, "The Helper, the Holy Spirit, whom the Father will send in My name, He will teach you all things, and bring to your remembrance all that I said to you" (John 14:26). Now the truth that the Holy Spirit teaches us is not, I am convinced, Christian doctrine. There are too many Spirit-filled Christians who differ doctrinally for that to be the case. What

John is talking about is the inner assurance the Holy Spirit gives of the basic truths of the Christian faith. This assurance does not come from arguments of men but directly from the Holy Spirit himself.

John also underlines other teachings of Jesus on the work of the Holy Spirit. For example, according to Jesus it is the indwelling Holy Spirit that gives the believer certainty of knowing that Jesus lives in him and that he is in Jesus, in the sense of being united with Him.

> And I will ask the Father, and He will give you another Helper, that He may be with you forever; that is the Spirit of truth, whom the world cannot receive, because it does not behold Him or know Him, but you know Him because He abides with you, and will be in you. . . . In that day you shall know that I am in my Father, and you in Me, and I in you.
>
> (John 14:16-17, 20)

John teaches the same thing: "We know by this that He abides in us, by the Spirit whom He has given us. . . . By this we know that we abide in Him and He in us, because He has given us of His Spirit" (1 John 3:24; 4:13). John uses his characteristic phrase "by this we know" to emphasize that as Christians we have absolute assurance that our faith is true, that we really do abide in God, and God really does live in us. As Christians we have the testimony of God living within us, the Holy Spirit who bears witness with our spirit that we are children of God (1 John 5:7-10a).

Thus, although arguments may be used to support the believer's faith, they are never the basis of that faith. For the believer, God is not the conclusion of a syllogism; He is the living God of Abraham, Isaac, and Jacob dwelling within us. How then does the believer know that Christianity is true? He knows because of the self-authenticating witness of God's Spirit who lives within him.

     1.13112 *For the unbeliever.* But what about the role of the Holy Spirit in the life of an unbeliever? Since the Holy Spirit does not indwell him, does this mean that he must rely only upon arguments to convince him that Christianity is true? No, not at all. According to the Scripture, God has a different ministry of the Holy Spirit especially geared to the needs of the unbeliever. Jesus describes this ministry in John 16:7-11.

> It is to your advantage that I go away; for if I do not go away, the Helper shall not come to you; but if I go, I will send Him to you. And He, when He comes, will convict the world concerning sin, and righteousness, and judgment; concerning sin, because they do not believe in Me; and concerning righteousness, because I go to the Father, and you no longer behold Me; and concerning judgment, because the ruler of this world has been judged.

Here the Holy Spirit's ministry is three-fold: He convicts the believer of his own sin, of God's righteousness, and of his condemnation before God.

This is the way it has to be. For if it were not for the work of the Holy Spirit, no one would *ever* become a Christian. According to Paul, natural man left to himself does not even seek God: "There is none righteous, not even one; There is none who understands, There is none who seeks for God" (Rom. 3:10). Man in himself cannot understand spiritual things: "A natural man does not accept the things of the Spirit of God; for they are foolishness to him, and he cannot understand them, because they are spiritually appraised" (1 Cor. 2:14). And he is hostile to God: "The mind set on the flesh is hostile toward God; for it does not subject itself to the law of God, for it is not even able to do so" (Rom. 8:7). As Jesus said, men love darkness rather than light. Left to himself, natural man would never come to God.

The fact that we do find people who are seeking God and are ready to receive Christ is evidence that the Holy Spirit has already been at work, convicting them and drawing them to Him. As Jesus said, "No one can come to Me, unless the Father who sent Me draws him" (John 6:44). Therefore, when a person refuses to come to Christ it is never just because of lack of evidence or because of intellectual difficulties: at root, he refuses to come simply because he willingly ignores and rejects the drawing of God's Spirit on his heart. No one really fails to become a Christian because of lack of arguments; he fails to become a Christian because he loves darkness rather than light and wants nothing to do with God. But anyone who responds to the drawing of God's Spirit with an open mind and an open heart can know with certainty that Christianity is true, because God's Spirit will convict him that it is. Jesus said, "My teaching is not Mine, but His who sent Me. If any man is willing to do His will, he shall know of the teaching, whether it is of God, or whether I speak from myself" (John 7:16-17). Jesus says that if any man is truly seeking God, then he will know that Jesus' teaching is truly from God.

So then for the unbeliever as well as for the believer, it is the testimony of God's Spirit that ultimately assures him of the truth of Christianity. The unbeliever who is truly seeking God will be convinced of the truth of the Christian message.

Therefore, we find that for believer and unbeliever alike it is the self-authenticating work of the Holy Spirit that supplies assurance of Christianity's truth. Thus I would agree that belief in the God of the Bible is a properly basic belief, and emphasize that it is the ministry of the Holy Spirit that supplies the circumstance for its proper basicality. And because this belief is from God, it is not merely rational, but definitely true. We can be confident of Christianity's truth.

1.1312 *Role of reason.* But what about the second point: the role of reason in knowing Christianity to be true? We have already said that it is the Holy Spirit who gives us the ultimate assurance of Christianity's truth. Therefore, the only role left for reason to play is a subsidiary role. I think Martin Luther correctly distinguished between the magisterial and ministerial use of reason. The *magisterial use* of reason occurs when reason stands over and above the gospel like a magistrate and judges it. The *ministerial use* of reason occurs when reason submits to and serves the gospel. Only the ministerial use of reason can be allowed. Philosophy is rightly the handmaid of theology. Reason is a tool to help us better understand and defend our faith; as Anselm put it, ours is a faith that seeks understanding. Should faith and reason conflict, it is reason that must submit to faith, not vice versa.

1.1313 *Danger.* Now there is a danger in all this so far. Some persons might say that we should never seek to defend the faith. Just preach the gospel and let the Holy Spirit work! But this attitude is unbalanced and unscriptural, as we shall see in a moment. For now, let us just note in passing that as long as reason is a minister of the faith, Christians should employ it.

1.1314 *Objection.* Some people disagree with what I have said about the role of reason. They would say that reason can be used in a magisterial role, at least by the unbeliever. They ask how else we could determine which is true, the Bible, the Koran, or the *Baghavad-Gita,* unless we use reason to judge them? Now I have already answered that question: The Holy Spirit teaches us directly which teaching is really from God. But let me suggest two other reasons I think those who support the magisterial role of reason are wrong.

First, such a role is inconsistent with their own practice. Divinity schools are full of young men trying to work out a sound apologetic for the Christian faith. According to the magisterial role of reason, these young men should not believe in Christ until they have finished their apologetic. Otherwise, they would be believing for insufficient reasons. I asked one fellow student, "How do you know Christianity is true?" He replied, "I really don't know." Does that mean he should give up Christianity until he finds rational arguments to ground his faith? Of course not! He knew Christianity was true because he knew Jesus, regardless of rational arguments. The fact is that we can know the truth whether we have rational arguments or not.

Second, if the magisterial role of reason were valid, then a person who had been given poor arguments for Christianity would have just excuse before God for not believing in Him. Suppose someone had been told to believe in God because of an invalid argument. Could he stand before God on the judgment day and say, "God, those Christians only gave me a lousy argument for believing in you. That's why I didn't believe." Of course not! The Bible says all men are without excuse. Even men who are given no good reason to believe and many persuasive reasons to disbelieve have no excuse, because the ultimate reason they do not believe is that they have deliberately rejected God's Holy Spirit.

Therefore, the role of reason in knowing Christianity to be true is the role of a servant. A person knows Christianity is true because the Holy Spirit tells him it is true, and while reason can be used to support this conclusion, reason cannot overrule it.

1.132 SHOWING CHRISTIANITY TO BE TRUE

Such is the role of the Holy Spirit and of reason in *knowing* Christianity is true. But what about their role in *showing* Christianity is true? Here things are somewhat reversed.

1.1321 *Role of reason: systematic consistency.* Let us look first at the role of reason in showing Christianity is true. Here we are concerned about how to prove to another person that our faith is true. Accordingly, we are going to need a test for truth. May I suggest to you that the test for truth is systematic consistency? Let me define what I mean. By *consistency* I mean obedience to the laws of logic. Nothing can be true if it is self-contradictory or otherwise illogical. By *systematic* I mean fitting all the facts of experience. To be true, something must not only be logical, but it must also have the support of facts, whether historical, personal, or scientific. Somebody may have an airtight logical system, but if it does not explain the facts, we have no reason to regard it as true.

In showing Christianity to be true, we seek to demonstrate that it is systematically consistent, that is, that it is logical and that it fits the facts of experience. Since it passes the test for truth, we have shown it to be true, and any reasonable man should believe in it. Now this type of knowledge is only probable knowledge. Because new facts can always be discovered, we can only show something to be probably true, although to different degrees of probability. Therefore, it is the aim of the apologist to prove that Christianity possesses a high degree of probability. The fact that this type of knowledge cannot be absolutely certain should not discourage us, for virtually all our knowledge is based on probability, even the knowledge that other people exist or that the earth is round. So while the Holy Spirit gives us certain spiritual conviction of the truth of the gospel, systematic consistency can give us probable rational conviction of the truth of the gospel.

1.1322 *Role of the Holy Spirit.* But turn now to the second point: the role of the Holy Spirit in showing Christianity to be true. The role of the Holy Spirit is to use our arguments to convince the unbeliever of the truth of Christianity. When one presents reasons for his faith, one is not working apart from or against the Holy Spirit. To return to a point mentioned earlier: it is unbalanced and unscriptural to simply preach the gospel *if* the unbeliever has questions or objections.

1.13221 *Unbalanced to reject argumentation.* First, it is unbalanced because it assumes the Holy Spirit works only through preaching. But He can work through rational proofs, too. We must appeal to the head as well as the heart. As one writer has put it, the "prepared heart" alone will respond to the reasons, but there must be reasons to which it can respond. If an unbeliever objects that the Bible is unreliable because it is a translation of a translation of a translation, the answer is not to tell him to get right with God. The answer is to explain that we have excellent manuscripts of the Bible in the original Greek and Hebrew languages—and *then* tell him to get right with God!

1.13222 *Unscriptural to reject argumentation.* But second, it is unscriptural to refuse to reason with an unbeliever. Look at Paul. It was Paul's standard procedure to present reasons for the truth of the gospel and so defend the faith:

> According to Paul's custom, he went to them, and for three Sabbaths reasoned with them from the Scriptures, explaining and giving evidence that Christ had to suffer and rise again from the dead . . . So he was reasoning in the synagogue with the Jews and the God-fearing Gentiles, and in the market-place every day with those who happened to be present.

> And he entered the synagogue and continued speaking out boldly for three months, reasoning and persuading them about the kingdom of God.

> He was explaining to them by solemnly testifying about the kingdom of God, and trying to persuade them concerning Jesus, from both the law of Moses and the Prophets, from morning until evening. And some were being persuaded by the things spoken, but others would not believe.
> (Acts 17:2-3, 17; 19:8; 28:23-4)

Indeed, Scripture actually *commands* us to be prepared to give such a defense to an unbeliever: ". . . always being ready to make a defense to everyone who asks you to give an account for the hope that is in you" (1 Pet. 3:15*b*). So as Christians, we are to have an apologetic case ready to show that Christianity is true. To ignore the unbeliever's questions or objections is therefore both unbalanced and unscriptural. Of course it is true that we can never *argue* anyone into the kingdom of God. Conversion is exclusively the role of the Holy Spirit. But the Holy Spirit uses our arguments to draw men to Him.

1.1323 *Danger.* Now there is also a danger in all this. There is the danger that we may focus our attention on the argument instead of on the sinner. We must never let apologetics distract us from our primary aim of communicating the gospel. Indeed, I would say that with most people there is no need to use apologetics at all. Only use rational proofs after sharing the gospel and when the unbeliever still has questions. If you tell him, "God loves you and has a wonderful plan for your life," and He says He doesn't believe in God, do not get bogged down at that point in trying to prove the existence of God to him. Tell him, "Well, at this point I'm not trying to convince you what the Bible says is *true*; I'm just trying to share with you what the Bible *says*. After I've done that, then perhaps we can come back to whether there are good reasons to believe what it says is true." Remember our primary aim is to present Christ.

1.1324 *Objection.* Some would disagree with what I have said about the role of the Holy Spirit in showing Christianity to be true. They would contend that the believer and the unbeliever have no common ground on which to discuss; therefore it is futile to try to convince an unbeliever that Christianity is true. I think I have already indicated what our common ground with unbelievers is: the laws of logic and the facts of experience. Starting from these, we build our case for Christianity.

But in addition, I think that the example of Jesus and the apostles confirms the validity of this approach. Jesus appealed to miracles and to fulfilled prophecy to prove that His claims were true (Luke 24:25-27; John 14:11). What about the apostles? In dealing with Jews, they appealed to fulfilled prophecy, Jesus' miracles, and especially Jesus' resurrection. A model apologetic for Jews is Peter's sermon on the Day of Pentecost in Acts, chapter two. In verse 22 he appeals to Jesus' miracles. In verses 25-31 he appeals to fulfilled prophecy. In verse 32 he appeals to Christ's resurrection. By means of these arguments the apostles sought to show the Jews that Christianity is true. In dealing with non-Jews, the apostles sought to show the existence of God through His handiwork in nature (Acts 14:17). In Romans, chapter one, Paul says that from nature alone all men can know God exists. (Rom. 1:20) According to Michael Greene in his book *Evangelism in the Early Church*, the standard procedure of the apostles in dealing with Gentiles was to point to nature to show God's existence. Paul also appealed to eyewitness testimony of the resurrection of Jesus to show further that Christianity is true. (1 Cor. 15:3-8) So it is quite apparent, I think, that both Jesus and the apostles were not afraid to argue for the truth of Christianity. This does not mean they did not trust the Holy Spirit to bring men to God. Rather, they trusted the Holy Spirit to use their arguments to bring men to God.

Therefore, in showing Christianity to be true, it is the role of reason to construct arguments to show that the Christian *Weltanschauung* is the most systematically consistent position one can hold. And it is the role of the Holy Spirit to use these arguments, as we lovingly present them, to bring men to Him.

1.133 CONCLUSION

In summary, we have seen that in answering the question "How do I know Christianity is true?" we must make a distinction between *knowing* it is true and *showing* it is true. We *know* Christianity is true by the self-authenticating witness of God's Spirit. We *show* Christianity is true by demonstrating that it is systematically consistent.

What, then, should be our approach in apologetics? It should be something like this: "My friend, I know Christianity is true because God's Spirit lives in me and assures me undeniably that it is true. And you can know it is true, too, because God is knocking at the door of your heart, telling you the same thing. If you are sincerely seeking God, then God will give you assurance the gospel is true. Now to try to show you it is true, I will share with you some arguments that I really find convincing. But should my arguments seem weak and unconvincing to you, that is my fault, not God's. It only shows that I am a poor arguer, not that the gospel is untrue. Whatever you think of my arguments, God still loves you and holds you accountable. I will do my best to present good arguments to you. But ultimately you have to deal, not with arguments, but with God Himself."

1.14 PRACTICAL APPLICATION

The foregoing discussion has profound practical application both in our Christian walk and in our evangelism. With regard to our Christian walk, it helps us to have a proper assurance of the truth of our faith. A student once remarked to me after class, "I find this view so liberating!" He had struggled for some time to sort out the relation between faith and reason, but without success. Christians often fall into the extremes of fideism or theological rationalism. But the view just expounded enables us to hold to a rational faith without having reason as the foundation of that faith. It is tremendously liberating to be able to commend our faith to an unbeliever as rational and to know that our faith is rational, without being dependent upon the vagaries of reason for the assurance that our faith is true; while at the same time we know without embarrassment or apology that our faith is true and that the unbeliever can know this, too, without falling into relativistic subjectivism.

This view also underlines the vital importance of cultivating the ministry of the Holy Spirit in our lives. For though all Christians are indwelt by the Spirit, not all are filled with the Spirit. The New Testament teaches that we can grieve the Holy Spirit of God by sin (Eph. 4:30) and quench the Spirit by repressing His working in our lives (1 Thess. 5:19). The Christian who is not filled with the Spirit may often be wracked with doubts concerning his faith. I can testify personally that my intellectual doubts seem most poignant when I am in a carnal condition. But when a Christian is walking in the Spirit, then, although his intellectual questions may remain, he can *live* with those questions, without their robbing his faith of its vitality. As the source of the assurance that our faith is true, the Holy Spirit's ministry in our lives needs to be cultivated by spiritual activities that help us to walk close to God, such as Bible study, prayer, devotional reading, inspirational music, witnessing, and Spirit-filled worship.

In evangelism, too, this view enables us to give the unbeliever rational arguments and evidence for the truth of the Gospel, instead of challenging him to "just have faith." I have met many non-Christians who came from conservative Christian backgrounds and were turned off to the gospel by having their honest questions squelched and being told to just believe. By contrast, let me tell you of one university student to whom I related the gospel. After I finshed, he asked, "But how do you know this is all true?" I replied, "Well, we need to have some test for truth. What is your test for truth?" When he confessed he did not have one, I continued, "What about systematic consistency?" I explained that notion to him, and to my surprise that was enough—he did not even ask me to show him that Christianity was true! It was sufficient for him just to hear a test for truth that could be applied to Christianity. With tears in his eyes, he then prayed with me to receive Christ.

At the same time, however, this view reminds us that unbelief is at root a spiritual, not an intellectual, problem. Sometimes an unbeliever will throw up an intellectual smoke screen so that he can avoid personal, existential involvement with the gospel. In such a case, further argumentation may be futile and counterproductive, and we need to be sensitive to moments when apologetics is and is not appropriate. If we sense the unbeliever's arguments and questions are not sincere, we may do better to simply break off the discussion and ask him, "If I answered that objection, would you then really be ready to become a Christian?" Tell him lovingly and forthrightly that you think he is throwing up an intellectual smoke screen to keep from confronting the real issue: his sin before God. Apologetics is thus most appropriate and effective when the unbeliever is spiritually open and sincerely seeking to know the truth.

That leads to a final point. Many times a person will say, "That argument was not effective because the unbeliever I shared it with was not convinced." Here we have to be very careful. Being "convincing" is person-relative. Some people will simply refuse to be convinced. Hence, an argument cannot be said to be ineffective because some people remain unconvinced by it. When one reflects on the fact that "the gate is small, and the way is narrow that leads to life, and few are those who find it" (Matt. 7:14), it should not surprise us if most people find our apologetic unconvincing. But that does not mean that our apologetic is ineffective. Of course, if *nobody* finds our arguments convincing, then they may be said to be ineffective, even if they are cogent. What we need to develop is an apologetic that is both cogent and persuasive to as many people as possible. But we must not be discouraged and think our apologetic is ineffective if many or even most people find our arguments unconvincing. Success in witnessing is simply communicating Christ in the power of the Holy Spirit and leaving the results to God. Similarly, effectiveness in apologetics is presenting cogent and persuasive arguments for the gospel in the power of the Holy Spirit, and leaving the results to God.

2.0 DE HOMINE

2.1 THE ABSURDITY OF LIFE WITHOUT GOD

One of the apologetic questions that contemporary Christian theology must treat in its doctrine of man is what has been called "the human predicament," that is to say, the significance of human life in a post-theistic universe. Logically, this question ought, it seems to me, to be raised prior to and as a prelude to the question of the existence of God.

2.11 LITERATURE CITED OR RECOMMENDED

2.111 HISTORICAL BACKGROUND

Dostoyevsky, Fyodor. *The Brothers Karamazov.* Translated by C. Garnett, foreword by M. Komroff. New York: New American Library, Signet Classics, 1957.

———. *Crime and Punishment.* Translated by C. Garnett, introduction by E. Simmons. New York: Modern Library, 1950.

Kierkegaard, Søren. *Either/Or.* Translated by D. F. Swenson and L. M. Swenson. Princeton: Princeton U., 1944. Volume 1 describes the first stage of life, and Volume 2 the second.

———. *Fear and Trembling.* Edited and translated with an introduction and notes by H. V. Hong and E. H. Hong. Princeton: Princeton U., 1983. This handles the religious stage.

Pascal, Blaise. *Pensées.* Edited by Louis Lafuma, translated by John Warrington. Everyman's Library. London: Dent, 1960.

Schaeffer, Francis. *Escape from Reason.* Downers Grove, Ill.: Inter-Varsity Press, 1968.

————. *The God Who Is There*. Chicago: Inter-Varsity Press, 1968.

————. *How Should We Then Live?* Old Tappan, N.J.: Fleming H. Revell, 1976.

2.112 ASSESSMENT

Beckett, Samuel. *Waiting for Godot*. New York: Grove, 1956.

Bloch, Ernst. *Das Prinzip Hoffnung*. 2d ed. 2 vols. Frankfurt am Main. Suhrkamp Verlag, 1959.

Camus, Albert. *The Myth of Sisyphus and other essays*. Translated by J. O'Brien. New York: Vintage, 1959.

————. *The Stranger*. Translated by S. Gilbert. New York: Vintage, 1958.

Crick, Francis. "Why I Study Biology." *Washington University Magazine*, Spring 1971, pp. 20-4.

Eliot, T. S. "The Hollow Men." In *The Complete Poems and Plays*. New York: Harcourt, Brace, 1934.

Encyclopaedia Britannica, 15th ed. *Propaedia*, s.v. "The Cosmic Orphan," by Loren Eiseley.

Hesse, Hermann. *Steppenwolf*. Translated by Basil Creighton. New York: Holt, Rinehart and Winston, 1961.

Hocking, W. E. *Types of Philosophy*. New York: Scribner's, 1959.

Hoyle, Fred. *From Stonehenge to Modern Cosmology*. San Francisco: W. H. Freeman, 1972.

Kaufmann, Walter. "Existentialism from Dostoyevsky to Sartre." In *Existentialism from Dostoyevsky to Sartre*. 2d ed. Edited by W. Kaufmann. New York: New American Library, Meridian, 1975. Pp. 11-51.

Monod, Jacques. *Chance and Necessity*. Translated by A. Wainhouse. New York: Alfred A. Knopf, 1971.

Nietzsche, Friedrich. "The Gay Science." In *The Portable Nietzsche*. Edited and translated by W. Kaufmann. New York: Viking, 1954. Pp. 93-102.

————. "The Will to Power." Translated by Walter Kaufmann. In *Existentialism from Dostoyevsky to Sartre*. 2d ed. Edited with an introduction by W. Kaufmann. New York: New American Library, Meridian, 1975. Pp. 130-2.

Novikov, I.D., and Zeldovich, Ya.B. "Physical Processes Near Cosmological Singularities." *Annual Review of Astronomy and Astrophysics* 11 (1973): 387-410.

Russell, Bertrand. "A Free Man's Worship." In *Why I Am Not a Christian*. Edited by P. Edwards. New York: Simon & Schuster, 1957. Pp. 104-16.

————. Letter to the *Observer*, 6 October 1957.

Sagan, Carl. *Cosmos*. New York: Random House, 1980.

Sartre, Jean-Paul. *Being and Nothingness*. Translated with an introduction by H. E. Barnes. New York: Washington Square, 1966.

──────. "Existentialism Is a Humanism." Translated by P. Mairet. In *Existentialism from Dostoyevsky to Sartre.* 2d ed. Edited with an introduction by W. Kaufmann. New York: New American Library, Meridian, 1975. Pp. 345-69.

──────. *Nausea.* Translated by L. Alexander. London: H. Hamilton, 1962.

──────. *No Exit.* Translated by S. Gilbert. New York: Alfred A. Knopf, 1963.

──────. "Portrait of the Antisemite." Translated by M. Guggenheim. In *Existentialism from Dostoyevsky to Sartre.* 2d ed. Edited with an introduction by W. Kaufmann. New York: New American Library, Meridian, 1975. Pp. 329-45.

──────. "The Wall." Translated by L. Alexander. In *Existentialism from Dostoyevsky to Sartre.* 2d ed. Edited with an introduction by W. Kaufmann. New York: New American Library, Meridian, 1975. Pp. 281-99.

Wells, H. G. *The Time Machine.* New York: Berkeley, 1957.

2.12 HISTORICAL BACKGROUND

The apologetic for Christianity based on the human predicament is an extremely recent phenomenon, associated primarily with Francis Schaeffer. Often it is refered to as "cultural apologetics" because of its analysis of post-Christian culture. This approach constitutes an entirely different sort of apologetics, since it is not concerned with epistemological issues (hence Lewis's silence on this approach in *Testing Christianity's Truth Claims*). Indeed, in a sense it does not even attempt to show in any positive sense that Christianity is true; it simply explores the disastrous consequences for human existence, society, and culture if Christianity should be false. In this respect, this approach is somewhat akin to existentialism: the precursors of this approach were also precursors of existentialism, and much of its analysis of the human predicament is drawn from the insights of recent atheistic existentialism.

2.121 BLAISE PASCAL

One of the earliest examples of a Christian apology appealing to the human predicament is the *Penseés* of the French mathematician and physicist Blaise Pascal (1623-62). Having come to a personal faith in Christ in 1654, Pascal had planned to write a defense of the Christian faith entitled *L'Apologie de la religion chrétienne,* but died of a debilitating disease at the age of only 39 years, leaving behind hundreds of notes for the work, which were then published posthumously as the

Pensées.[1] Pascal's approach is thoroughly Christocentric. The Christian religion, he claims, teaches two truths: that there is a God whom men are capable of knowing, and that there is an element of corruption in men that renders them unworthy of God. Knowledge of God without knowledge of man's wretchedness begets pride, and knowledge of man's wretchedness without knowledge of God begets despair, but knowledge of Jesus Christ furnishes man knowledge of both simultaneously. Pascal invites us to look at the world from the Christian point of view and see if these truths are not confirmed. His *Apology* was evidently to comprise two divisions: in the first part he would display the misery of man without God (that man's nature is corrupt) and in the second part the happiness of man with God (that there is a Redeemer).[2] With regard to the latter, Pascal appeals to the evidences of miracle and especially fulfilled prophecy. In confirming the truth of man's wretchedness Pascal seeks to unfold the human predicament.

For Pascal the human condition is an enigma. For man is at the same time miserable and yet great. On the one hand, his misery is due principally to his uncertainty and insignificance. Writing in the tradition of the French skeptic Montaigne, Pascal repeatedly emphasizes the uncertainty of conclusions reached via reason and the senses. Apart from intuitive first principles, nothing seems capable of being known with certainty. In particular, reason and nature do not seem to furnish decisive evidence as to whether God exists or not. As man looks out around him, all he sees is darkness and obscurity. Moreover, insofar as his scientific knowledge is correct, man learns that he is an infinitesimal speck lost in the immensity of time and space. His brief life is bounded on either side by eternity, his place in the universe is lost in the immeasurable infinity of space, and he finds himself suspended, as it were, between the infinite microcosm within and the infinite macrocosm without. Uncertain and untethered, man flounders in his efforts to lead a meaningful and happy life. His condition is characterized by inconstancy, boredom, and anxiety. His relations with his fellow men are warped by self-love; society is founded on mutual deceit. Man's justice is fickle and relative, and no fixed standard of value may be found.

Despite their predicament, however, most men, incredibly, refuse to seek an answer or even to think about their dilemma, but instead lose themselves in escape. Listen to how Pascal describes the reasoning of such a man:

1. The definitive ordering and numbering of these notes is that of Louis Lafuma, and the *Pensées* are cited in reference to the number of each fragment.
2. Blaise Pascal, *Pensées* 29.

I know not who sent me into the world, nor what the world is, nor what I myself am. I am terribly ignorant of everything. I know not what my body is, nor my senses, nor my soul and that part of me which thinks what I say, which reflects upon itself as well as upon all external things, and has no more knowledge of itself than of them.

I see the terrifying immensity of the universe which surrounds me, and find myself limited to one corner of this vast expanse, without knowing why I am set down here rather than elsewhere, nor why the brief period appointed for my life is assigned to me at this moment rather than another in all the eternity that has gone before and will come after me. On all sides I behold nothing but infinity, in which I am a mere atom, a mere passing shadow that returns no more. All I know is that I must soon die, but what I understand least of all is this very death which I cannot escape.

As I know not whence I come, so I know not whither I go. I only know that on leaving this world I fall for ever into nothingness or into the hands of a wrathful God, without knowing to which of these two states I shall be everlastingly consigned. Such is my condition, full of weakness and uncertainty. From all this I conclude that I ought to spend every day of my life without seeking to know my fate. I might perhaps be able to find a solution to my doubts; but I cannot be bothered to do so, I will not take one step towards its discovery.[3]

Pascal can only regard such indifference as insane. Man's condition ought to impel him to seek to discover whether there is a God and a solution to his predicament. But men preoccupy their time and their thoughts with trivialities and distractions, so as to avoid the despair, boredom, and anxiety that would inevitably result if those diversions were removed.

Such is the misery of man. But mention must also be made of the greatness of man. For although man is miserable, he is at least capable of *knowing* that he is miserable. The greatness of man consists in thought. Man is a mere reed, yes, but he is a *thinking* reed. The universe might crush him like a gnat; but even so, man is nobler than the universe because he *knows* that it crushes him, and the universe has no such knowledge. Man's whole dignity consists therefore, in thought. "By space the universe encompasses and swallows me up like a mere speck; by thought I comprehend the universe." Man's greatness, then, lies not in his having the solution to his predicament, but in the fact that he alone in all the universe is aware of his wretched condition.

What a chimaera then is man, what a novelty, what a monster, what chaos, what a subject of contradiction, what a prodigy! Judge of all things, yet an

3. Ibid. 11.

imbecile earthworm; depositary of truth, yet a sewer of uncertainty and error; pride and refuse of the universe. Who shall resolve this tangle?[4]

Pascal hopes that by explaining man's greatness as well as his misery, he might shake men out of their lethargy to *think* about their condition and to seek a solution.

Pascal's analysis of the human predicament leads up to his famous Wager argument, by means of which he hopes to tip the scales in favor of theism.[5] The founder of probability theory, Pascal argues that when the odds that God exists are even, then the prudent man will gamble that God exists. This is a wager that all men must make—the game is in progress and a bet must be laid. There is no option: you have already joined the game. Which then will you choose—that God exists or that He does not? Pascal argues that since the odds are even, reason is not violated in making either choice; therefore, reasons cannot determine which bet to make. Therefore, the choice should be made pragmatically in terms of maximizing one's happiness. If one wagers that God exists and He does, one has gained eternal life and infinite happiness. If He does not exist, one has lost nothing. On the other hand, if one wagers that God does not exist and He does, then one has suffered infinite loss. If He does not in fact exist, then one has gained nothing. Hence, the only prudent choice is to believe that God exists.

Now Pascal does believe that there is a way of "getting a look behind the scenes" to rationally determine how one should bet, namely, the proofs of Scripture of miracle and prophecy, which he discusses in the second half of his work. But for now, he wants to emphasize that wholly in the absence of such evidence, one still ought to believe in God. For given the human predicament of being cast into existence and facing either eternal annihilation or eternal wrath, the only reasonable course of action is to believe in God: "for if you win, you win all; if you lose, you lose nothing."[6]

2.122　FYODOR DOSTOYEVSKY

Another apologetic based on the human predicament may be found in the magnificent novels of the great Russian writer of the last century Fyodor Dostoyevsky (1821-81). (May I add that I think the obsession of contemporary evangelicals with the writings of authors like C. S. Lewis to the neglect of writers like Dostoyevsky is a great shame? Dostoyevsky is a far, far grander writer.) The problem that tortured Dostoyevsky was the problem of evil: How can a good and loving God exist

4. Ibid. 217, 246.
5. Ibid. 343.
6. Ibid.

when the world is filled with so much suffering and evil? Dostoyevsky presented this problem in his works so persuasively, so poignantly, that certain passages of his, notably "The Grand Inquisitor" section from his *Brothers Karamazov*, are often reprinted in anthologies as classic statements of the problem of evil. As a result, some people are under the impression that Dostoyevsky was himself an atheist and that the viewpoint of the Grand Inquisitor is his own.

Actually, he sought to carry through a two-pronged defense of theism in the face of the problem of evil. Positively, he argued that innocent suffering may perfect character and bring one into a closer relation with God. Negatively, he tried to show that if the existence of God is denied, then one is landed in complete moral relativism, so that no act, regardless of how dreadful or heinous, can be condemned by the atheist. To live consistently with such a view of life is unthinkable and impossible. Hence, atheism is destructive of life and ends logically in suicide.

Dostoyevsky recognizes that this constitutes no positive proof of Christianity. Indeed, he rejects that there could be such. Men demand of Christ that he furnish them "bread and circuses," but He refuses to do so. The decision to follow Christ must be made in loneliness and anxiety. Each man must face for himself the anguish of a world without God and in the solitude of his own heart give himself to God in faith.

2.123 SØREN KIERKEGAARD

The Danish existentialist of the late nineteenth century, Søren Kierkegaard (1813-55), also presents a sort of negative apologetic for the Christian faith. He thinks of life as being lived on three different planes or stages: the aesthetic stage, the ethical stage, and the religious stage. Man in the aesthetic stage lives life only on the sensual level, a life that is self- and pleasure-centered. This need not be a gross hedonism. Man on this level could be very cultivated and even circumspect; but nevertheless his life revolves around himself and those material things—whether sex, art, music, or whatever—that bring him pleasure. The paradox of life on this level is that it leads ultimately to unhappiness. The self-centered, aesthetic man finds no ultimate meaning in life and no true satisfaction. Thus, the aesthetic life leads finally to despair, a sort of sickness with life.

But this is not the end, for only at this point is a man ready to live on the second plane of existence, the ethical plane. The transition to the ethical stage of life is a sort of leap motivated by despair to a higher level, where one affirms trans-personal moral values and guides life by those objective standards. No longer is life lived only for self and for pleasure; rather one is constrained to seek the ethical good and to change one's conduct to bring it into conformity with that good. Thus, man in the ethical stage is the moral man. But life on this level, too, ends in unhappiness. For the more one tries sincerely to bring one's life into conformity with the objective standards of good, the more painfully aware one is that one cannot do it. Thus, the ethical life, when earnestly pursued, leads ultimately to guilt and despair.

But there is one more stage along life's way: the religious stage. Here one finds forgiveness of sins and a personal relationship with God. Only here, in intimate communion with one's Creator, does man find authentic existence and true fulfillment. Again Kierkegaard represents the transition to this stage from the ethical as a leap. The decision to believe is a criterionless choice, a leap of faith into the dark. But although man can be given no rational grounds to leap, unless he does so he will remain in despair and inauthentic existence.

2.124 FRANCIS SCHAEFFER

As I remarked earlier, Francis Schaeffer is the thinker responsible for drafting a Christian apologetic based on the modern predicament. According to Schaeffer, there can be traced in recent Western culture a "line of despair," which penetrates philosophy, literature, and the arts in succession. He believes the root of the problem lies in Hegelian philosophy, specifically in its denial of absolute truths. Hegel developed the famous triad of thesis-antithesis-synthesis, in which contradictions are seen not as absolute opposites, but as partial truths, which are synthesized in the whole. Ultimately, all is One, which is absolute and noncontradictory. In Schaeffer's view, Hegel's system undermined the notion of particular absolute truths (such as "That act is morally wrong" or "This painting is aesthetically ugly") by synthesizing them into the whole. This denial of absolutes has gradually made its way through Western culture. In each case, it results in despair, because without absolutes man's endeavors degenerate into absurdity. Schaeffer believes that the Theater of the Absurd, abstract modern art, and modern music such as is composed by John Cage are all indications of what happens below the line of despair. Only by reaffirming belief in the absolute God of Christianity can man and his culture avoid inevitable degeneracy, meaninglessness, and despair.

Schaeffer's efforts against abortion may be seen as a logical extension of this apologetic. Once God is denied, human life becomes worthless, and we see the fruit of such a philosophy in the abortion and infanticide now taking place. Schaeffer warns that unless Western man returns to the Christian world and life view, nothing will stop the trend from degenerating into population control and human breeding. Only a theistic world view can save the human race from itself.

2.131 THE NECESSITY OF GOD AND IMMORTALITY

Man, writes Loren Eiseley, is the Cosmic Orphan. He is the only creature in the universe who asks, "Why?" Other animals have instincts to guide them, but man has learned to ask questions.

"Who am I?" man asks. "Why am I here? Where am I going?" Since the Enlightenment, when he threw off the shackles of religion, man has tried to answer these questions without reference to God. But the answers that came back were not exhilarating, but dark and terrible. "You are the accidental by-product of nature," he is told, "a result of matter plus time plus chance. There is no reason for your existence. All you face is death."

Modern man thought that when he had got rid of God, he had freed himself from all that repressed and stifled him. Instead, he discovered that in killing God, he had also killed himself.

For if there is no God, then man's life becomes absurd.

If God does not exist, then both man and the universe are inevitably doomed to death. Man, like all biological organisms, must die. With no hope of immortality, man's life leads only to the grave. His life is but a spark in the infinite blackness, a spark that appears, flickers, and dies forever. Compared to the infinite stretch of time, the span of man's life is but an infinitesmal moment; and yet this is all the life he will ever know. Therefore, all men must come face to face with what theologian Paul Tillich has called "the threat of non-being." For though I know now that I exist, that I am alive, I also know that someday I will no longer exist, that I will no longer be, that I will die. This thought is staggering and threatening: to think that the person I call "myself" will cease to exist, that I will be no more.

I remember vividly the first time my father told me that someday I would die. Somehow as a child the thought had just never occurred to me. When he told me, I was filled with fear and unbearable sadness. And though he tried repeatedly to reassure me that this was a long way off, that did not seem to matter. Whether sooner or later, the undeniable fact was that I would die and be no more, and the thought overwhelmed me. Eventually, like all of us, I grew to simply accept the fact. We learn to live with the inevitable. But the child's insight remains true. As the French existentialist Jean-Paul Sartre observed, several hours or several years make no difference once you have lost eternity.

Whether it comes sooner or later, the prospect of death and the threat of non-being is an inconceivable horror. I met a student once who did not feel this threat. He said he had been raised on the farm and was used to seeing the animals being born and dying. Death was for him simply natural—a part of life, so to speak. I was puzzled by how different our two perspectives on death were and found it difficult to understand why he did not feel the threat of non-being. Years later, I think I found my answer in reading Sartre. Sartre observed that death is not threatening so long as we view it as the death of the other, from a third-person standpoint, so to speak. It is only when we internalize it and look at it from the first person perspective—"*my* death: *I* am going to die"—that the threat of non-being becomes real. As Sartre points out, many people never assume this first-person perspective in the midst of life; one can even look at one's own death from the third-person standpoint, as if it were the death of another or even of an animal, as did my friend. But the true existential significance of *my death* can only be appreciated from the first-person perspective, as I realize that I am going to die and forever cease to exist. My life is just a momentary transition out of oblivion into oblivion.

And the universe, too, faces death. Scientists tell us that the universe is expanding, and everything in it is growing farther and farther apart. As it does so, it grows colder and colder, and its energy is used up. Eventually, all the stars will burn out and all matter will collapse into dead stars and black holes. There will be no light at all; there will be no heat; there will be no life; only the corpses of dead stars and galaxies, everexpanding into the endless darkness and the cold recesses of space—a universe in ruins. The entire universe marches irreversibly toward its grave. So not only is the life of each individual man doomed; the entire human race is doomed. The universe is plunging toward inevitable extinction—death is written throughout its structure. There is no escape. There is no hope.

2.132 THE ABSURDITY OF LIFE WITHOUT GOD AND IMMORTALITY

If there is no God, then man and the universe are doomed. Like prisoners condemned to death, we await our unavoidable execution. There is no God, and there is no immortality. And what is the consequence of this? It means that life itself is absurd. It means that the life we have is without significance, value, or purpose. Let us look at each of these.

2.1321 *Life has no ultimate meaning . . .*

2.13211 *without immortality.* If each individual person passes out of existence when he dies, then what ultimate meaning can be given to his life? Does it really matter whether he ever existed at all? It might be said that his life was important because it influenced others or affected the course of history. But this only shows a relative significance to his life, not an ultimate significance. His life may be important relative to certain other events, but what is the ultimate significance of any of those events? If all the events are meaningless, then what can be the ultimate meaning of influencing any of them? Ultimately it makes no difference.

Look at it from another perspective: Scientists say that the universe originated in an explosion called the "big bang" about 15 billion years ago. Suppose the big bang had never occurred. Suppose the universe had never existed. What ultimate difference would it make? The universe is doomed to die anyway. In the end it makes no difference whether the universe ever existed or not. Therefore, it is without ultimate significance.

The same is true of the human race. Mankind is a doomed race in a dying universe. Because the human race will eventually cease to exist, it makes no ultimate difference whether it ever did exist. Mankind is thus no more significant than a swarm of mosquitos or a barnyard of pigs, for their end is all the same. The same blind cosmic process that coughed them up in the first place will eventually swallow them again.

And the same is true of each individual man. The contributions of scientist to the advance of human knowledge, the researches of the doctor to alleviate pain and suffering, the efforts of the diplomat to secure peace in the world, the sacrifices of good men everywhere to better the lot of the human race—all these come to nothing. In the end they don't make one bit of difference, not one bit. Each man's life is therefore without ultimate significance. And because our lives are ultimately meaningless, the activities we fill our lives with are also meaningless. The long hours spent in study at the university, our jobs, our interests, our friendships—all these are, in the final analysis, utterly meaningless. This is the horror of modern man: because he ends in nothing, he *is* nothing.

2.13212 *without God.* But it is important to see that it is not just immortality that man needs if life is to be meaningful. Mere duration of existence does not make that existence meaningful. If man and the universe could exist forever, but if there were no God, their existence would still have no ultimate significance. To illustrate: I once read a science-fiction story in which an astronaut was marooned on a barren chunk of rock lost in outer space. He had with him two vials: one containing poison and the other a potion that would make him live forever. Realizing his predicament, he gulped down the poison. But then to his horror, he discovered he had swallowed the wrong vial—he had drunk the potion for immortality. And that meant that he was cursed to exist forever—a meaningless, unending life. Now if God does not exist, our lives are just like that: meaningless. They could go and on and on and still be utterly without meaning. We could still ask of life, "So what?" So it is not just immortality man needs if life is to be ultimately significant; he needs God *and* immortality. And if God does not exist, then he has neither.

Twentieth-century man understands this. Read *Waiting for Godot* by Samuel Beckett. During this entire play, two men carry on trivial conversation while waiting for a third man to arrive, who never does. Our lives are like that, Beckett is saying; we just kill time waiting—for what, we don't know. In a tragic portrayal of man, Beckett wrote another play in which the curtain opened revealing a stage littered with junk. For thirty long seconds, the audience sat and stared in silence at that junk. Then the curtain closed. That was all.

One of the most devastating novels I have ever read was *Steppenwolf*, by Hermann Hesse. At the novel's end, Harry Haller stands looking at himself in a mirror. During the course of his life he had experienced all the world offers. And now he stands looking at himself, and he mutters "Ah, the bitter taste of life!" He spits at himself in the looking-glass, and then he kicks it to pieces. His life has been futile and meaningless.

French existentialists Jean-Paul Sartre and Albert Camus understood this, too. Sartre portrayed life in his play *No Exit* as hell—the final line of the play are the words of resignation, "Well, let's get on with it." Hence, Sartre writes elsewhere of the "nausea" of existence. Camus, too, saw life as absurd. At the end of his brief novel *The Stranger*, Camus's hero discovers in a flash of insight that the universe has no meaning and there is no God to give it one. The French bio-chemist Jacques Monod seemed to echo those sentiments when he wrote in his work *Chance and Necessity*, "Man finally knows he is alone in the indifferent immensity of the universe."

Thus, if there is no God, then life itself becomes meaningless. Man and the universe are without ultimate significance.

2.1322 *Life has no ultimate value . . .*

2.13221 *without immortality.* If life ends at the grave, then it makes no difference whether one has lived as a Stalin or as a saint. As the Dostoyevsky put it: "If there is no immortality, then all things are permitted." On this basis, a writer like Ayn Rand is absolutely correct to praise the virtues of selfishness. Live totally for self; no one holds you accountable! Indeed, it would be foolish to do anything else, for life is too short to jeopardize it by acting out of anything but pure self-interest. Sacrifice for another person would be stupid.

2.13222 *without God.* But the problem becomes even worse. For, regardless of immortality, if there is no God, then there can be no absolute standards of right and wrong. All we are confronted with is, in Jean-Paul Sartre's words, the bare, valueless fact of existence. In a world without God, who is to say which values are right and which are wrong? Who is to judge that the values of Adolf Hitler are inferior to those of a saint? The concept of morality loses all meaning in a universe without God. There can be no right and wrong. This means that it is impossible to condemn war, oppression, or crime as evil. Nor can one praise brotherhood, equality, and love as good. For in a universe without God, good and evil do not exist—there is only the bare value-less fact of existence, and there is no one to say you are right and I am wrong.

      2.1323 *Life has no ultimate purpose . . .*

      2.13231 *without immortality.* If death stands with open arms at the end of life's trail, then what is the goal of life? To what end has life been lived? Is it all for nothing? Is there no reason for life? And what of the universe? Is it utterly pointless? If its destiny is a cold grave in recesses of outer space, the answer must be yes—it is point-less. There is no goal, no purpose, for the universe. The litter of a dead universe will just go on expanding and expanding—forever. And what of man? In the last half of the twentieth century, man seems to be faced with the imminent prospect of nuclear holocaust or world-wide fam-ine. Mankind may finally have reached the end of its rope, and its destruction is being pronounced not by prophets of doom but by intel-ligent persons in the scientific community. A dark shadow has fallen over the final half of this century. Henry Kissinger reported that in a personal meeting with Mao Tse-Tung shortly before his death, Mao delivered to him what Kissinger described as the most brilliant and cold-blooded analysis of the world's future: nuclear war will wipe out most of the world's population, and out of the ashes the remnant of the Chinese proletariat will arise and dominate the earth. But, one might ask, to what end will they have survived? Is there no purpose at all for the human race? Or will it simply peter out someday, lost in the obliv-ion of an indifferent universe?

The English writer H. G. Wells foresaw such a prospect. In his novel *The Time Machine* Well's time traveler journeys far into the future to discover the destiny of man. What he finds is a dead earth, save for a few lichens and moss, orbiting a gigantic red sun. The only sounds are the rush of the wind and the gentle ripple of the sea. "Beyond these lifeless sounds," writes Wells, "the world was silent. Silent? It would be hard to convey the stillness of it. All the sounds of man, the bleating of sheep, the cries of birds, the hum of insects, the stir that makes the background of our lives—all that was over."[7] And so Wells's time trav-eler returned. But to what?—to merely an earlier point on the purpose-less rush toward oblivion. When as a non-Christian I first read Wells's book, I thought, "No, no! It can't end that way!" But if there is no God, it *will* end that way, like it or not. This is reality in a universe without God: there is no hope; there is no purpose. It reminds me of T. S. Eliot's haunting lines:

---

7. H. G. Wells, *The Time Machine*, chap. 11.

This is the way the world ends
This is the way the world ends
This is the way the world ends
Not with a bang but a whimper.[8]

What is true of mankind as a whole is true of each of us individually: we are here to no purpose. If there is no God, then our life is not qualitatively different from that of a dog. I know that is harsh, but it is true. As the ancient writer of Ecclesiastes put it: "The fate of the sons of men and the fate of beasts is the same. As one dies so dies the other; indeed, they all have the same breath and there is no advantage for man over beast, for all is vanity. All go to the same place. All come from the dust and all return to the dust" (Eccles. 3:19-20). In this book, which reads more like a piece of modern existentialist literature than a book of the Bible, the writer shows the futility of pleasure, wealth, education, political fame, and honor in a life doomed to end in death. His verdict? "Vanity of vanities! All is vanity" (1:2). If life ends at the grave, then we have no ultimate purpose for living.

2.13232 *without God*. But more than that: even if it did not end in death, without God life would still be without purpose. For man and the universe would then be simple accidents of chance, thrust into existence for no reason. Without God the universe is the result of a cosmic accident, a chance explosion. There is no reason for which it exists. As for man, he is a freak of nature—a blind product of matter plus time plus chance. Man is just a lump of slime that evolved rationality. There is no more purpose in life for the human race than for a species of insect; for both are the result of the blind interaction of chance and necessity. As one philosopher has put it: "Human life is mounted upon a subhuman pedestal and must shift for itself alone in the heart of a silent and mindless universe."[9] What is true of the universe and of the human race is also true of us as individuals. Insofar as we are individual human beings, we are the results of certain combinations of heredity and environment. We are victims of a kind of genetic and environmental roulette. Psychologists following Sigmund Freud tell us our actions are the result of various repressed sexual tendencies. Sociologists following B. F. Skinner argue that all our choices are determined by conditioning, so that freedom is an illusion. Biologists like Francis Crick regard man as an electro-chemical machine that can be controlled by altering its genetic code. If God does not exist, then you

---

8. From "The Hollow Men," in *Collected Poems 1909-1962* by T. S. Eliot, copyright 1936 by Harcourt Brace Jovanovich, Inc., © 1963, 1964, by T. S. Eliot. Reprinted by permission of the publisher.
9. W. E. Hocking, *Types of Philosophy*, p. 27.

are just a miscarriage of nature, thrust into a purposeless universe to live a purposeless life.

So if God does not exist, that means that man and the universe exist to no purpose—since the end of everything is death—and that they came to be for no purpose, since they are only blind products of chance. In short, life is utterly without reason.

Do you understand the gravity of the alternatives before us? For if God exists, then there is hope for man. But if God does not exist, then all we are left with is despair. Do you understand why the question of God's existence is so vital to man? As one modern writer has put it, "If God is dead, then man is dead, too."

Unfortunately, the mass of men do not realize this fact. They continue on as though nothing has changed. I am reminded of Nietzsche's story of the madman who in the early morning hours burst into the marketplace, lantern in hand, crying, "I seek God! I seek God!" Since many of those standing about did not believe in God, he provoked much laughter. "Did God get lost?" they taunted him. "Or is he hiding? Or maybe he has gone on a voyage or emigrated!" Thus they yelled and laughed. Then, writes Nietzsche, the madman turned in their midst and pierced them with his eyes.

> 'Whither is God?' he cried, 'I shall tell you. *We have killed him*—you and I. All of us are his murderers. But how have we done this? How were we able to drink up the sea? Who gave us the sponge to wipe away entire horizon? What did we do when we unchained this earth from its sun? Whither is it moving now? Away from all suns? Are we not plunging continually? Backward, sideward, forward, in all directions? Is there any up or down left? Are we not straying as through an infinite nothing? Do we not feel the breath of empty space? Has it not become colder? Is not night and more night coming on all the while? Must not lanterns be lit in the morning? Do we not hear anything yet of the noise of the gravediggers who are burying God? . . . God is dead. . . . And we have killed him. How shall we, the murderers of all murderers, comfort ourselves?'[10]

The crowd stared at the madman in silence and astonishment. At last he dashed his lantern to the ground. "I have come too early," he said. "This tremendous event is still on its way—it has not yet reached the ears of man." Men did not yet truly comprehend the consequences of what they had done in killing God. But Nietzsche predicted that someday men would realize the implications of their atheism; and this realization would usher in an age of nihilism—the destruction of all meaning and values in life. The end of Christianity means the advent of nihilism. This most gruesome of guests is standing already at the door.

10. Friedrich Nietzsche, "The Gay Science," p. 95.

"Our whole European culture is moving for some time now," wrote Nietzsche, "with a tortured tension that is growing from decade to decade, as toward a catastrophe: restlessly, violently, headlong, like a river that wants to reach the end, that no longer reflects, that is afraid to reflect."[11]

Most men still do not reflect on the consequences of atheism and so, like the crowd in the marketplace, go unknowingly on their way. But when we realize, as did Nietzsche, what atheism implies, then his question presses hard upon us: how *shall* we, the murderers of all murderers, comfort ourselves?

2.133 THE PRACTICAL IMPOSSIBILITY OF ATHEISM

About the only solution the atheist can offer is that we face the absurdity of life and live bravely. Bertrand Russell, for example, wrote that we must build our lives upon "the firm foundation of unyielding despair."[12] Only by recognizing that the world really is a terrible place can we successfully come to terms with life. Camus said that we should honestly recognize life's absurdity and then live in love for one another.

2.1331 *Impossible to live consistently and happily.* The fundamental problem with this solution, however, is that it is impossible for man to live consistently and happily within such a world view. If he lives consistently, he will not be happy; if he lives happily, it is only because he is not consistent. Francis Schaeffer has explained this point well. Modern man, says Schaeffer, resides in a two-story universe. In the lower story is the finite world without God; here life is absurd, as we have seen. In the upper story are meaning, value, and purpose. Now modern man lives in the lower story because he believes there is no God. But he cannot live happily in such an absurd world; therefore, he continually makes leaps of faith into the upper story to affirm meaning, value, and purpose, even though he has no right to, since he does not believe in God. Modern man is totally inconsistent when he makes this leap, because these values cannot exist without God, and man in his lower story does not have God.

2.1332 *Exposure of inconsistencies.* Now I will look at each of the three areas in which we saw life was absurd without God, to show how modern man cannot live consistently and happily in his atheism.

2.13321 *Meaning of life.* First, the area of meaning. We saw that without God, life has no meaning. Yet philosophers continue to live as though life does have meaning. For example, Jean-Paul Sartre argued that one may create meaning for his life by freely choosing to follow a certain course of action. Sartre himself chose Marxism.

11. Friedrich Nietzsche, "The Will to Power," pp. 130-31.
12. Bertrand Russell, "A Free Man's Worship," p. 107.

Now that is utterly inconsistent. It is inconsistent to say life is absurd and then to say one may create meaning for his life. If life is absurd, then man is trapped in the lower story. To try to create meaning in life represents a leap to the upper story. But Sartre has no basis for this leap. Without God, there can be no meaning in life. Sartre's program is actually an exercise in self-delusion. For the universe does not really acquire meaning just because I give it one. This is easy to see: for suppose I give the universe one meaning, and you give it another. Who is right? The answer, of course, is neither one. For the universe without God remains meaningless, no matter how we regard it. Sartre is really saying, "Let's *pretend* the universe has meaning." And this is just fooling ourselves. The point is this: if God does not exist, then life is meaningless; but man cannot live consistently and happily knowing that life is meaningless; so in order to be happy, he pretends life has meaning. But this is, of course, entirely inconsistent—for without God, man and the universe are without significance.

2.13322 *Value of life.* Turn now to the problem of value. Here is where the most blatant inconsistencies occur. First of all, atheistic humanists are totally inconsistent in pushing their values of love and brotherhood. Camus has been rightly criticized for inconsistently holding to the absurdity of life and the ethics of human love and brotherhood. The two are logically incompatible. Bertrand Russell, too, was inconsistent. For though he was an atheist, he was an outspoken social critic, denouncing war and restrictions on sexual freedom. Russell admitted that he could not live as though ethical values were simply a matter of personal taste, and that he therefore found his own views "incredible." "I do not know the solution," he confessed.[13] The point is that if there is no God, then absolute right and wrong cannot exist. As Dostoyevsky said, "All things are permitted."

But Dostoyevsky also showed that man cannot live this way. He cannot live as though it is perfectly all right for soldiers to slaughter innocent children. He cannot live as though it is all right for dictatorial regimes to follow a systematic program of physical torture of political prisoners. He cannot live as though it is all right for rulers like Idi Amin or Pol Pot to exterminate millions of their own countrymen. Everything in him cries out to say these acts are wrong—really wrong. But if there is no God, he cannot. So he makes a leap of faith and affirms values anyway. And when he does so, he reveals the inadequacy of a world without God.

The horror of a world devoid of value was brought home to me with new intensity recently as I viewed a BBC television documentary called "The Gathering." It concerned the reunion of survivors of the Holocaust in Jerusalem, where they rediscovered lost friendships and shared

13. Bertrand Russell, Letter to the *Observer,* 6 October 1957.

their experiences. Now, I had heard stories of the Holocaust before and had even visited Dachau and Buchenwald, and I thought I was beyond shocking by further tales of horror. But I found that I was not. Perhaps I had been made more sensitive by the recent birth of our beautiful baby girl, so that I applied the situations to her as they were related on the television. In any case, one woman prisoner, a nurse, told of how she was made the gynecologist at Auschwitz. She observed that pregnant women were grouped together by the soldiers under the direction of Dr. Mengele and housed in the same barracks. Some time passed, and she noted that she no longer saw any of these women. She made inquiries. "Where are the pregnant women who were housed in that barracks?" "Haven't you heard?" came the reply. *"Dr. Mengele used them for vivisection."*

Another woman told of how Mengele had bound up her breasts so that she could not suckle her infant. The doctor wanted to learn how long an infant could survive without nourishment. Desperately this poor woman tried to keep her baby alive by giving it pieces of bread soaked in coffee, but to no avail. Each day the baby lost weight, a fact that was eagerly monitored by Dr. Mengele. A nurse then came secretly to this woman and told her, "I have arranged a way for you to get out of here, but you cannot take your baby with you. I have brought a morphine injection that you can give to your child to end its life." When the woman protested, the nurse was insistent: "Look, your baby is going to die anyway. At least save yourself." And so *this mother took the life of her own baby.* Dr. Mengele was furious when he learned of it because he had lost his experimental specimen, and he searched among the dead to find the baby's discarded corpse so that he could have one last weighing.

My heart was torn by these stories. One rabbi who survived the camp summed it up well when he said that at Auschwitz it was as though there existed a world in which all the Ten Commandments were reversed. Mankind had never seen such a hell.

And yet, if God does not exist, then in a sense, our world *is* Auschwitz: there is no absolute right and wrong; *all things* are permitted. But no atheist, no agnostic, can live consistently with such a view. Nietzsche himself, who proclaimed the necessity of living "beyond good and evil," broke with his mentor Richard Wagner precisely over the issue of the composer's anti-Semitism and strident German nationalism. Similarly Sartre, writing in the aftermath of the Second World War, condemned anti-Semitism, declaring that a doctrine that leads to extermination is not merely an opinion or matter of personal taste, of equal value with its opposite.[14] In his important essay "Existentialism Is a

14. Jean Paul Sartre, "Portrait of the Antisemite," p. 330.

Humanism," Sartre struggles vainly to elude the contradiction between his denial of divinely pre-established values and his urgent desire to affirm the value of human persons. Like Russell, he could not live with the implications of his own denial of ethical absolutes.

A second problem is that if God does not exist and there is no immortality, then all the evil acts of men go unpunished and all the sacrifices of good men go unrewarded. But who can live with such a view? Richard Wurmbrand, who has been tortured for his faith in communist prisons, says,

> The cruelty of atheism is hard to believe when man has no faith in the reward of good or the punishment of evil. There is no reason to be human. There is no restraint from the depths of evil which is in man. The communist torturers often said, 'There is no God, no Hereafter, no punishment for evil. We can do what we wish.' I have heard one torturer even say, 'I thank God, in whom I don't believe, that I have lived in this hour when I can express all the evil in my heart.' He expressed it in unbelievable brutality and torture inflicted on prisoners.[15]

The English theologian Cardinal Newman once said that if he believed that all evils and injustices of life throughout history were not to be made right by God in the afterlife, "Why, I think I should go mad." Rightly so.

And the same applies to acts of self-sacrifice. A couple of years ago, a terrible mid-winter air disaster occurred in which a plane leaving the Washington, D.C., airport smashed into a bridge spanning the Potomac River, plunging its passengers into the icy waters. As the rescue helicopters came, attention was focused on one man who again and again pushed the dangling rope ladder to another passenger rather than be pulled to safety himself. Six times he passed the ladder by. When they came again, he was gone. He had freely given his life that others might live. The whole nation turned its eyes to this man in respect and admiration for the selfless and good act he had performed. And yet, if the atheist is right, that man was not noble—he did the stupidest thing possible. He should have gone for the ladder first, pushed others away if necessary in order to survive. But to die for others he did not even know, to give up all the brief existence he will ever have—what for? For the atheist there can be no reason. And yet he like the rest of us instinctively reacts with praise for this man's selfless action. Indeed, one will probably never find an atheist who lives consistently with his system. For a universe without moral accountability and devoid of value is unimagineably terrible.

          2.13323 *Purpose of life.* Finally, let us look at the

---

15. Richard Wurmbrand, *Tortured for Christ* p. 34.

problem of purpose in life. The only way most people who deny purpose in life live happily is either by making up some purpose, which amounts to self-delusion as we saw with Sartre, or by not carrying their view to its logical conclusions. Take the problem of death, for example. According to Ernst Bloch, the only way modern man lives in the face of death is by subconsciously borrowing the belief in immortality that his forefathers held to, even though he himself has no basis for this belief, since he does not believe in God. Bloch states that the belief that life ends in nothing is hardly, in his words, "sufficient to keep the head high and to work as if there were no end." By borrowing the remnants of a belief in immortality, writes Bloch, "modern man does not feel the chasm that unceasingly surrounds him and that will certainly engulf him at last. Through these remnants, he saves his sense of self-identity. Through them the impression arises that man is not perishing, but only that one day the world has the whim no longer to appear to him." Bloch concludes, "This quite shallow courage feasts on a borrowed credit card. It lives from earlier hopes and the support that they once had provided."[16] Modern man no longer has any right to that support, since he rejects God. But in order to live purposefully, he makes a leap of faith to affirm a reason for living.

We often find the same inconsistency among those who say that man and the universe came to exist for no reason or purpose, but just by chance. Unable to live in an impersonal universe in which everything is the product of blind chance, these persons begin to ascribe personality and motives to the physical processes themselves. It is a bizarre way of speaking and represents a leap from the lower to the upper story. For example, the brilliant Russian physicists Zeldovich and Novikov, in contemplating the properties of the universe, ask, Why did "Nature" choose to create this sort of universe instead of another? This language is quite incredible for Marxist scientists who are supposed to be atheists. "Nature" has obviously become a sort of God-substitute, filling the role and function of God. Francis Crick, halfway through his book *The Origin of the Genetic Code* begins to spell nature with a capital "N" and elsewhere speaks of natural selection as being "clever" and as "thinking" of what it will do. Fred Hoyle, the English astronomer, attributes to the universe itself the qualities of God. For Carl Sagan the "Cosmos," which he always spells with a capital letter, obviously fills the role of a God-substitute. Though all these men profess not to believe in God, they smuggle in a God-substitute through the back door because they cannot bear to live in a universe in which everything is the chance result of impersonal forces.

16. Ernst Bloch, *Das Prinzip Hoffnung*, 2:360-61.

And it is interesting to see many thinkers betray their views when they are pushed to their logical conclusions. For example, proponents of women's rights are raising a storm of protest over Freudian sexual psychology because it is chauvinistic and degrading to women. And some psychologists are knuckling under and revising their theories. Now that is totally inconsistent. If Freudian psychology is really true, then it does not matter if it is degrading to women. You cannot change the truth because you don't like what it leads to. But people cannot live consistently and happily in a world where other persons are devalued. Yet if God does not exist, then nobody has any value. Only if God exists can a person consistently support women's rights. For if God does not exist, then natural selection dictates that the male of the species is the dominant and aggressive one. Women would have no rights any more than a female goat or chicken. In nature whatever is, is right. But who can live with such a view? Apparently not even Freudian psychologists, who betray their theories when pushed to their logical conclusions.

Or take the sociological behaviorism of a man like B. F. Skinner. This view leads to the sort of society envisioned in George Orwell's *1984*, where the government controls and programs the thoughts of everybody. If Pavlov's dog can be made to salivate when a bell rings, so can a human being. If Skinner's theories are right, then there can be no objection to treating people like the rats in Skinner's rat-box as they run through their mazes, coaxed on by food and electric shocks. According to Skinner, all our actions are determined anyway. And if God does not exist, then no moral objection can be raised against this kind of programming, for man is not qualitatively different from a rat, since both are just matter plus time plus chance. But again, who can live with such a dehumanizing view?

Or finally, take the biological determinism of a man like Francis Crick. The logical conclusion is that man is like any other laboratory specimen. The world was horrified when it learned that at camps like Dachau the Nazis had used prisoners for medical experiments on living humans. But why not? If God does not exist, there can be no objection to using people as human guinea pigs. A memorial at Dachau says *Nie Wieder*—"Never Again"—but this sort of thing is still going on. It was recently revealed that in the United States several people had been injected, unknown to themselves, with a sterilization drug by medical researchers. Must we not protest that this is wrong—that man is more than an electro-chemical machine? The end of this view is population control in which the weak and unwanted are killed off to make room for the strong. But the only way we can consistently protest this view is if God exists. Only if God exists can there be purpose in life.

Do you see why it is that if God is dead, man is dead, too? Man cannot live consistently as though life were without meaning, value, or purpose. The atheistic world view is insufficient to maintain a happy and consistent life.

2.134 THE SUCCESS OF BIBLICAL CHRISTIANITY

But if atheism fails in this regard, what about biblical Christianity? According to the Christian world view, God does exist, and man's life does not end at the grave. In the resurrection body, man may enjoy eternal life and fellowship with God. Biblical Christianity therefore provides the two conditions necessary for a meaningful, valuable, and purposeful life for man: God and immortality. Because of this, man can live consistently and happily. Thus, biblical Christianity succeeds precisely where atheism breaks down. Atheism cannot provide a world view that enables man to live consistently and happily.

2.135 CONCLUSION

Now I want to make clear that I have not yet shown biblical Christianity to be true. But what I have done is clearly spell out the alternatives. If God does not exist, then life is futile. If the God of the Bible does exist, then life is meaningful. Only the second of these two alternatives enables man to live happily and consistently. Therefore, it seems to me that even if the evidence for these two options were absolutely equal, a rational man ought to choose biblical Christianity. It seems to me positively irrational to prefer death, futility, and destruction to life, meaningfulness, and happiness. As Pascal said, we have nothing to lose and infinity to gain.

2.14 PRACTICAL APPLICATION

The foregoing discussion makes clear the role I conceive cultural apologetics to play: it is not a whole apologetic but rather an introduction to positive argumentation. It serves to lay out in a dramatic way the alternatives facing the unbeliever, in order to create a felt need in him. When he realizes the predicament he is in, he will see why the gospel is so important to him; and many a non-Christian will be impelled by these considerations alone to give his life to Christ.

In sharing this material with an unbeliever, we need to push him to the logical conclusions of his position. If I am right, no atheist or agnostic really lives consistently with his world view. In some way he affirms meaning, value, or purpose without an adequate basis. It is our job to discover those areas and lovingly show him where those beliefs are groundless. We need not attack his values themselves—for these are probably largely correct—but we may agree with him concerning these, and then point out only that he lacks any foundation for those values, whereas the Christian has such a foundation. Thus, we need not make him defensive by a frontal attack on his personal values; rather we offer him a foundation for the values he already possesses.

In dealing with unbelievers, it is important also to ask ourselves exactly what part of our case his objections are meant to refute. Thus, if he says that values are merely social conventions pragmatically adopted to ensure mutual survival, what does this purport to refute? Not that life really is without value, for this the objection admits. Therefore, it would be a mistake to react by arguing that values are not social conventions but are grounded in God. Rather the objection is really aimed at the claim that one cannot live as though values do not exist; it holds one may live by social conventions alone. Seen in this light, however, the objection is entirely implausible, for we have argued precisely that man cannot live as though morality were merely a matter of social convention. Man believes certain acts to be genuinely wrong or right. Therefore, we ought to respond to the unbeliever on this score by saying, "You're exactly right: if God does not exist, then values are merely social conventions. But the point I'm trying to make is that it is impossible to live consistently and happily with such a world view." Push him on the holocaust or some issue of popular appeal like the arms race or child abuse. Bring it home to him personally, and if he is honest and you are not threatening, I think he will admit that he does hold to some absolutes. Thus, it is very important to analyze exactly what the unbeliever's objection actually attacks before we answer.

I believe that this mode of apologetics can be very effective in helping to bring people to Christ because it does not concern neutral matters but cuts to the heart of the unbeliever's own existential situation. I remember that once, when I was delivering a series of talks at the University of Birmingham in England, the audience the first night was very hostile and aggressive. The second night I spoke on the absurdity of life without God. This time the largely same audience was utterly subdued: the lions had turned to lambs, and now their questions were no longer attacking but sincere and searching. The remarkable transformation was due to the fact that the message had penetrated their intellectual façade and struck at the core of their existence. I would encourage you to employ this material in evangelistic dorm meetings and fraternity/sorority meetings, where you can compel people to really *think* about the desperate human predicament in which we all find ourselves.

3.0 DE DEO

3.1 THE EXISTENCE OF GOD

We have seen that only if God exists can there be hope for a solution to the human predicament. Therefore, the question of the existence of God is vital for modern man. Now most people today would probably agree that this question does have great existential significance, but at the same time deny that it is a question to which rational argumentation is relevant. Most people would say that it is impossible to "prove" the existence of God and that therefore if one is going to believe in God, he must "take it by faith" that God exists. I have heard many students say this as an excuse for not believing in God. "Nobody can prove that God exists and nobody can prove that He doesn't," they say with a smile, "So I just don't believe in Him." I have already argued that such a blithe attitude fails to appreciate the depth of modern man's existential predicament in a universe without God. The rational man ought to believe in God even when the evidence is equally balanced, rather than the reverse.

But is it in fact the case that there is no compelling evidence that a Supreme Being exists? This was not the opinion of the biblical writers. The Psalmist said, "The heavens are telling of the glory of God; and their expanse is declaring the work of His Hands" (Ps. 19:1), and the apostle Paul declared, "Since the creation of the world His invisible attributes, His eternal power and divine nature, have been clearly seen, being understood through what has been made, so that they [men] are without excuse" (Rom. 1:20). Nor can it be said that this evidence is so ambiguous as to admit of equally plausible counter-explanations—for then men would not be "without excuse." Thus, men are without excuse for not believing in God's existence, not only because of the internal testimony of the Holy Spirit, but also because of the external witness of nature. I think that there are good reasons for believing that God exists. Accordingly we shall in this *locus* examine various arguments for the existence of God.

This question has an extreme importance at the present juncture in history. Atheism and agnosticism are widespread in Europe and have become influential in the United States as well, particularly in the universities. Most philosophers would probably adhere to one of those world views. Humanism has become remarkably aggressive in the United States, with an almost evangelical fervor. I am not talking about low-brow atheists like Madeleine Murray O'Hare, but sophisticated and intelligent humanists who are opposing theism and Christianity with rational argument. Not only do they publish several magazines in the tradition of free thought, such as *The Humanist* or *The Sceptical Inquirer*, but they have founded a publishing house, appropriately called Prometheus Press, which disseminates anti-theistic literature. In perusing Prometheus Press's book displays at philosophical conventions, I observed a very clever strategy: they publish anti-theistic books, which serve to undermine belief in God, ethics books on sex and love, which aim to undercut absolutist morality, and parapsychological books, which afford a sort of mystical substitute for religion. I was saddened to see that they even publish a child's primer aimed at destroying or insulating the child against belief in God. How it tore my heart to watch one woman purchase that book to take home, no doubt, to her children! Their approach is rationally argumentative. As Christians, we simply cannot afford to stand by, exhorting people to believe in God, without dealing with the problem on the rational level.

Rational argumentation will not, of course, save people, but as J. G. Machen once observed, it provides an intellectual, cultural context in which the gospel cannot be dismissed simply as a logical absurdity and is therefore given an honest chance to be heard. There are signs that point in the direction of such a re-shaping of our intellectual milieu. For example, not too long ago *Time* carried a lengthy article on the renewed interest among philosophers in all the traditional arguments for God's existence. That is an encouraging sign that the question of God's existence will not be abandoned to the fideists and the atheists.

3.11 LITERATURE CITED OR RECOMMENDED

3.111 HISTORICAL BACKGROUND

Al-Ghāzālī. *Kitab al-Iqtisad fi'l-I'tiqad*. Cited in Beaurecueil, S. de. "Gazzali et S. Thomas d' Aqin: Essai sur la preuve de l'existence de

Dieu proposée dans l'Iqtisad et sa comparison avec les 'voies' Thomistes." *Bulletin de l'Institut Francais d' Archaeologie Orientale* 46 (1947): 199-238.

———. "The Jerusalem Tract." Translated and edited by A. L. Tibawi. *The Islamic Quarterly* 9 (1965): 95-122.

———. *Tahafut al-Falasifah [Incoherence of the Philosophers]*. Translated by Sabih Ahmad Kamali. Lahore, Pakistan: Pakistan Philosophical Congress, 1958.

Anselm. *Proslogion*. In *Anselm of Canterbury.* 4 vols. Edited and translated by Jaspar Hopkins and Herbert Richardson. London: SCM, 1974. See particularly 2, 3.

Aristotle. *The Works of Aristotle*. 12 vols. Edited by W. D. Ross. Oxford: Clarendon, 1908-1952.

Chroust, Anton-Hermann. "A Cosmological (Teleological) Proof for the Existence of God in Aristotle's *On Philosophy.*" In *Aristotle: New Light on His Lost Works*. London: Routledge & Kegan Paul, 1972. 2:159-74.

Craig, William Lane. *The Cosmological Argument from Plato to Leibniz*. New York: Barnes & Noble, 1980.

Leibniz, G. W. F. von. "Monadology." In *Leibniz Selections*. Edited by P. Wiener. New York: Scribner's, 1951. Pp. 533-52.

———. "On the Ultimate Origin of Things." In *Leibniz Selections*. Edited by P. Wiener. New York: Scribner's, 1951. Pp. 345-55.

———. "The Principles of Nature and of Grace, Based on Reason." In *Leibniz Selections*. Edited by P. Wiener. New York: Scribner's, 1951. Pp. 522-33.

———. *Theodicy: Essays on the Goodness of God, the Freedom of Man, and the Origin of Evil*. Translated by E. M. Huggard. London: Routledge & Kegan Paul, 1951.

Paley, William. *Natural Theology: Selections*. Edited with an introduction by F. Ferré. Indianapolis: Bobbs-Merrill, 1963.

Plato. *The Dialogues of Plato*. 4 vols. 4th ed., rev. Translated with introductions and analyses by B. Jowett. Oxford: Clarendon, 1953.

Stephen, Leslie. *History of English Thought in the Eighteenth Century.* 2 vols. 2d ed. London: Smith, Elder, 1881.

Thomas Aquinas. *On the Truth of the Catholic Faith*. Edited and translated by Anton C. Pegis et al. Notre Dame, Ind.: U. of Notre Dame, 1975. See particularly 1.13.

———. *Summa theologiae*. 60 vols. London: Eyre & Spottiswoode for Blackfriars, 1964. See particularly 1a.2, 3.

3.112 ASSESSMENT

Bore, Rick. "The Once and Future Universe." *National Geographic*, June 1983, pp. 704-49.

Craig, William Lane. *The Kalām Cosmological Argument.* New York: Barnes & Noble, 1979.

Davies, P. C. W. *The Physics of Time Asymetry.* London: Surrey U., 1974.

Dicke, R. H. et al. "Cosmic Black-Body Radiation." *Astrophysical Journal* 142 (1965): 414-19.

Dicus, Duane et al. "Effects of Proton Decay on the Cosmological Future." *Astrophysical Journal* 252 (1982): 1-9.

———. et al. "The Future of the Universe." *Scientific American,* March 1983, pp. 90-101.

Gamow, George. *One, Two, Three, . . . Infinity.* London: Macmillan, 1946.

Gott, J. Richard et al. "Will the Universe Expand Forever?" *Scientific American,* March 1976, pp. 62-79.

Gribbin, John. "Oscillating Universe Bounces Back." *Nature* 259 (1976): 15-16.

Hackett, Stuart. *The Resurrection of Theism.* 2d ed. Grand Rapids: Baker, 1982.

Hoyle, Fred. *Astronomy Today.* London: Heinemann, 1975.

Hume, David. *The Letters of David Hume.* 2 vols. Edited by J. Y. T. Greig. Oxford: Clarendon, 1932.

Iben, Jr., Icko. "Globular Cluster Stars." *Scientific American,* July 1970, pp. 26-39.

Jaki, Stanley L. *Science and Creation.* Edinburgh: Scottish Academic, 1974.

Jastrow, Robert. *God and the Astronomers.* New York: W. W. Norton, 1978.

Kenny, Anthony. *The Five Ways.* New York: Schocken, 1969.

King, Ivan. *The Universe Unfolding.* San Francisco: W. H. Freeman, 1976.

Mackie, J. L. *The Miracle of Theism.* Oxford: Clarendon, 1982.

Melott, Adrian L. "Massive Neutrinos in Large-Scale Gravitational Clustering." *Astrophysical Journal* 264 (1983): 59-86.

Narlikar, J. V. "Singularity and Matter Creation in Cosmological Models." *Nature: Physical Science* 242 (1973): 135-36.

Novikov, I. D., and Zeldovich, Ya. B. "Physical Processes Near Cosmological Singularities." *Annual Review of Astronomy and Astrophysics* 11 (1973): 387-410.

Plantinga, Alvin. *The Nature of Necessity.* Oxford: Clarendon, 1974. See particularly the section on the ontological argument.

Physics Today. "Do Neutrinos Oscillate from One Variety to Another?" July 1980, pp. 17-19.

Russell, Bertrand. *Our Knowledge of the External World.* 2d ed. New York: W. W. Norton, 1929.

Sandage, Allan, and Tammann, G. A. "Steps Toward the Hubble Constant. I-VIII." *Astrophysical Journal* 190 (1974): 525-38; 191 (1974): 603-21; 194 (1974): 223-43, 559-68; 196 (1975): 313-28; 197 (1975): 265-80; 210 (1976): 7-24; 256 (1982): 339-45.

Schlegel, Richard, "Time and Thermodynamics." Fraser, J. T. ed., *The Voice of Time.* London: Penguin, 1968.

Schramm, David N., and Steigman, Gary. "Relic Neutrinos and the Density of the Universe." *Astrophysical Journal* 243 (1981): 1-7.

Stecker, F. W., and Brown, R. W. "Astrophysical Tests for Radiative Decay of Neutrinos and Fundamental Physics Implications." *Astrophysical Journal* 257 (1982): 1-9.

Tennant, F. R. *Philosophical Theology.* 2 vols. Cambridge: Cambridge U., 1930. His teleological argument is in volume 2.

Tinsley, Beatrice. "From Big Bang to Eternity?" *Natural History Magazine*, October 1975, pp. 102-5.

Trefil, James S. "How the Universe Began." *Smithsonian*, May 1983, pp. 132-51.

———. "How the Universe Will End." *Smithsonian*, June 1983, pp. 72-83.

Vishniac, Ethan T. "Relativistic Collisionless Particles and the Evolution of Cosmological Perturbations." *Astrophysical Journal* 257 (1982): 456-72.

Wainright, William J. Review of *The Kalām Cosmological Argument*, by William Lane Craig. *Nous* 16 (1982): 328-34.

Webster, Adrian. "The Cosmic Background Radiation." *Scientific American*, August 1974, pp. 26-33.

3.12 HISTORICAL BACKGROUND

Ever since Plato, men have tried to provide a rational basis for belief in God. In this section, we shall briefly survey some of the traditional theistic arguments as developed by various thinkers.

3.121 ONTOLOGICAL ARGUMENT

The ontological argument attempts to prove from the very concept of God that God exists: if God is conceivable, then He must actually exist. This argument was formulated by Anselm and defended by Scotus, Descartes, Spinoza, Leibniz, and, in modern times, Norman Malcolm, Charles Hartshorne, and Alvin Plantinga, among others. We shall examine the Anselmian argument.

3.1211 *Anselm of Canterbury.* Anselm (1033-1109) wanted to find a single argument that would prove not only that God exists, but also that He has all the superlative attributes Christian doctrine ascribes to Him. Having almost given up the project, Anselm landed upon the following reasoning:[1] God is the greatest conceivable being. This is true by definition, for if we could conceive of something greater than God, then *that* would be God. So nothing greater than God can be conceived. It is greater to exist in reality than merely in the mind. Anselm gives the example of a painting. Which is greater, the artist's idea of the painting or the painting itself as it really exists? Obviously the latter; for the painting itself exists not only in the artist's mind, but in reality as well. Similarly, if God existed only in the mind, then something greater than Him could be conceived, namely, His existence not only in the mind, but in reality as well. But God is the greatest conceivable being. Hence, He must not exist merely in the mind, but in reality as well. Therefore, God exists.

Another way of putting this, says Anselm, is the following: a being whose non-existence is inconceivable is greater than a being whose non-existence is conceivable. But God is the greatest conceivable being. Therefore, God's non-existence must be inconceivable. There is no contradiction involved in this notion. Therefore, God must exist.

This deceptively simple argument is still hotly debated today.

3.122 COSMOLOGICAL ARGUMENT

In contrast to the ontological argument, the cosmological argument assumes that something exists and argues from the existence of that thing to the existence of a First Cause or a Sufficient Reason of the cosmos. This argument has its roots in Plato and Aristotle and was developed by medieval Islamic, Jewish, and Christian thinkers. It has been defended by such great minds as Plato, Aristotle, ibn Sīna, al-Ghāzālī, ibn Rushd, Maimonides, Anselm, Aquinas, Scotus, Descartes, Spinoza, Berkeley, Locke, and Leibniz. The cosmological argument is really a family of different proofs, which can be conveniently grouped under three main types.

3.1221 *Al-Ghāzālī.* The *kalām* cosmological argument originated in the attempts of Christian thinkers to rebut Aristotle's doctrine of the eternity of the universe and was developed by medieval Islamic theologians into an argument for the existence of God. Let us look at the formulation of this argument by al-Ghāzālī (1058-1111). He reasons, "Every being which begins has a cause for its beginning; now the world is a being which begins; therefore, it possesses a cause for its beginning."[2] In support of the first premise, that every being that begins has a cause for its beginning, Ghāzālī reasons: anything that begins to exist does so at a certain moment of time. But since, prior to the thing's existence, all moments are alike, there must be some cause that

---

1. Anselm *Proslogion* 2, 3.
2. Al-Ghāzālī, *Kitab al-Iqtisad fi'l-I'tiqad*, p. 203.

determines that the thing comes to exist at that moment rather than earlier or later. Thus, anything that comes to exist must have a cause.

The second premise is that the world, or the universe, began to exist. In support of this premise Ghāzālī argues that it is impossible that there should be an infinite regress of events in time, that is to say, that the series of past events should be beginningless. He gives several reasons for this conclusion. For one thing, the series of past events comes to an end in the present—but the infinite cannot come to an end. It might be pointed out that even though the series of events has one end in the present, it can still be infinite in the other direction because it has no beginning. But Ghāzālī's point may be that if the series is infinite going back into the past, then how could the present moment arrive? For it is impossible to cross the infinite to get to today. So today could never arrive, which is absurd, for here we are! Second, if the number of past events were infinite, that would lead to infinites of different sizes. For suppose Jupiter completes an orbit once every twelve years and Saturn once every thirty years and the sphere of the stars once every thirty-six thousand years. If the universe is eternal, then each of these bodies has completed an infinite number of orbits, and yet one will have completed twice as many or thousands of times as many orbits as another, which is absurd. Finally, if we take the orbits completed by just one of these planets, we may ask, is the number of orbits it has completed odd or even? It would *have* to be one or the other, and yet it is absurd to say the infinite is odd or even. For these reasons, the universe must have had a beginning.

Therefore, the universe must have a cause of its beginning, which Ghāzālī identifies with God, the Eternal.

3.1222 *Thomas Aquinas.* The Thomist cosmological argument is based on the impossibility of an infinite regress of simultaneously operating causes. It seeks a Cause that is First, not in the temporal sense, but in the sense of rank or source. Although Thomas Aquinas (1225-74) did not originate this line of reasoning, he is famous for his clear summary of it in his Five Ways of proving that God exists.[3] We shall look at his first three ways, which are different versions of the argument for a First Cause.

The First Way is the proof for an Unmoved Mover based on motion. We see in the world that things are in motion. But anything that is in motion is being moved by something else. For a thing that has the potential to move cannot actualize its own potential; some other thing must cause it to move. But this other thing is also being moved by something else, and that is also being moved by something else, and so on. Now this series of things being moved by other things cannot go on

---

3. Thomas Aquinas *Summa Theologiae* 1a.2, 3; cf. idem *Summa contra gentiles* 1.13.

to infinity. For in such a series, the intermediate causes have no power of their own but are mere instruments of a first cause. It is important to keep in mind that Aquinas is thinking here of causes that all act simultaneously, like the gears of a machine, not successively, like falling dominoes. So if you take away the first cause, all you have left are the powerless instrumental causes. It does not matter if you have an infinity of such causes; they still could not cause anything. Aquinas contends, in effect, that a watch could not run without a spring even if it had an infinite number of gears, or that a train could not move without an engine even if it had an infinite number of box cars. There must be a first cause of motion in every causal series. For all self-moving things—including humans, animals, and plants—this would be the individual soul, which is an unmoved mover. But souls themselves come to be and pass away and thus cannot account for the eternal motion of the heavenly spheres. In order to account for this cosmic motion, we must postulate an absolutely Unmoved Mover, the First Cause of all motion, and this is God.

The Second Way attempts to prove the existence of a First Cause of existence based on causation in the world. We observe that causes are ordered in series. Now nothing can be self-caused, because then it would have to bestow existence on itself, which is impossible. Everything that is caused is therefore caused by something else. Aquinas thinks here of the same sort of simultaneous causal series as he did in the First Way, except that here the causes are of existence, not motion. The existence of any object depends on a whole array of contemporary causes, of which each in turn depends on other causes, and so forth. But such a causal series cannot go on to infinity, for the same reason I explained above. Therefore, there must be a First Cause of the existence of everything else, which is simply uncaused; and this everyone calls "God."

The Third Way is the proof for an Absolutely Necessary Being based on the existence of possible beings. We see in the world beings whose existence is not necessary but only possible. That is to say, these beings do not have to exist, for we see them come to be and pass away. If they were necessary, they would always exist. But all beings cannot be merely possible beings, for if everything were merely possible, then at some point in time everything would cease to exist. Aquinas here presupposes the past eternity of the world and appears to reason that in infinite time all possibilities would be realized. Hence, if every being, including matter itself, were only a possible being, then it is possible that nothing would exist. Thus, given infinite past time, this possibility would be realized and nothing would exist. But then nothing would now exist either, since out of nothing, nothing comes. Since this is obviously absurd, not all beings must be possible beings. Some being or beings must be necessary. In fact, Aquinas believed that there were many necessary beings: the heavenly bodies, angels, even matter itself. Now, he continues, where do these necessary beings get their necessity—from themselves or from another? Thomas here distinguishes between a thing's essence and existence. A thing's essence is its nature, that set of properties which it must possess in order to be what it is. For example, the essence of man is "rational animal." If anything lacked either of these properties, it would not be a man. A thing's existence, on the other hand, is its being. Now if a being is not necessary in itself, this means that its essence is distinct from its existence. It does not belong to its nature to exist. For example, I could think of the nature of an angel without ever knowing whether or not an angel actually exists. Its essence is distinct from its existence. Hence, if such a being is to exist, something else must conjoin to its essence an act of existence. Then it would exist. But there cannot be an infinite regress of necessary beings that get their existence from another. (The reasoning is the same as that in the First Way, against an infinite regress.) So there must be a First Being, which is absolutely necessary in itself. In this Being, essence and existence are not distinct; in some mysterious way its nature *is* existence. Hence, according to Aquinas, God is Being itself subsisting *(ipsum esse subsistens)*. God is pure Being and is the source of being to everything else, whose essences do not involve their existing.

3.12.2.3 *G. W. F. Leibniz.* The Leibnizian cosmological argument was developed by the German mathematician and philosopher G. W. F. Leibniz (1646-1716) and is often confused with the Thomist cosmological argument. But Leibniz does not argue for the existence of an Uncaused Cause, but for the existence of a Sufficient Reason for the universe.[4] The difference will become clear as we proceed.

"The first question which should rightly be asked," wrote Leibniz, "will be, *Why is there something rather than nothing?*" That is, why does anything at all exist? There must be an answer to this question, because "*nothing happens without a sufficient reason.*"[5] Leibniz's famous Principle of Sufficient Reason holds that there must be a reason or rational explanation for the existence of one state of affairs rather than another. Why does the universe exist? The reason cannot be found in any single thing in the universe, for these are contingent themselves and do not have to exist. Nor is the reason to be found in the whole aggregate of such things, for the world is just the collection of these contingent beings and is therefore itself contingent. Nor can the reason be found in the prior causes of things, for these are just past states of the universe and do not explain why there are any such states, any

---

4. G. W. F. von Leibniz, "On the Ultimate Origin of Things," pp. 527-28; idem, "Monadology," p. 540; idem, *Theodicy,* p. 127.
5. Leibniz, "Nature and Grace," p. 527.

universe, at all. Leibniz asks us to imagine that a series of geometry books has been copied from eternity; such an infinite regress would still not explain why such books exist at all. But the same is true with regard to past states of the world: even should these be infinite, there is no sufficient reason for the existence of an eternal universe. Therefore, the reason for the universe's existence must be found outside the universe, in a being whose sufficient reason is self-contained; it is its own sufficient reason for existing and is the reason the universe exists as well. This Sufficient Reason of all things is God, whose own existence is to be explained only by reference to Himself. That is to say, God is a metaphysically necessary being.

This proof is clearly different from the Thomist argument: there is no reference to the distinction between essence and existence, nor to the argument against an infinite causal regress. Indeed, Leibniz is not seeking a cause at all but an explanation for the world. Thomas concludes to an Uncaused Cause, but Leibniz to a Self-Explanatory Being. Many philosophers have confused these and come up with God as a Self-Caused Being, which neither Aquinas nor Leibniz defended.

Thus, there is a variety of cosmological arguments, which need to be kept distinct, for arguments against one version may prove inapplicable to another.

3.123 TELEOLOGICAL ARGUMENT

Perhaps the oldest and most popular of all the arguments for the existence of God is the teleological argument. It is the famous argument from design, inferring an intelligent designer of the universe just as we infer an intelligent designer for any product in which we discern evidence of purposeful adaptation of means to some end *(telos)*.

   3.1231 *Plato and Aristotle.* The ancient Greek philosophers were impressed with the order that pervades the cosmos, and many of them ascribed that order to the work of an intelligent mind who fashioned the universe. The heavens in constant revolution across the sky were especially awesome to the ancients. Plato's Academy lavished extensive time and thought on the study of astronomy because, Plato believed, it was the science that would awaken man to his divine destiny. According to Plato, there are two things that "lead men to believe in the Gods": the argument based on the soul, and the argument "from the order of the motion of the stars, and of all things under the dominion of the mind which ordered the universe."[6] What a lovely statement of the divine design evident throughout the universe! Plato employed both of these arguments to refute atheism and concluded that there must be a "best soul" who is the "maker and father of all," the

6. Plato *Laws* 12.966e.

"King," who ordered the primordial chaos into the rational cosmos we observe today.[7]

An even more magnificent statement of divine teleology is to be found in a fragment from a lost work of Aristotle's entitled *On Philosophy.* Aristotle, too, was struck with wonder by the majestic sweep of the glittering host across the night sky of ancient Greece. Philosophy, he said, begins with this sense of wonder about the world:

> For it is owing to their wonder that men both now begin and at first began to philosophize; they wondered originally at the obvious difficulties, then advanced little by little and stated difficulties about greater matters, e.g. about the phenomena of the moon and those of the sun, and about the stars and about the genesis of the universe.[8]

Anyone who has himself studied the heavens must lend a sympathetic ear to these men of antiquity who gazed up into the night sky, as yet undimmed by pollution and the glare of city lights, and watched the slow but irresistable turn of the cosmos, replete with its planets, stars, and familiar constellations, across their view and wondered—what is the cause of all this? Aristotle concluded that the cause was divine intelligence. He imagined the impact that the sight of the world would have on a race of men who had lived underground and never beheld the sky:

> When thus they would suddenly gain sight of the earth, seas, and the sky; when they should come to know the grandeur of the clouds and the might of the winds; when they should behold the sun and should learn its grandeur and beauty as well as its power to cause the day by shedding light over the sky; and again, when the night had darkened the lands and they should behold the whole of the sky spangled and adorned with stars; and when they should see the changing lights of the moon as it waxes and wanes, and the risings and settings of all these celestial bodies, their courses fixed and changeless throughout all eternity—when they should behold all these things, most certainly they would have judged both that there exist gods and that all these marvellous works are the handiwork of the gods.[9]

In his *Metaphysics* Aristotle proceeded to argue that there must be a First Unmoved Mover which is God, a living, intelligent, incorporeal, eternal, and most good being who is the source of order in the cosmos. Hence, from earliest times men, wholly removed from the biblical revelation, have concluded to the existence of divine mind on the basis of design in the universe.

7. Plato *Laws* 10.893b-899c; idem *Timaeus.*
8. Aristotle *Metaphysica* Λ.1.982610-15.
9. Aristotle *On Philosophy.*

3.1232 *Thomas Aquinas.* We have already seen that Thomas Aquinas in his first three Ways argues for the existence of God via the cosmological argument. His Fifth Way, however, represents the teleological argument. He notes that we observe in nature that all things operate toward some end, even when those things lack consciousness. For their operation hardly ever varies and practically always turns out well, which shows that they really do tend toward a goal and do not hit upon it merely by accident. Thomas is here expressing the conviction of Aristotelian physics that everything has not only a productive cause but also a final cause, or goal toward which it is drawn. To use an example of our own, poppy seeds always grow into poppies and acorns into oaks. Now nothing, Aquinas reasons, that lacks consciousness tends toward a goal, unless it is under the direction of someone with consciousness and intelligence. For example, the arrow does not tend toward the bull's eye unless it is aimed by the archer. Therefore, everything in nature must be directed toward its goal by someone with intelligence, and this we call "God."

3.1233 *William Paley.* Undoubtedly, the high point in the development of the teleological argument came with William Paley's brilliant formulation in his *Natural Theology* of 1804. Paley combed the sciences of his time for evidences of design in nature and produced a staggering catalogue of such evidences, based, for example, on the order evident in bones, muscles, blood vessels, comparative anatomy, and particular organs throughout the animal and plant kingdoms. So conclusive was Paley's evidence that Leslie Stephen in his *History of English Thought in Eighteenth Century* wryly remarked that "if there were no hidden flaw in the reasoning, it would be impossible to understand, not only how any should resist, but how anyone should ever have overlooked the demonstration."[10] Although most philosophers— who have undoubtedly never read Paley—believe that his sort of argument was dealt a crushing and fatal blow by David Hume's critique of the teleological argument, Paley's argument, which was written nearly thirty years after the publication of Hume's critique, is in fact not vulnerable to most of Hume's objections, as Frederick Ferré has pointed out.[11] Paley opens with a statement of the famous "watch-maker argument":

> In crossing a heath, suppose I pitched my foot against a stone, and were asked how the stone came to be there; I might possibly answer, that, for anything I knew to the contrary, it had lain there forever: nor would it perhaps be very easy to show the absurdity of this answer. But suppose I had found a *watch* upon the ground, and it should be inquired how the

10. Leslie Stephen, *History of English Thought in the Eighteenth Century,* 1:408.
11. Frederick Ferré, Introduction to *Natural Theology: Selections,* by William Paley, pp. xi-xxxii.

watch happened to be in that place; I should hardly think of the answer which I had before given, that, for anything I knew, the watch might have always been there. Yet why should not this answer serve for the watch as well as for the stone? Why is it not as admissible in the second case, as in the first? For this reason, and for no other, viz. that, when we come to inspect the watch, we perceive (what we could not discover in the stone) that its several parts are framed and put together for a purpose, e.g. that they are so formed and adjusted as to produce motion, and that motion so regulated as to point out the hour of the day; that if the different parts had been differently shaped from what they are, of a different size from what they are, or placed after any other manner, or in any other order, than that in which they are placed, either no motion at all would have been carried on in the machine, or none which would have answered the use that is now served by it. To reckon up a few of the plainest of these parts, and of their offices, all tending to one result: We see a cylindrical box containing a coiled elastic spring, which, by its endeavor to relax itself, turns round the box. We next observe a flexible chain (artificially wrought for the sake of flexure) communicating the action of the spring from the box to the fusee. We then find a series of wheels, the teeth of which catch in, and apply to each other, conducting the motion from the fusee to the balance, and from the balance to the pointer; and at the same time, by the size and shape of those wheels, so regulating that motion, as to terminate in causing an index, by an equable and measured progression, to pass over a given space in a given time. We take notice that the wheels are made of brass in order to keep them from rust; the springs of steel, no other metal being so elastic; that over the face of the watch there is placed a glass, a material employed in no other part of the work; but in the room of which, if there had been any other than a transparent substance, the hour could not be seen without opening the case. This mechanism being observed (it requires indeed an examination of the instrument, and perhaps some previous knowledge of the subject, to perceive and understand it; but being once, as we have said, observed and understood,) the inference, we think, is inevitable; that the watch must have had a maker; that there must have existed, at sometime, and at some place or other, an artificer or artificers, who formed it for the purpose which we find it actually to answer; who comprehended its construction, and designed its use.[12]

This conclusion, Paley continues, would not be weakened if I had never actually seen a watch being made nor knew how to make one. For we recognize the remains of ancient art as the products of intelligent design without having even seen such things made, and we know the products of modern manufacture are the result of intelligence even though we may have no inkling how they are produced. Nor would our conclusion be invalidated if the watch sometimes went wrong. The purpose of the mechanism would be evident even if the machine did

12. Paley, *Natural Theology*, pp. 3-4.

not function perfectly. Nor would the argument become uncertain if we were to discover some parts in the mechanism that did not seem to have any purpose, for this would not negate the purposeful design in the other parts. Nor would anyone in his right mind think that the existence of the watch was accounted for by the consideration that it was one out of many possible configurations of matter and that some possible configuration had to exist in the place where the watch was found. Nor would it help to say that there exists in things a principle of order, which yielded the watch. For one never knows a watch to be so formed, and the notion of such a principle of order that is not intelligent seems to have little meaning. Nor is it enough to say the watch was produced from another watch before it and that one from yet a prior watch, and so forth to infinity. For the design is still unaccounted for. Each machine in the infinite series evidences the same design, and it is irrelevant whether one has ten, a thousand, or an infinite number of such machines—a designer is still needed.

Now the point of the analogy of the watch is this: just as we infer a watchmaker as the designer of the watch, so ought we to infer an intelligent designer of the universe:

> For every indication of contrivance, every manifestation of design, which existed in the watch, exists in the works of nature, of being greater and more, and that in a degree which exceeds all computation. I mean, that the contrivances of nature surpass the contrivances of art, in the complexity, subtilty, and curiosity of the mechanism; and still more, if possible, do they go beyond them in number and variety: yet, in a multitude of cases, are not less evidently contrivances, not less evidently accommodated to their end, or suited to their office, than are the most perfect products of human ingenuity.[13]

Here Paley begins his cataloging of the contrivances of nature bespeaking divine design. He concludes that an intelligent designer of the universe exists, and closes with a discussion of some of the attributes of this cosmic architect.

3.124 MORAL ARGUMENT

The moral argument for the existence of God argues for the existence of a Being that is the embodiment of the ultimate Good, which is the source of the objective moral values we experience in the world. The reasoning at the heart of the moral argument goes all the way back to Plato, who argued that things have goodness insofar as they stand in some relation to the Good, which subsists in itself. With the advent of Christian theism, the Good became identified with God Himself.

13. Ibid., p. 13.

3.1241 *Thomas Aquinas.* Aquinas's Fourth Way is a type of moral argument. He observes that we find in the world a gradation of values: some things are more good, more true, more noble, and so forth, than other things. Such comparative terms describe the varying degrees to which things approach a superlative standard: the most good, most true, and so forth. There must therefore exist something that is the best and truest and noblest thing of all. Aquinas believed that whatever possesses a property more fully than anything else is the cause of that property in other things. Hence, there is some being that is the cause of the existence, goodness, and any other perfection of finite beings, and this being we call "God."

3.1242 *William Sorley.* Perhaps the most sophisticated development of the moral argument is that of William Sorley (1855-1935), professor of moral philosophy at Cambridge University until 1933, in his Gifford Lectures, *Moral Values and the Idea of God* (1918). Sorley believed that ethics provides the key to metaphysics, and he argues that God as the ground of the natural and moral orders best provides for a rational, unified view of reality. He begins by arguing that reality is characterized by an objective moral order, which is as real and independent of our recognition of it as the natural order of things is. He admits that in a sense one cannot prove that objective values exist but insists that in this same sense one cannot prove that the external world exists either! Thus, the moral order and the natural order are on equal footing. On the same ground that we assume the reality of the world of objects, we assume the reality of the moral order of objective value. Now obviously Sorely does not mean we perceive value with our five senses, in the way we do physical objects. We discern value in some non-empirical way, and just as we are rational to assume that some objective natural order lies behind our sense perceptions, so we are rational to assume that some objective moral order lies behind our perceptions of value. Our perceptions of both value and physical objects are simply givens of experience.

Our perception of a realm of objective value does not mean for Sorley that everyone has an innate and accurate knowledge of specific moral values. In his *The Ethics of Naturalism* (1885) he had refuted the historical, evolutionary approach to ethics, and now he turns to refute psychological, sociological explanations of value. The fundamental error of all these approaches is that they confuse the subjective origin of our moral judgments and the objective value to which the judgments refer. Just because the origin of our moral judgments can be historically or sociologically explained does not mean there are no objective, corresponding values in reality. In fact, Sorely argues that our moral judgments are not infallible and that we do not know the content of the moral ideal that we ever seek to approach.

Where, then, does objective moral value reside? Sorley answers: In persons. The only beings that are bearers of intrinsic moral value are persons; non-personal things have merely instrumental value in relation to persons. Only persons have intrinsic value, because meaningful moral behavior requires purpose and will. The foregoing analysis of moral value provides the ground for Sorley's moral argument for God. We have seen that the natural order and the moral order are both part of reality. Therefore, the question is: what world-view can combine these two orders into the most coherent explanatory form? According to Sorley, there are three competing world-views: theism, pluralism, and monism.

Turning first to theism, Sorley believes that the most serious objection to this world view is the problem of evil. Basically, the problem here is that the natural order and the moral order seem to be working at cross-purposes with each other: the natural order often fails to realize the good that ought to be realized. Sorley, however, thinks this objection is answerable. The objection, he says, tends to confuse moral purpose with personal happiness; because personal happiness is often not realized, it is assumed that moral purpose has been frustrated. But Sorley points out that the realization of moral purpose cannot be equated with the realization of personal happiness. In other words, just because we are not happy about some situation does not imply that the situation ought not to be. In general Sorley argues that suffering and evil are possible in a theistic world view if finite minds are gradually recognizing moral ends that they are free to accept or reject.

Indeed, Sorley argues that the theistic account of the natural and moral orders is the superior world view. For we have seen that moral values or ideals are an objective part of reality and that they reside in persons. The problem is that no finite person has ever fully realized all moral value. The moral ideal is nowhere fully actualized in the finite world, though it is presently valid, that is, binding and obligatory, for the finite world. But how can something be objective and valid if it does not exist? Physical laws, by contrast, are fully realized in the world. So no further explanation of their validity is required. Therefore if the moral ideal is to be valid for reality, it must be fully realized in an existent that is both personal and eternal, that is, God.

Sorley then proceeds to refute the other two alternatives, pluralism and monism. Against pluralism, which holds that the moral ideal resides in a plurality of finite beings, Sorley argues that the moral values are eternally valid and so cannot reside in temporally finite persons. Against monism, which holds that the universe is constituted by a non-personal reality of which minds are mere modes, Sorely maintains that it leaves no room for purposeful endeavor or real freedom, because "is" and "ought to be" are identical and everything simply is as it is.

Hence, although not a rigid demonstration, this reasoning, concludes Sorely, shows that theism offers the most reasonable and unified explanation of reality. The moral order is the order of an infinite, eternal Mind who is the architect of nature and whose moral purpose man and the universe are slowly fulfilling.

3.13 ASSESSMENT

All of these arguments have been criticized and defended by modern philosophers. The ontological argument was rejected by Immanuel Kant, and many thinkers have followed him in this regard. On the other hand, Alvin Plantinga defends the argument against Kant's criticisms via the notion of possible worlds. Plantinga contends that God is by definition a being that exists supremely, with maximum greatness, in all possible worlds; and since the actual world is a possible world, God must actually exist. So if God's existence is possible, He must exist.

The teleological argument is widely regarded as having been refuted by Hume, with the Darwinian theory of evolution supplying the nails in the coffin. But F. R. Tennant and Stuart Hackett, in full cognizance of Hume's objections, have argued that on the very assumption of evolution, there is a cosmic teleology that points to a divine designer. Moreover, the gradualism of classical evolutionary theory, based upon the mechanism of minor mutations and natural selection, has been radically called into question by the proponents of "punctuated equilibrium," who argue that the transitional forms are absent from the fossil record because they never existed. Rather, they say, evolution occurs by leaps from one form to another. Insofar as this new theory fails to account for these leaps and must appeal to "hopeful monsters"—massive mutations that produce new forms without transitional forms—the hypothesis of design becomes more plausible. On a broader scope, current science is wrestling with the so-called "anthropic principle," according to which the entire universe and its history are fine-tuned with incredible precision to produce man on earth. These cosmic considerations have also breathed new life into the argument from design.

For my part, however, I find the *kalām* cosmological argument for a temporal first cause of the universe to be the most plausible argument for God's existence. I have defended this argument in two books, *The Kalām Cosmological Argument* and *The Existence of God and the Beginning of the Universe*. Let me explain and supplement what I say there. The argument is basically this: both philosophical reasoning and scientific evidence show that the universe began to exist. Anything that begins to exist must have a cause that brings it into being. So the universe must have a cause. The argument may be formulated in three simple steps:

- Whatever begins to exist has a cause.

- The universe began to exist.

- Therefore, the universe has a cause.

The logic of the argument is valid and very simple: it is the same as when we reason, "All men are mortal; Socrates is a man; therefore, Socrates is mortal." So the question is, are there good reasons to believe that each of the steps is true? I think there are.

3.131 WHATEVER BEGINS TO EXIST HAS A CAUSE

The first step is so intuitively obvious that I think scarcely anyone could sincerely believe it to be false. I therefore think it somewhat unwise to argue in favor of it, for any proof of the principle is likely to be less obvious than the principle itself. And as Aristotle remarked, one ought not to try to prove the obvious via the less obvious. The old axiom that "out of nothing, nothing comes" remains as obvious today as ever. In a sense, I find it an attractive feature of this argument that it allows the atheist a way of escape: he can always deny the first premise and assert that the universe sprang into existence uncaused out of nothing. For he thereby exposes himself as a man interested only in an academic refutation of the argument and not in really discovering the truth about the universe.

The late J. L. Mackie appears to have been such a man. In refuting the *kalām* cosmological argument, he turns his main guns on this first step: "there is *a priori* no good reason why a sheer origination of things, not determined by anything, should be unacceptable, whereas the existence of a god [sic] with the power to create something out of nothing is acceptable."[14] Indeed, *creatio ex nihilo* raises problems: (i) If God began to exist at a point in time, then this is as great a puzzle as the beginning of the universe. (ii) Or if God existed for infinite time, then the same arguments would apply to His existence as would apply to the infinite duration of the universe. (iii) If it be said that God is timeless, then this, says Mackie, is a complete mystery.

Now notice that Mackie never *refutes* the principle that whatever begins to exist has a cause. Rather, he simply demands what good reason there is *a priori* to accept it. He writes, "As Hume pointed out, we can certainly conceive an uncaused beginning-to-be of an object; if what we can thus conceive is nevertheless in some way impossible, this still requires to be shown."[15] But, as many philosophers have pointed out, Hume's argument in no way makes it plausible to think that something could really come into being without a cause. Just because I can

14. J. L. Mackie, *The Miracle of Theism*, p. 94.
15. Ibid., p. 89.

imagine an object, say a horse, coming into existence from nothing, that in no way proves that a horse really could come into existence that way. The defender of the *kalām* argument is claiming that it is *really* impossible for something to come uncaused from nothing. Does Mackie sincerely believe that things can pop into existence uncaused, out of nothing? Does anyone in his right mind really believe that, say, a raging tiger could suddenly come into existence uncaused, out of nothing, in this room right now? The same applies to the universe: if there were originally absolute nothingness—no God, no space, no time—how could the universe possibly come to exist?

In fact, Mackie's appeal to Hume at this point is counterproductive. For Hume himself clearly believed in the causal principle. In 1754 he wrote to John Stewart, "But allow me to tell you that I never asserted so absurd a Proposition as *that anything might arise without a cause:* I only maintain'd, that our Certainty of the Falsehood of that Proposition proceeded neither from Intuition nor Demonstration, but from another source."[16] Even Mackie confesses, "Still this [causal] principle has some plausibility, in that it is constantly confirmed in our experience (and also used, reasonably, in interpreting our experience.)"[17] So why not accept the truth of the causal principle as plausible and reasonable—at the very least more so than its denial?

Because, Mackie thinks, in this particular case the theism implied by affirming the principle is even more unintelligible than the denial of the principle. But is this really the case? Certainly the proponent of the *kalām* argument would not hold (i) that God began to exist or (ii) that God has existed for infinite time. But what is wrong with (iii), that God is, prior to creation, timeless? I would argue that God exists timelessly prior to creation and in time subsequent to creation. This may be "mysterious" in the sense of "wonderful" or "awe-inspiring," but it is not, so far as I can see, unintelligible; and Mackie gives us no reason to think that it is. It seems to me, therefore, that Mackie is entirely unjustified in rejecting the first step of the argument as not intuitively obvious, implausible, and unreasonable.

3.132 THE UNIVERSE BEGAN TO EXIST

If we agree that whatever begins to exist has a cause, what evidence is there to support the crucial second step in the argument, that the universe began to exist? I think that this step is supported by both philosophical arguments and scientific confirmation of those arguments.

3.1321 *Philosophical arguments.*

3.13211 *Argument from the impossibility of an actually infinite number of things.* An actually infinite number of things

16. David Hume, *The Letters of David Hume,* 1:187.
17. Mackie, *Theism,* p. 89.

cannot exist, because this would involve all sorts of absurdities, which I shall illustrate in a moment. And if the universe never had a beginning, then the series of all past events is actually infinite. That is to say, an actually infinite number of past events exists. Because an actually infinite number of things cannot exist, then an actually infinite number of past events cannot exist. The number of past events is finite; therefore the series of past events had a beginning. Since the history of the universe is identical to the series of all past events, the universe must have begun to exist. This argument can also be formulated in three steps:

- An actually infinite number of things cannot exist.

- A beginningless series of events in time entails an actually infinite number of things.

- Therefore, a beginningless series of events in time cannot exist.

Let us examine each step together.

3.132111 *An actually infinite number of things cannot exist.* In order to understand this first step, we need to understand what an actual infinite is. There is a difference between a potential infinite and an actual infinite. A potential infinite is a collection that is increasing toward infinity as a limit but never gets there. Such a collection is really indefinite, not infinite. An actual infinite is a collection in which the number of members really is infinite. The collection is not growing toward infinity; it *is* infinite, it is "complete." This sort of infinity is used in set theory to designate sets that have an infinite number of members, such as $\{1, 2, 3 \ldots\}$. Now I am arguing, not that a potentially infinite number of things cannot exist, but that an actually infinite number of things cannot exist. For if an actually infinite number of things could exist, this would spawn all sorts of absurdities.

Perhaps the best way to bring this home is by means of an illustration. Let me use one of my favorites, Hilbert's Hotel, a product of the mind of the great German mathematician David Hilbert.[18] Let us imagine a hotel with a finite number of rooms. Suppose, furthermore, that all the rooms are full. When a new guest arrives asking for a room, the proprietor apologizes, "Sorry, all the rooms are full." But now let us imagine a hotel with an infinite number of rooms and suppose once more that *all the rooms are full.* There is not a single vacant room throughout the entire infinite hotel. Now suppose a new guest shows up, asking for a room. "But of course!" says the proprietor, and he

---

18. The story of Hilbert's Hotel is related in George Gamow, *One, Two, Three, . . . Infinity*, p. 17.

immediately shifts the person in room #1 into room #2, the person in room #2 into room #3, the person in room #3 into room #4, and so on, out to infinity. As a result of these room changes, room #1 now becomes vacant and the new guest gratefully checks in. But remember, before he arrived, all the rooms were full! Equally curious, according to the mathematicians, there are now no more persons in the hotel than there were before: the number is just infinite. But how can this be? The proprietor just added the new guest's name to the register and gave him his keys—how can there not be one more person in the hotel than before? But the situation becomes even stranger. For suppose an infinity of new guests show up at the desk, asking for a room. "Of course, of course!" says the proprietor, and he proceeds to shift the person in room #1 into room #2, the person in room #2 into room #4, the person in room #3 into room #6, and so on out to infinity, always putting each former occupant into the room number twice his own. As a result, all the odd numbered rooms become vacant, and the infinity of new guests is easily accommodated. And yet, before they came, all the rooms were full! And again, strangely enough, the number of guests in the hotel is the same after the infinity of new guests check in as before, even though there were as many new guests as old guests. In fact, the proprietor could repeat this process *infinitely many times* and yet there would never be one single person more in the hotel than before.

But Hilbert's Hotel is even stranger than the German mathematician made it out to be. For suppose some of the guests start to check out. Suppose the guest in room #1 departs. Is there not now one less person in the hotel? Not according to the mathematicians—but just ask the woman who makes the beds! Suppose the guests in rooms ##1, 3, 5, . . . check out. In this case an infinite number of people have left the hotel, but according to the mathematicians there are no less people in the hotel—but don't talk to that laundry woman! In fact, we could have every other guest check out of the hotel and repeat this process infinitely many times, and yet there would never be any less people in the hotel. But suppose that the persons in rooms ##4, 5, 6, . . . checked out. At a single stroke the hotel would be virtually emptied, the guest register would be reduced to three names, and the infinite would be converted to finitude. And yet it would remain true that the *same number* of guests checked out this time as when the guests in rooms ##1, 3, 5, . . . checked out. Can anyone believe that such a hotel could exist in reality?

Hilbert's Hotel is absurd. As one person remarked, if Hilbert's Hotel could exist, it would have to have a sign posted outside: NO VACANCY—GUESTS WELCOME. The above sorts of absurdities show that it is impossible for an actually infinite number of things to exist. There is simply no way to avoid these absurdities once we admit the possibility of the existence of an actual infinite. William J. Wainwright has suggested that we could reduce the force of these paradoxes by translating them into mathematical terms; for example, an actually infinite set has a proper subset with the same cardinal number as the set itself.[19] But this amounts only to a way of *concealing* the paradoxes; it was to bring out the paradoxical character of these mathematical concepts that Hilbert came up with his illustration in the first place. And the whole purpose of philosophical analysis is to bring out what is entailed by unanalyzed notions and not to leave them at face value.

But does the possibility of an actual infinite really *entail* that such absurdities are possible, or could an actual infinite be possible, as Wainwright suggests, without thereby implying that such absurdities are possible? The answer to that question is simple: the possibility of the existence of an actual infinite *entails*, that is, necessarily implies, that such absurdities could exist. Hilbert's illustration merely serves to bring out in a practical and vivid way what the mathematics necessarily implies; for if an actual infinite number of things is possible, then a hotel with an actually infinite number of rooms must be possible. Hence, it logically follows that if such a hotel is impossible, then so is the real existence of an actual infinite.

These considerations also show how superficial Mackie's analysis of this point is.[20] He thinks that the absurdities are resolved by noting that for infinite groups the axiom that *the whole is greater than its part* does not hold, as it does for finite groups. But far from being the solution, this is precisely the problem. Because in infinite set theory this axiom is denied, one gets all sorts of absurdities, like Hilbert's Hotel, when one tries to translate that theory into reality. Hence, I conclude that an actually infinite number of things cannot exist.

3.132112 *A beginningless series of events in time entails an actually infinite number of things.* This second point is pretty obvious. If the universe never began to exist, then the series of events would be infinite. If the universe never began to exist, then prior to the present there have existed an actually infinite number of previous events. Thus, a beginningless series of events in time entails an actually infinite number of things, namely, events.

3.132113 *Therefore, a beginningless series of events in time cannot exist.* If the above two premises are true, then the conclusion follows logically. The series of past events must be finite and have a beginning. Since, as I said, the universe is not distinct from the series of events, the universe therefore began to exist.

3.13212 *Argument from the impossibility of forming*

19. William J. Wainwright, review of The Kalām Cosmological Argument, pp. 328-34.
20. Mackie, Theism, p. 93.

an actually infinite collection of things by adding one member after another. It is very important to note that this argument is distinct from the foregoing argument (3.13211), for it does not deny that an actually infinite number of things can exist. It denies that a collection containing an actually infinite number of things can be *formed* by adding one member after another. Basically, the argument goes like this: you cannot form an actually infinite collection of things by adding one member after another because it would be impossible to get to infinity. The series of past events is a collection that has been formed by adding one event after another. Therefore, the series of past events up till now can only be finite, not infinite. Otherwise, it would be an actually infinite collection formed by adding one member after another. This argument, too, can be formulated in three steps:

- The series of events in time is a collection formed by adding one member after another.
- A collection formed by adding one member after another cannot be actually infinite.
- Therefore, the series of events in time cannot be actually infinite.

Let us take a look at each step.

3.132121 *The series of events in time is a collection formed by adding one member after another.* This is rather obvious. The past did not spring into being whole and entire but was formed sequentially, one event occurring after another. Notice, too, that the direction of this formation is "forward," in the sense that the collection grows with time. Although we sometimes speak of an "infinite regress" of events, in reality an infinite past would be an "infinite progress" of events with no beginning and its end in the present.

3.132112 *A collection formed by adding one member after another cannot be actually infinite.* This is the crucial step. It is important to realize that this impossibility has nothing to do with the amount of time available: no matter how much time one has available, an actual infinite cannot be formed.

Now someone might say that while an infinite collection cannot be formed by beginning at a point and adding members, nevertheless an infinite collection could be formed by never beginning but ending at a point, that is to say, ending at a point after having added one member after another from eternity. But this method seems even more unbelievable than the first method. If one cannot count to infinity, how can one count down from infinity? If one cannot traverse the infinite by moving in one direction, how can one traverse it by moving in the opposite direction?

Indeed, the idea of a beginningless series ending in the present seems absurd. To give just one illustration: suppose we meet a man who claims to have been counting from eternity and who is now finishing: . . ., -3, -2, -1, 0. We could ask, why didn't he finish counting yesterday or the day before or the year before? By then an infinite time had already elapsed, so that he should already have finished by then. Thus, at no point in the infinite past could we ever find the man finishing his countdown, for by that point he should already be done! In fact, no matter how far back into the past we go, we can never find the man counting at all, for at any point we reach he will already have finished. But if at no point in the past do we find him counting, this contradicts the hypothesis that he has been counting from eternity. This illustrates that the formation of an actual infinite by never beginning but reaching an end is as impossible as beginning at a point and trying to reach infinity.

Hence, set theory has been purged of all temporal concepts; as Russell says, "classes which are infinite are given all at once by the defining properties of their members, so that there is no question of 'completion' or of 'successive synthesis.' "[21] The only way an actual infinite could come to exist in the real world would be by being created all at once, simply in a moment. It would be a hopeless undertaking to try to form it by adding one member after another.

Mackie's objections to this step are off the target.[22] He thinks that the argument illicitly assumes an infinitely distant starting point in the past and then pronounces it impossible to travel from that point to today. If we take the notion of infinity "seriously," he says, we must say that in the infinite past there would be no starting point whatever, not even an infinitely distant one. Yet from any given point in the past, there is only a finite distance to the present.

Now I know of no proponent of the kalām argument who assumed that there was an infinitely distant starting point in the past. On the contrary, the beginningless character of the series of past events only serves to underscore the difficulty of its formation by adding one member after another. The fact that there is no beginning at all, not even an infinitely distant one, makes the problem worse, not better. It is not the proponent of the kalām argument who fails to take infinity seriously. To say the infinite past could have been formed by adding one member after another is like saying someone has just succeeded in writing down all the negative numbers, ending at -1. And, we may ask, how is Mackie's point that from any given moment in the past there is only a finite distance to the present even relevant to the issue? The defender of the kalām argument could agree to this without batting an eye. For the

21. Bertrand Russell, Our Knowledge of the External World, p. 170.
22. Mackie, Theism, p. 93.

issue is how the *whole* series can be formed, not a finite portion of it. Does Mackie think that because every *finite* segment of the series can be formed by adding one member after another that the whole *infinite* series can be so formed? That is as logically fallacious as saying because every part of an elephant is light in weight, the whole elephant is light in weight. Mackie's point is therefore irrelevant. It seems that this step of the argument, that an actually infinite collection cannot be formed by adding one member after another, remains unrefuted.

        3.132123 *Therefore, the series of events in time cannot be actually infinite.* Given the truth of the premises, the conclusion logically follows. If the universe did not begin to exist a finite time ago, then the present moment would never arrive. But obviously, it has arrived. Therefore, we know that the universe is finite in the past and began to exist.

We thus have two separate arguments to prove that the universe began to exist, one based on the impossibility of an actually infinite number of things and one on the impossibility of forming an actually infinite collection by successive addition. If one wishes to deny the beginning of the universe, he must refute, not one, but both of these arguments.

        3.1322 *Scientific confirmation.* Now some people find philosophical arguments difficult to follow; they prefer empirical evidence. So I should now like to turn to an examination of two remarkable scientific confirmations of the conclusion already reached by philosophical argument alone. This evidence comes from what is undoubtedly one of the most exciting and rapidly developing fields of science: astronomy and astrophysics.

        3.13221 *Confirmation from the big-bang model of the universe.*

        3.132211 *The big-bang model.* Prior to the 1920s, scientists had always assumed that the universe was stationary. But in 1929 an alarming thing happened. An astronomer named Edwin Hubble discovered that the light from distant galaxies appears to be redder than it should. The startling conclusion to which Hubble was led was that the light is redder because the universe is *growing apart*; it is expanding! The light from the stars is affected because they are moving away from us. But this is the interesting part: Hubble not only showed that the universe is expanding, but that *it is expanding the same in all directions.* To get a picture of this, imagine a balloon with dots painted on it. As you blow up the balloon, the dots get farther and farther apart. Now those dots are just like the galaxies in space. Everything in the universe is expanding outward. The staggering implication of this is that at some point in the past *the entire known universe was contracted down to a single mathematical point,* from which it has been expanding ever since. The farther back one goes in the past, the denser the universe becomes, so that one finally reaches a point of infinite density from which the universe began to expand. That initial event has come to be known as the "big bang."

How long ago did the big bang occur? Only since the 1970s have accurate estimates become available. In a very important series of six articles published in 1974 and 1975, two scientists, Allan Sandage and G. A. Tammann, estimated that the big bang occurred about 15 billion years ago. More recent studies conducted at Harvard University suggest that it may have occurred only nine billion years ago. Therefore, according to the big-bang theory the universe began to exist with a great explosion from a state of infinite density about 9-15 billion years ago. Four of the world's most famous astronomers describe that event in these words:

> The universe began from a state of infinite density. . . . Space and time were created in that event and so was all the matter in the universe. It is not meaningful to ask what happened before the Big Bang; it is like asking what is north of the North Pole. Similarly, it is not sensible to ask where the Big Bang took place. The point-universe was not an object isolated in space; it was the entire universe, and so the only answer can be that the Big Bang happened everywhere.[23]

Thus, the term *big bang* and the terminology associated with an explosion can be misleading, because it is not correct to suppose that the expansion can be visualized from the outside. There is no external vantage point from which the expansion could be observed because what is expanding is the entire universe. Space itself is expanding in the sense that the separation between any two galaxies grows with time.

The event that marked the beginning of the universe becomes all the more amazing when one reflects on the fact that a state of "infinite density" is synonymous to "nothing." There can be no object that possesses infinite density, for if it had any size at all, it could be even more dense. Therefore, as astronomer Fred Hoyle points out, the big-bang theory requires the creation of matter from nothing. This is because as one goes back in time, one reaches a point at which, in Hoyle's words, the universe was "shrunk down to nothing at all."[24] Thus what the big-bang model requires is that the universe had a beginning and was created out of nothing.

Now some people were deeply disturbed with the idea that the universe began from nothing.[25] That is too close to the Christian doctrine of creation to allow atheistic minds to be comfortable. Einstein wrote

---

23. J. Richard Gott, et al., "Will the Universe Expand Forever?" p. 65.
24. Fred Hoyle, *Astronomy and Cosmology,* p. 658.
25. See Robert Jastrow, *God and the Astronomers,* pp. 28, 112-13.

privately, "This circumstance of an expanding universe irritates me. . . . To admit such possibilities seems senseless." Another scientist, Arthur Eddington, wrote, "I have no axe to grind in this discussion, but the notion of a beginning is repugnant to me. . . . I simply do not believe that the present order of things started off with a bang. . . . The expanding universe is preposterous . . . incredible . . . It leaves me cold." The German chemist Walter Nernst declared, "To deny the infinite duration of time would be to betray the very foundations of science." Phillip Morrison of the Massachusetts Institute of Technology said, "I find it hard to accept the Big Bang theory; I would like to reject it, but I have to face the facts."

3.132212 *Alternative models.* But if one rejects the big-bang model, he has only two alternative theories: the steady-state model or the oscillating model. Let us examine each of these.

3.1322121 *The steady-state model.* The steady-state model holds that the universe never had a beginning but has always existed in the same state. Ever since this model was first proposed in 1948, it has never been very convincing. According to S. L. Jaki, this theory never secured "a single piece of experimental verification." It always seemed to be trying to explain away the facts rather than explain them. According to Jaki, the proponents of this model were actually motivated by "openly anti-theological, or rather anti-Christian motivations."[26]

Against this theory is the fact that a count of galaxies emitting radio waves indicates that there were once more radio sources than there are today. Therefore, the universe is not in a steady state after all. But the theory was decisively discredited when in 1965 A. A. Penzias and R. W. Wilson discovered that the entire universe is bathed with a background of microwave radiation. This radiation background shows that the universe was once in a very hot and very dense state. In the steady state model no such state could have existed, since the universe is supposed to be the same from eternity. Therefore, the steady state model has been abandoned by virtually everyone. According to Ivan King, "The steady-state theory has now been laid to rest, as a result of clear-cut observations of how things have changed with time."[27]

3.1322122 *The oscillating model.* John Gribbin describes this model:

> The biggest problem with the Big Bang theory of the origin of the universe is philosophical—perhaps even theological—what was there before the bang? This problem alone was sufficient to give a great initial impetus to the steady state theory; but with that theory now sadly in conflict with the observations, the best way round this initial difficulty is provided by a

26. Stanley L. Jaki, *Science and Creation*, p. 347.
27. Ivan R. King, *The Universe Unfolding*, p. 462.

model in which the universe expands, collapses back again, and repeats the cycle indefinitely.[28]

According to this model, the universe is sort of like a spring, expanding and contracting from eternity. This model has become a sort of "Great White Hope" for atheistic scientists, who terribly want it to be true so as to avoid an absolute beginning of the universe. You may have seen Carl Sagan, for example, in his popular "Cosmos" program on public television propounding this model and reading from the Hindu scriptures about cyclical Brahman years in order to illustrate the oscillating universe. There are, however, at least two very well-known difficulties with the oscillating model, which Sagan did not mention.

First, the oscillating model is physically impossible. That is to say, for all the talk about such a model, the fact remains that it is only a *theoretical* possibility, not a *real* possibility. You can draft such models on paper, but they cannot be descriptive of the real universe because they contradict the known laws of physics. As the late Professor Tinsley of Yale explains, in oscillating models "even though the mathematics *says* that the universe oscillates, there is no known physics to reverse the collapse and bounce back to a new expansion. The physics seems to say that those models start from the Big Bang, expand, collapse, then end."[29] More recently four other scientists, themselves obviously in sympathy with the oscillating model, admitted, in describing the contraction of the universe, "The major difficulty for the bounce model is to understand how an extraordinarily inhomogeneous . . . universe of isolated, coalescing black holes can be smoothed out [after the bounce]; for that matter, there is no understanding of how a bounce can take place. . . . We have nothing to contribute to the question of whether and/or how the universe bounces."[30] In order for the oscillating model to be correct, the known laws of physics would have to be revised.

Second, the observational evidence is contrary to the oscillating model. Let me explain two respects in which the observational evidence does not support the oscillating model. The first was alluded to in the quotation just cited, namely, there is no way to account for the observed even distribution of matter in the universe on the basis of an oscillating model. This is because as the universe contracts, black holes begin to suck everything up, so that matter becomes very unevenly distributed. But when the universe supposedly rebounds from its contracting phase, there is no mechanism to "iron out" these lumps and

28. John Gribbin, "Oscillating Universe Bounces Back," p. 15.
29. Beatrice Tinsley, personal letter.
30. Duane Dicus et al., "The Future of the Universe," p. 100; idem, "Effects of Proton Decay on the Cosmological Future," pp. 1-9.

make the distribution smooth. Hence, the scientists cited above confess that even if there is some unknown mechanism that could cause the universe to bounce back to a new expansion, it is still not clear that it would prevent the unevenness that would result from the black holes formed during the contraction phase.[31] The present evenness of matter distribution simply cannot be explained using models in which the universe begins with matter unevenly distributed.[32] The oscillating model therefore cannot satisfactorily account for the presently observed evenness of the distribution of matter in the universe.

A second respect in which the observational evidence is contrary to the oscillating model concerns the question of whether the universe is "open" or "closed." If the universe is closed, that means that the expansion will reach a certain point, halt, and then gravity will pull everything back together again. But if the universe is open, that means that the force of the expansion is greater than the force of gravity, so that the expansion will never stop but will just go on and on forever. An illustration of this difference concerns the escape velocity needed by a rocket to escape earth's gravity. If a certain speed is not attained, the force of gravity will pull the ship back to earth again. But if the rocket attains or exceeds escape velocity, then the force of the earth's gravity cannot prevent its flying off into space. Similarly, if the universe is expanding, so to speak, at escape velocity or faster, then it will overcome the internal pull of its own gravity and will expand forever. Now clearly, the oscillating model, even in order to be a *possibility*, must posit a closed universe, one that is expanding slower than escape velocity. But is it?

The crucial factor in answering that question is the density of the universe. For density determines the gravitational force of an object. Scientists have estimated that if there are more than about three hydrogen atoms per cubic meter on the average throughout the universe, then the universe will be closed. Now that may not sound like very much, but remember that most of the universe is just empty space. The scientific evidence up to the time of writing of my earlier works on this subject indicated that the universe would have to be about ten times denser than it is in order for the universe to be closed. Since that time, however, scientists have embarked on a quest to find the "missing mass" needed to close the universe, and have discovered more mass in the universe than was previously known. A halo of non-luminous matter (matter that does not give off light) has been discovered surrounding our galaxy. This halo is one to two times the mass of the galaxy itself. The non-luminous matter associated with each of the galaxies might

31. Dicus, "Cosmological Future," p. 8.
32. Ethan T. Vishniac, "Relativistic Collisionless Particles and the Evolution of Cosmological Perturbations," p. 472.

supply an additional 5 to 10 percent of the mass needed to close the universe. Clusters of galaxies may also have associated with them additional halos of non-luminous matter, which could raise the total density of the universe to about one-half of the density needed for closure. Thus, according to current evidence we may say that the universe would have to be twice as dense as it is in order for it to be closed.

Those who hope that the universe is closed have been holding out for the possibility that neutrinos (sub-atomic particles that have no electrical charge and travel at the speed of light) may have mass, and that this mass could supply the additional 50% of the mass necessary for closure. The speculation that neutrinos may have mass has been around for some time. But new interest in the possibility has been generated by experiments conducted at the Institute of Theoretical and Experimental Physics in Moscow and at the University of California at Irvine, which indicated that neutrinos may indeed have a small mass. The results have, however, been disputed, and the question is fraught with uncertainty. More than that, even if neutrinos do have some mass, it is very uncertain how much mass they have: neutrinos that have been discovered appear to have masses too light to close the universe, and although scientists suspect that a species of heavier neutrino may also exist, no one is certain exactly how much mass it would have. Hence, it is to a great extent speculative whether such particles would be massive enough to close the universe. Finally, even if heavy neutrinos do exist, there are certain constraints on them that indicate they would not close the universe. Stecker and Brown calculate that the neutrino mass would have to be somewhere between 25 and 100 electron volts in order to close the universe.[33] So high a mass, however, seems unlikely.

You will recall the halos of non-luminous material surrounding the clusters and groups of galaxies. What are these halos made of? The evidence indicates that they cannot be made up of ordinary matter. For then the universe would be too dense to permit the observed quantities of the element deuterium in the universe. Let me explain. Within a few minutes after the big bang, subatomic particles began to interract via nucleosynthesis to form the lighter elements. The simplest of these is deuterium, which is formed by the synthesis of one proton and one neutron. Deuterium nuclei then combined to form helium, which is composed of two protons and two neutrons. The proportion of deuterium to helium is closely related to the density of the universe at that time. If the universe possessed a closure density, most or all of the deuterium would have been converted into helium. But, in fact, this was not the case, for deuterium is abundant in the present universe

33. F. W. Stecker and R. W. Brown, "Astrophyhsical Tests for Radiative Decay of Neutrinos and Fundamental Physics Implications," pp. 1-9.

(4 x 10^{-31} grams per cubic centimeter in nearby interstellar space). In order for the universe to be closed, the amount of deuterium would have to be less than 20 percent of the observed lower limit. Hence, if there were in the universe a great deal of non-luminous ordinary matter in addition to the luminous matter, we would have much less deuterium and much more helium than is observed. Neutrinos, if they have mass, would not affect the ratio of deuterium to helium. As one scientist points out, if the non-luminous material were in the form of ordinary matter, "standard big-bang nucleosynthesis calculations would be in gross conflict with observation. . . . This is not the case if the missing mass were in the form of massive neutrinos."[34] This has led to the hypothesis that the non-luminous material may actually be neutrinos. If that is the case, however, light neutrinos with a mass of four electron volts or less would not have been pulled into galactic halos. On the other hand, heavy neutrinos with a mass of 20 electron volts or more could have been pulled into such halos, but then there would be more non-luminous mass than there actually is. Hence, only neutrinos with a mass between 4 and 20 electron volts could supply the non-luminous mass around groups and clusters of galaxies. But if Stecker and Brown's estimates are correct, this is insufficient mass to close the universe.

Therefore, Schramm and Steigman calculate, that after adding up the contributions of ordinary matter, heavy neutrinos, and light neutrinos, the best estimate for the density of the universe is that it is about one-half needed for closure.[35] And remember, this assumes that unknown "heavy" neutrinos exist and that neutrinos have mass. Physicist James Trefil reports in a recent article,

> A few years ago . . . it appeared that the neutrino . . . might have a small mass after all. Cosmologists have speculated that if such were the case, there might be enough invisible mass in the form of neutrinos to close the universe. . . . Unfortunately, a new generation of experiments has weakened the evidence, and the question of what, if anything, will provide the unseen mass remains unanswered.[36]

Therefore, although we await eagerly further developments in this area, it does not seem that neutrinos suffice to close the universe.

I might mention, too, that further work on the speed of the expansion re-confirms previous evidence that the universe is expanding at escape velocity and will therefore not re-contract. The findings of Sandage and Tammann still stand: "Hence, we are forced to decide that . . .

34. Adrian L. Melott, "Massive Neutrinos in Large Scale Gravitational Clustering," p. 59.
35. David N. Schramm and Gary Steigman, "Relic Neutrinos and the Density of the Universe," p. 6.
36. James S. Trefil, "How the Universe Will End," p. 78.

it seems inevitable that the Universe will expand forever." Therefore, they conclude, "the Universe has happened only once."[37]

The oscillating model, therefore, is seriously flawed. It contradicts both the known laws of physics and the current observational evidence. It therefore provides no plausible escape from the beginning of the universe.

            3.13222 *Confirmation from thermodynamics.* Now if this were not enough, there is a second scientific confirmation for the beginning of the universe, the evidence from thermodynamics. According to the second law of thermodynamics, processes taking place in a closed system always tend toward a state of equilibrium. In other words, unless energy is constantly being fed into a system, the processes in the system will tend to run down and quit. For example, if I had a bottle that was a sealed vacuum inside, and I introduced into it some molecules of gas, the gas would spread itself out evenly inside the bottle. It is virtually impossible for the molecules to retreat, for example, into one corner of the bottle and remain. This is why when you walk into a room, the air in the room never separates suddenly into oxygen at one end and nitrogen at the other. It is also why when you step into your bath you may be confident that it will be an even temperature instead of frozen solid at one end and boiling at the other. It is clear that life would not be possible in a world in which the second law of thermodynamics did not operate.

            3.132221 *Heat death of the universe.* Now our interest in the law is what happens when it is applied to the universe as a whole. The universe is a gigantic closed system (closed in the thermodynamic sense, not in the sense of expansion and re-contraction), since it is everything there is and there is nothing outside it. What this seems to imply then is that, given enough time, the universe and all its processes will run down, and the entire universe will come to equilibrium. This is known as the heat death of the universe. Once the universe reaches this state, no further change is possible. The universe is dead.

            3.1322211 *"Hot" death.* There are two possible types of heat death for the universe. If the universe is "closed," it will die a hot death. Dr. Tinsley describes such a state:

> If the average density of matter in the universe is great enough, the mutual gravitational attraction between bodies will eventually slow the expansion to a halt. The universe will then contract and collapse into a hot fireball. There is no known physical mechanism that could reverse a catastrophic big crunch. Apparently, if the universe becomes dense enough, it is in for a hot death.[38]

37. Allan Sandage and G. A. Tammann, "Steps Toward the Hubble Constant VII," pp. 23, 7. See also idem, "Steps Toward the Hubble Constant. VIII."
38. Beatrice Tinsley, "From Big Bang to Eternity?" p. 103.

If the universe is closed, then as it contracts the stars gain energy, causing them to burn more rapidly so that they finally explode or evaporate. As everything in the universe grows closer together, the black holes begin to gobble up everything around them, and eventually begin themselves to coalesce. In time, "All the black holes finally coalesce into one large black hole that is coextensive with the universe,"[39] from which the universe will never re-emerge.

        3.1322212 *"Cold" death.* But suppose, as is more likely, that the universe is "open." Dr. Tinsley describes the final state of this universe:

> If the universe has a low density, its death will be cold. It will expand forever, at a slower and slower rate. Galaxies will turn all of their gas into stars, and the stars will burn out. Our own sun will become a cold, dead remnant, floating among the corpses of other stars in an increasingly isolated Milky Way.[40]

At 10^{30} years the universe will consist of 90 percent dead stars, and 9 percent supermassive black holes formed by the collapse of galaxies, and 1 percent atomic matter, mainly hydrogen. Elementary particle physics suggests that thereafter protons will decay into electrons and positrons, so that space will be filled with a rarefied gas so thin that the distance between an electron and a positron will be about the size of the present galaxy. At 10^{100} years, some scientists believe that the black holes themselves will dissipate by a strange effect predicted by quantum mechanics. The mass and energy associated with a black hole so warp space that they are said to create a "tunnel" or "worm-hole" through which the mass and energy are ejected in another region of space. As the mass of a black hole decreases, its energy loss accelerates, so that it is eventually dissipated into radiation and elementary particles. Eventually all black holes will completely evaporate and all the matter in the ever-expanding universe will be reduced to a thin gas of elementary particles and radiation. Equilibrium will prevail throughout, and the entire universe will be in its final state, from which no change will occur.

    Now the question that needs to be asked is this: if given enough time the universe will reach heat death, then why is it not in a state of heat death now if it has existed forever, from eternity? If the universe did not begin to exist, then it should now be in a state of equilibrium. Its energy should be all used up. My wife and I have a very loud wind-up alarm clock. If I hear that the clock is ticking—which is no problem,

---

39. Dicus, "Future of the Universe," p. 99.
40. Tinsley, "Big Bang," p. 105.

believe me—then I know that at some point in the recent past it was wound up and has been running down since then. It is the same with the universe. Since it has not yet run down, this means, in the words of one baffled scientist, "In some way the universe must have been *wound up*."[41]

3.132222 *Oscillating model.* Some scientists have tried to escape this conclusion by arguing that the universe oscillates back and forth from eternity, and so never reaches a final state of equilibrium. Now I have already observed that such a model of the universe is a physical impossibility. But suppose it were possible. The fact is that the thermodynamic properties of this model imply the very beginning of the universe that its proponents seek to avoid. For as several scientists have pointed out, each time the model universe expands it would expand a little farther than before. Therefore, if you traced the expansions back in time they would get smaller and smaller and smaller. One scientific team explains "The effect of entropy production will be to enlarge the cosmic scale, from cycle to cycle. . . . Thus, looking back in time, each cycle generated less entropy, had a smaller cycle time, and had a smaller cycle expansion factor then [sic] the cycle that followd it."[42] Therefore, in the words of another scientific team, "the multicycle model has an infinite future, but only a finite past."[43] As another writer points out, this implies that the oscillating model of the universe still requires an origin of the universe prior to the smallest cycle.[44]

So whether you choose a closed model, an open model, or an oscillating model, thermodynamics implies that the universe had a beginning. According to the English scientist P. C. W. Davies, the universe must have been created a finite time ago and is in the process of winding down. Prior to the creation, the universe simply did not exist. Therefore, Davies concludes, even though we may not like it, we must conclude that the universe's energy was somehow simply "put in" at the creation as an initial condition.[45]

So we have two scientific confirmations that the universe began to exist. First, the expansion of the universe implies the universe had a beginning. Second, thermodynamics shows the universe began to exist.

3.13223 *God and the astronomers.* But that brings us back full circle to Leibniz's question: Why? It is futile to say the universe just exists and never had a beginning, for that is contrary to all the

---

41. Richard Schlegel, "Time and Thermodynamics," p. 511.
42. Dicus, "Cosmological Future," pp. 1, 8.
43. I. D. Novikov and Ya. B. Zeldovich, "Physical Processes Near Cosmological Singularities," pp. 401-2.
44. Gribbin, "Oscillating Universe," p. 16.
45. P. C. W. Davies, *The Physics of Time Asymmetry,* p. 104.

evidence. Now this is very embarrassing for atheistic scientists. When I was at the 16th World Congress on Philosophy in Düsseldorf in 1978, I found that the only scientists who opposed the big-bang theory were Marxists from communist nations. They were committed to the doctrine of materialism and *had* to maintain, in spite of and contrary to all the evidence, that the universe was eternal. They could not explain away the evidence; rather, they accepted the eternity of the universe *by faith*. Never before had I so clearly seen the religious nature of Marxist beliefs.

But if we are honest and accept that the universe did begin to exist, how are we to explain it? The atheist has no explanation. As Anthony Kenny of Oxford University urges, "a proponent of the Big Bang theory, at least if he is an atheist, must believe that the matter of the universe came from nothing and by nothing."[46]

Because of this, most scientists simply ignore the question. Fred Hoyle explains that the big-bang theory cannot explain either where matter came from or why the big bang occurred. Then he comments, "It is not usual in present day cosmological discussions to seek an answer to this question; the question and its answer are taken to be outside the range of scientific discussion."[47] Another scientist admits that the big-bang theory only *describes* the initial conditions of the universe, but it cannot *explain* them.[48] An astronomer concludes, "The question, 'How was the matter created in the first place?' is left unanswered."[49] The scientific team that discovered the microwave background radiation sums it up: "we cannot understand the origin of matter or of the universe."[50]

This then is the question that the scientists cannot and will not answer: *Why does the universe exist?*

Robert Jastrow, director of NASA's Goddard Institute for Space Studies, in his book *God and the Astronomers* explains that many scientists are simply running away from God. He writes:

> There is a kind of religion in science. . . . Every event can be explained in a rational way as the product of some previous event. . . . there is no First Cause. This religious faith of the scientist is violated by the discovery that the world had a beginning . . . as a product of forces or circumstances we cannot discover. When that happens, the scientist has lost control. If he really examined the implications, he would be traumatized. As usual when faced with trauma, the mind reacts by ignoring the implications—in science this is known as "refusing to speculate"— or trivializing the origin of

46. Anthony Kenny, *The Five Ways*, p. 66.
47. Fred Hoyle, *Astronomy Today*, p. 166.
48. Adrian Webster, "The Cosmic Background Radiation," p. 31.
49. J. V. Narlikar, "Singularity and Matter Creation in Cosmological Models," p. 136.
50. R. H. Dicke, et. al., "Cosmic Black-Body Radiation," p. 414.

the world by calling it the Big Bang, as if the universe were a firecracker.

Consider the enormity of the problem. Science has proven that the universe exploded into being at a certain moment. It asks, what cause produced this effect? Who or what put the matter and energy into the universe? . . . And science cannot answer these questions. . . . The scientist's pursuit of the past ends in the moment of creation.[51]

I do not mean to imply that all scientists are running away from God. For example, another scientist, Sir Edmund Whittaker, said, "It is simpler to postulate creation *ex nihilo*—Divine will constituting nature from nothingness." The British scientist Edward Milne wrote, "As to the first cause of the universe, . . . that is left for the reader to insert, but our picture is incomplete without Him."[52] And astronomer Icko Iben asserts that when we remember that at the beginning most of the energy of the universe was in the form of radiation or photons, it gives "added meaning to the phrase, 'And God said, "Let there be light." ' "[53] The discovery that the universe began to exist, Jastrow says, surprised everybody except the theologians. The Bible says, "In the beginning God created the heavens and the earth" (Gen. 1:1). For thousands of years, those who believed what the Bible says have known the truth that scientists have discovered only within the last fifty years. Or as Jastrow puts it,

> For the scientist who has lived by his faith in the power of reason, the story ends like a bad dream. He has scaled the mountains of ignorance; he is about to conquer the highest peak; as he pulls himself over the final rock, he is greeted by a band of theologians who have been sitting there for centuries.[54]

Thus science points us to the Creator God of the Bible. It is interesting that this fact has even been inadvertently endorsed by the U.S. judiciary. In ruling against the Arkansas law allowing creation science to be taught in public schools, the judge wrote:

> The argument that creation from nothing . . . does not involve a supernatural deity has no evidentiary or rational support. . . . Indeed, creation of the world "out of nothing" is the ultimate religious statement because God is the only actor. . . . The idea of sudden creation from nothing, or *creatio ex nihilo*, is an inherently religious concept.[55]

51. Jastrow, *God and the Astronomers*, pp. 113-15.
52. Cited in ibid., pp. 111-12.
53. Icko Iben, Jr. "Globular Cluster Stars," p. 39.
54. Jastrow, *God and the Astronomers*, p. 116.
55. Memorandum Opinion, *Maclean v. Arkansas*, 1981. Judge Overton's opinion is reprinted in full in Norman Geisler, *The Creator in the Courtroom* (Milford, Mich.: Mott Media, 1982), pp. 165-89.

Since this is precisely what modern cosmology teaches, then, if the judge is right, the existence of God is inherently implied by the standard model of the universe.

3.133 THEREFORE, THE UNIVERSE HAS A CAUSE OF ITS EXISTENCE

Both philosophical reasoning and scientific evidence point to a beginning of the universe. But since whatever begins to exist has a cause, the universe must have a cause. From what we have already said this cause would have to be uncaused, eternal, changeless, timeless, and immaterial. Moreover, I would argue, it must also be personal. For how else could a temporal effect arise from an eternal cause? If the cause were present from eternity, why would not the effect also be present from eternity? To give an example, if a heavy ball's resting on a cushion is the cause of a depression in the cushion, then if the ball is resting on the cushion from eternity, the cushion should be depressed from eternity. However, the only way to have an eternal cause but an effect that begins at a point in time is if the cause is a *personal agent* who freely decides to create an effect in time. For example, a man sitting from eternity may will to get up; hence, a temporal effect may be caused by an eternally existing agent. In fact, the agent may have purposed eternally to do some act in time. Thus, the Bible speaks of the *eternal* plan, hidden for ages in God who created all things, which God has *realized* in Christ Jesus our Lord (Eph. 3:11). Therefore, we are brought, not merely to a First Cause of the universe, but to the Personal Creator of the universe.

3.14 PRACTICAL APPLICATION

Having just completed this section, some of you may wonder, "How could I possibly share all this in an evangelistic contact?" Here we must simply exercise a little common sense and be sensitive to where the other person is in his thinking. Of course you do not lay all this material about actual and potential infinity, the expanding universe, infinite density, thermodynamics, black holes, and neutrinos on the poor non-Christian at once! You need to understand how deep his thinking and background concerning these subjects are in order to know just what to relate to him. You start simple and go deep as he has further questions. I know this material is effective because I have seen God use it when it is communciated with sensitivity.

For example, my wife, Jan, was once talking to a girl in the student union and this girl said that she did not believe in God. Jan replied, "Well, what do you think of the argument for a first cause?" "What's that?" said the girl. My wife explained, "Everything we see has a cause, and those causes have causes, and so on. But this can't go back forever.

There had to be a beginning and a first cause which started the whole thing. This is God." Now that was obviously a very simple statement of the argument we have been discussing. The girl responded, "I guess God exists after all." She was not ready to receive Christ at that point, but at least she had moved one step closer, away from her atheism. On another occasion I was talking to a guy who thought he was very clever; he said smugly, "If God created the universe, then where did God come from?" I think he thought this was an unanswerable question. But I replied, "God didn't come from anywhere. He is eternal and has always existed. So He doesn't need a cause. But now let me ask you something. The universe has not always existed but had a beginning. So *where did the universe come from?*" He was utterly dumbfounded. Again, he did not become a Christian, but I hope that at least he was shaken out of his intellectual lethargy so as to be more open to the gospel. Here again the insights of the argument we have been discussing were capable of being shared in a very simple way to speak to the man in the street on his own level.

When one talks with a person who has a deeper understanding of these issues, then of course one must go deeper. For example, when we were studying in West Germany we met a physicist from behind the Iron Curtain. As we chatted, he mentioned that physics had destroyed his belief in God and that life had become meaningless to him. "When I look out at the universe all I see is blackness," he explained, "and when I look in myself all I see is blackness within." What a poignant statement of the modern predicament! Well, at that point my wife popped, "Oh, you should read Bill's doctoral dissertation! He uses physics to prove God exists." So we lent him my dissertation on the cosmological argument to read. Over the ensuing days, he became progressively more excited. When he got to the section on astronomy and astrophysics, he was positively elated. "I *know* these scientists that you are quoting!" he exclaimed in amazement. By the time he reached the end, his faith had been restored. "Thank you for helping me to believe that God exists," he said. We answered, "Would you like to know Him in a personal way?" Then we made an appointment to meet him that evening at a restaurant. Meanwhile we prepared from memory our own hand-printed Four Spiritual Laws. After supper we opened the booklet and began, "Just as there are physical laws that govern the physical universe, so there are spiritual laws that govern your relationship to God. . . ." "Why, physical laws! Spiritual laws!" he exclaimed. "This is just for me!" When we got to the circles at the end representing two lives and asked him which circle represented his life, he put his hand over the circles and said, "Oh, this is so personal! I cannot answer now." So we encouraged him to take the booklet home and to give his life to Christ. When we saw him the next day, his face was radiant with joy.

He told us of how he had gone home and in the privacy of his room prayed to receive Christ. He then flushed all the wine and tranquilizers that he had been on down the toilet. He was a truly transformed individual. We gave him a *Good News for Modern Man* and explained the importance of maintaining a devotional life with God. Our paths then parted for several months. But when we saw him again he was still enthusiastic in his faith, and his most precious possessions were his Good News Bible and hand-made Four Spiritual Laws. So it was a great victory for God. This illustration shows how the Holy Spirit can use arguments and evidence to draw men to a saving knowledge of God.

So I encourage you to master this material and learn to communicate with sensitivity. As Clark Pinnock once remarked to us, "We should know our subject profoundly and share it simply." If you cannot answer an unbeliever's objection on some point, admit it and refer him to literature on the subject that can satisfy his question. In an age of increasing atheism and agnosticism, we cannot afford to forgo an apologetic for this most basic of all Christian beliefs: the existence of God.

4.0 DE CREATIONE

4.1 THE PROBLEM OF MIRACLES

Before we can even examine the evidence to see whether the Creator God of the universe has revealed Himself in some special way in the world, we must first deal with the problem of whether such divine action is possible in the first place. And if it is, how can it be identified? That is to say, we are confronted with the problem of miracles.

Undoubtedly one of the major stumbling blocks to becoming a Christian is for many people today that Christianity is a religion of miracles. It asserts that God became incarnate in Jesus of Nazareth, being born of a virgin, that He performed various miracles, exorcised demonic beings, and that, having died by crucifixion, He rose from the dead. But the problem is that these sorts of miraculous events seem to belong to a world view foreign to modern man—a pre-scientific, superstitious world view belonging to the ancient and middle ages. Some theologians have been so embarrassed by this fact that many of them, following Rudolf Bultmann, have sought to demythologize the Bible, thereby removing the stumbling block to modern man. According to Bultmann, no one who uses the radio or electric lights should be expected to believe in the mythological world view of the Bible in order to become a Christian. He insists that he is not trying to make Christianity more palatable to modern man but is trying merely to remove a false stumbling block so that the true stumbling block—the call to authentic existence symbolized by the cross—might become evident. But in so doing, Bultmann reduces Christianity to little more than the existentialist philosophy of Martin Heidegger. Indeed, some Bultmann disciples like Herbert Braun or Schubert Ogden have pushed Bultmann's views to their logical conclusion and have propounded a Christless and even atheistic Christianity. If, on the other hand, one is convinced that biblical Christianity is to be preserved, he must present a defense of the miraculous element in the Christian faith.

4.11 LITERATURE CITED OR RECOMMENDED

4.111 HISTORICAL BACKGROUND

Brown, Colin. *Miracles and the Critical Mind.* Grand Rapids: Eerdmans, 1984.

Clarke, Samuel. *A Discourse concerning the Unchangeable Obligations of Natural Religion and the Truth and Certainty of the Christian Revelation.* London: W. Botham, 1706.

Diderot, Denis. "Philosophical Thoughts." In *Diderot's Early Philosophical Works.* Translated by M. Jourdain. Open Court Series of Classics of Science and Philosophy 4. Chicago: Open Court, 1916.

Houtteville, Abbé. *La religion chrétienne prouvée par les faits.* 3 vols. Paris: Mercier & Boudet, 1740.

Hume, David. *Enquiries Concerning Human Understanding and Concerning the Principles of Morals.* 3d ed. Edited by P. H. Nidditch. Oxford: Clarendon, 1975. Chapter 10 of the first enquiry constitutes his case against miracles.

Le Clerc, Jean. *Five Letters Concerning the Inspiration of the Holy Scriptures.* London: [n. p.], 1690.

Less, Gottfried. *Wahrheit der christlichen Religion.* 4th ed. Göttingen: Georg Ludewig Förster, 1776.

Paley, William. *A View of the Evidences of Christianity.* 2 vols. 5th ed. London: R. Faulder, 1796; rep. ed.: Westmead, England: Gregg International, 1970.

Sherlock, Thomas. *The Tryal of the Witnesses of the Resurrection of Jesus.* London: J. Roberts, 1729.

Spinoza, Benedict de. *Tractatus theologico-politicus.* 2d ed. London: N. Trubner, 1868.

Stephen, Leslie. *History of English Thought in the Eighteenth Century.* 2 vols. 3d ed. New York: Harcourt, Brace, & World; Harbinger, 1962.

Turrettin, J. Alph. *Traité de la vérité de la religion chrétienne.* 2d ed. 7 vols. Translated by J. Vernet. Geneva: Henri-Albert Gosse, 1745-55.

Voltaire, Marie Francois. *A Philosophical Dictionary.* 2 vols. New York: Harcourt, Brace, & World; Harbinger, 1962. See particularly the article on miracles.

4.112 ASSESSMENT

Bilinskyj, Stephen S. "God, Nature, and the Concept of Miracle." Ph.D. dissertation, University of Notre Dame, 1982.

Dickens, Charles. "A Christmas Carol." In *Christmas Books*, by Charles Dickens. Introduced by E. Farejon. London: Oxford U., 1954.

Encyclopedia of Philosophy. S.v. "Miracles," by Antony Flew.

Hesse, Mary. "Miracles and the Laws of Nature." In *Miracles.* Edited by C. F. D. Moule. London: A. R. Mowbray, 1965.

Pannenberg, Wolfhart. "Jesu Geschichte und unsere Geschichte." In *Glaube und Wirklichkeit.* München: Chr. Kaiser, 1975.

———. *Jesus—God and Man.* Translated by L. L. Wilkins and D. A. Priebe. London: SCM, 1968.

Schweitzer, Albert. *The Quest of the Historical Jesus.* 3d ed. Translated by W. Montgomery. London: Adam & Charles Black, 1954.

Strauss, David Friedrich. *The Life of Jesus Critically Examined.* Translated by G. Eliot. Edited with an Introduction by P. C. Hodgson. Lives of Jesus Series. London: SCM, 1973.

Swinburne, Richard. *The Concept of Miracle.* New York: Macmillan, 1970.

4.12 HISTORICAL BACKGROUND

4.121 DEIST OBJECTION TO MIRACLES

The skepticism of modern man with regard to miracles arose during the Enlightenment, or Age of Reason, which dawned in Europe during the seventeenth century. Thereafter, miracles simply became unbelievable for most of the intelligentsia. The attack upon miracles was led by the Deists. Although Deists accepted the existence of God and His general revelation in nature, they strenuously denied that He had revealed Himself in any special way in the world. They were therefore very exercised to demonstrate the impossibility of the occurrence of miracle, or at least of the identification of miracle. They were countered by a barrage of Christian apologetic literature defending the possibility and evidential value of miracle. Let us examine now the principal arguments urged by the Deists against miracles and the responses offered by their Christian opponents.

4.1211 *The Newtonian world-machine.* Although the most important opponents of miracles were Spinoza and Hume, much of the debate was waged against the backdrop of the mechanical worldview of Newtonian physics. In his *Philosophiae naturalis principia* (1687), Isaac Newton formulated his famous three laws of motion, from which together with some definitions, he was able to deduce the various theorems and corollaries of his physics. In regarding the world in terms of masses, motions, and forces operating according to these laws, Newton's *Principia* seemed to eliminate the need for God's providence and gave rise to a picture of the universe appropriately characterized as the "Newtonian world-machine."

Newton's model of mechanical explanation was enthusiastically received as the paradigm for explanation in all fields; this attitude reached its height in Pierre Simon de Laplace's belief that a Supreme Intelligence, equipped with Newton's *Principia* and knowing the present position and velocity of every particle in the universe, could deduce the exact state of the universe at any other point in time. Such a world view promoted the Deist conception of God as the creator of the world-machine, who wound it up like a clock and set it running under the laws of matter and motion, never to interfere with it again.

Indeed, this harmoniously functioning world-machine was thought to provide the best evidence that God exists. The eighteenth-century French *philosophe* Diderot exclaimed, "Thanks to the works of these great men, the world is no longer a God; it is a machine with its wheels, its cords, its pulleys, its springs, and its weights."[1] But equally, it was thought that such a world system also made incredible that God should interfere with its operation via miraculous interventions. Diderot's contemporary Voltaire said it was absurd and insulting to God to think that He would interrupt the operations of "this immense machine," since He designed it from the beginning to run according to His divinely decreed, immutable laws.[2] For eighteenth-century Newtonians, such miraculous interventions could only be described as violations of the laws of nature and were therefore impossible.

4.1212 *Benedict de Spinoza.* The philosophical attack upon miracles, however, actually preceded the publication of Newton's *Principia.* In 1670 the pantheistic, Jewish philosopher Benedict de Spinoza in his *Tractatus theologico-politicus* argued against both the possibility and evidential value of miracles. Two of his arguments are of special significance for our discussion.

4.12121 *Miracles violate the unchangeable order of nature.* First, he argues that nothing happens contrary to the eternal and unchangeable order of nature. He maintains that all that God wills is characterized by eternal necessity and truth. For since there is no difference between God's understanding and His will, it is the same to say that God knows a thing or that God wills a thing. Thus, the same necessity that characterizes God's knowledge characterizes His will. Therefore, the laws of nature flow from the necessity and perfection of

---

1. Denis Diderot, "Philosophical Thoughts," p. 18.
2. *A Philosophical Dictionary,* s.v. "Miracles," by Marie Francois Arouet de Voltaire.

the divine nature. If some event that was contrary to these laws could occur, then the divine will and knowledge would stand in contradiction to nature, which is impossible. To say God does something contrary to the laws of nature is to say God does something contrary to His own nature. Therefore, miracles are impossible.

4.12122 *Miracles are insufficient to prove God's existence.* Second, Spinoza believed that a proof of God's existence must be absolutely certain. It is by the unchangeable order of nature that we know that God exists. By admitting miracles, Spinoza warns, we break the laws of nature and thus create doubts about the existence of God, leading us right into the arms of atheism!

Spinoza also developed two sub-points under this objection. First, a miracle could not in any case prove God's existence, since a lesser being such as an angel or demon could be the cause of the event. Second, a so-called miracle is simply a work of nature not yet discovered by man. Our knowledge of nature's laws is limited, and just because we cannot explain the cause of a particular event does not mean it is a miracle having God as its supernatural cause.

4.1213 *David Hume.* While Spinoza attacked the possibility of the occurrence of a miracle, the eighteenth-century Scottish skeptic David Hume attacked the possibility of the identification of a miracle. In his essay "Of Miracles" he presents a two-pronged assault against miracles, which takes the form of an "Even if . . . but in fact . . ." argument; that is to say, in the first half he argues against miracles while granting certain concessions, and in the second half he argues on the basis of what he thinks is in fact the case. We may differentiate the two halves of his argument by referring to the first as his "in principle" argument and to the second as his "in fact" argument.

4.12131 *"In principle" argument.* Hume maintains that it is impossible in principle to prove that a miracle has occurred. A wise man, he says, proportions his belief to the evidence. If the evidence makes a conclusion virtually certain, then we may call this a "proof," and a wise man will give whole-hearted belief to that conclusion. If the evidence makes a conclusion more likely than not, then we may speak of a "probability," and a wise man will accept the conclusion as true with a degree of confidence proportionate to the probability. Now, Hume argues, even if we concede that the evidence for a particular miracle amounts to a *full proof,* it is still in principle impossible to identify that event as a miracle. Why? Because standing opposed to this proof is an equally full proof, namely the evidence for the unchangeable laws of nature, that the event in question is not a miracle.

Hume seems to imagine a scale in which the evidence is being weighed. On the one side of the scale is the evidence for miracle, which (he concedes for the sake of argument) amounts to a full proof. But on the other side of the scale stands the evidence from all men in all the ages for the regularity of the laws of nature, which also amounts to a full proof. He writes, "A miracle is a violation of the laws of nature, and as a firm and unalterable experience has established these laws, a proof against miracle, from the very nature of the fact, is as entire as any argument from experience can possibly be imagined."[3] Thus, proof stands against proof, and the scales are evenly balanced. Since the evidence does not incline in either direction, the wise man cannot hold to a miracle with any degree of confidence. Indeed, Hume continues, to prove a miracle has taken place, one would have to prove that it would be an even *greater* miracle for the testimony in support of the event in question to be false.

Thus, with regard to the resurrection, Hume asks, which would be the greater miracle: that a man should rise from the dead or that the witnesses should either be deceived or try to deceive? He leaves no doubt as to his answer: he asserts that even if all historians agreed that on January 1, 1600, Queen Elizabeth publicly died and was buried and her successor installed, but that a month later she reappeared, resumed the throne, and ruled England for three more years, Hume would not have the least inclination to believe so miraculous an event. He would accept the most extraordinary hypothesis for her pretended death and burial rather than admit such a striking violation of the laws of nature. Thus, even if the evidence for a miracle constituted a full proof, the wise man would not believe in miracles.

4.12132 *"In fact" arguments.* But in fact, says Hume, the evidence for miracles does not amount to a full proof. Indeed, the evidence is so poor, it does not even amount to a probability. Therefore, the decisive weight falls on the side of the scale containing the full proof for the regularity of nature, a weight so heavy that no evidence for miracle could ever hope to counter-balance it.

Hume gives four reasons that in fact the evidence for miracles is negligible: First, no miracle in history is attested by a sufficient number of educated and honest men, who are of such social standing that they would have a great deal to lose by lying. Second, people crave the miraculous and will believe the most absurd stories, as the abundance of false tales of miracles proves. Third, miracles occur only among barbarous peoples. And fourth, miracles occur in all religions and thereby cancel each other out, since they support contradictory doctrines.

Hume concludes that miracles can never be the foundation for any system of religion. "Our most holy religion is founded on *Faith*, not on reason," pontificates Hume, all the while laughing up his sleeve:

---

3. David Hume, *Enquiry concerning Human Understanding and concerning the Principles of Morals,* p. 114.

The Christian Religion not only was at first attended with miracles, but even at this day cannot be believed by any reasonable person without one. Mere reason is insufficient to convince us of its veracity: And whoever is moved by *Faith* to assent to it, is conscious of a continued miracle in his own person, which subverts all the principles of his understanding, and gives him a determination to believe what is most contrary to custom and experience.[4]

In other words, it is a miracle that anyone could be stupid enough to believe in Christianity!

4.122 CHRISTIAN DEFENSE OF MIRACLES

As I indicated earlier, the Christians of the seventeenth and eighteenth centuries were far from lax in responding to the Deists' attacks. Let us look therefore at their answers to Spinoza and Hume, as well as to the general Newtonian worldview.

4.1221 *Contra Spinoza.* First, we shall consider the response to Spinoza's two objections by several of the leading Christian thinkers of that era.

4.12211 *Jean Le Clerc.* One of the earliest progenitors of biblical criticism, the French theologian Jean Le Clerc, presented in his *Sentimens de quelques theologiens* (1685) an apologetic for Christianity that, he maintained, was invulnerable to Spinoza's attacks. He asserts that the empirical evidence for Jesus' miracles and resurrection is simply more convincing than Spinoza's a priori philosophical reasoning. Specifically, against Spinoza's contention that miracles may simply be natural events, Le Clerc rejoins that nobody could sincerely believe Jesus' resurrection and ascension to be natural events comparable to, say, a man's birth. Nor does it suffice to say these events could be caused by unknown natural laws, for why then are not more of these events produced, and how is it that at the very instant Jesus commanded a paralyzed man to walk "the Laws of Nature (unknown to us) were prepared and ready to cause the . . . Paralytic Man to walk"?[5] Both of these considerations serve to show that the miraculous events in the gospels, which can be established by ordinary historical methods, are indeed of divine origin.

4.12212 *Samuel Clarke.* Considerable analysis was brought to the concept of miracle by the English philosopher-theologian Samuel Clarke in his Boyle lectures of 1705. Reflecting Newtonian influence, Clarke asserts that matter only has the power to continue in either motion or rest. Anything that is *done* in the world is done either by God or by created intelligent beings. The so-called natural

4. Ibid., pp. 130-31.
5. Jean Le Clerc, *Five Letters Concerning the Inspiration of the Holy Scriptures,* pp. 235-36.

forces of matter, like gravitation, are properly speaking the effect of God's acting on matter at every moment. The upshot of this is that the so-called "course of nature" is a fiction—what we call the course of nature is in reality nothing other than God's producing certain effects in a continual and uniform manner. Thus, a miracle is not contrary to the course of nature, which does not really exist; it is simply an unusual event that God does. Moreover, since God is omnipotent, miraculous events are no more difficult for Him than regular events. So the regular order of nature proves the existence and attributes of God, and miracles prove the interposition of God into the regular order in which He acts.

From the miracle itself taken as an isolated event, it is impossible to determine whether it was performed directly by God or by an angel or a demonic spirit. But, according to Clarke, the key to distinguishing between demonic miracles and divine miracles (whether done directly or indirectly by God) is the *doctrinal context* in which the miracle occurs. If the miracle is done in support of a doctrine that is contrary to moral law, then we may be sure it is not a divine miracle. Thus, in order to be a divine miracle, the doctrinal context of the event must be *at least* morally neutral. If two miracles are performed in support of two contrary doctrines, each morally neutral in itself, then the doctrine supported by the greater miracle ought to be accepted as of divine origin. Hence, the correct theological definition of a miracle is: "a work effected in a manner unusual, or different from the common and regular Method of Providence, by the interposition of God himself, or of some intelligent Agent superior to Man, for the proof or Evidence of some particular Doctrine, or in attestation to the Authority of some particular Person." Jesus' miracles thus prove that he was "a Teacher sent from God" who had "a Divine Commission."[6]

4.12213 *Jacob Vernet.* The finest apologetic work written in French during the eighteenth century was in my opinion J. Alphonse Turrettin and Jacob Vernet's multi-volume *Traité de la vérité de la religion chrétienne* (1730-88). Turrettin, an esteemed professor of Protestant theology at Geneva, wrote the first volume in Latin; Vernet, also a member of the theological faculty at Geneva after 1756, translated Turrettin's volume and added nine of his own. The result was a sophisticated and informed response to French Deism based on internal and external Christian evidences. Vernet defines a miracle as "a striking work which is outside the ordinary course of nature and which is done by God's all-mighty will, such that witnesses thereof regard it as extraordinary and supernatural."[7] Vernet does not, like Clarke, deny that there is a course of nature, but he does insist that

6. Samuel Clarke, *A Discourse Concerning the Unchangeable Obligations of Natural Religion and the Truth and Certainty of the Christian Revelation*, pp. 367-68.
7. Alph. Turrettin, *Traité de la vérité de la religion chrétienne*, 5:2-3.

the so-called course or order of nature is really composed of incidental states of events, not necessary or essential states. They depend on the will of God, and it is only the constant and uniform procession of events that leads us to think the course of nature is invariable. But God can make exceptions to the general order of things when He deems it important. These miraculous events show that the course of nature "is not the effect of a blind necessity, but of a free Cause who interrupts and suspends it when He pleases."[8] Against the objection that miracles may be the result of an as yet undiscovered law of nature, Vernet replies that when the miracles are diverse and numerous, this possibility is minimized because it is hardly possible that all these unknown, marvelous operations of nature should occur at the same time. One might be able to explain away a single, isolated miracle on this basis but not a series of miracles of different sorts.

4.12214 *Claude François Houtteville.* The French Abbé Claude François Houtteville also argued for the possibility of miracles against Spinoza in his treatise *La religion chrétienne prouvée par les faits* (1740). He defines a miracle as "a striking action superior to all finite power" or more commonly as "a singular event produced outside the chain of natural causes."[9] Given the existence of God, it is at once evident that He can perform miracles, since He not only created the world but preserves it in being and directs all the laws of its operation by His sovereign hand. Against Spinoza's charge that miracles are impossible because natural law is the necessary decree of God's immutable nature, Houtteville responds that natural law is not necessary, but that God is free to establish whatever laws He wills. Moreover, God can change His decrees whenever He wishes. And even if He could not, miracles could be part of God's eternal decree for creation just as much as the natural laws, so that they represent no change in God. Houtteville even suggests that miracles may not be contrary to nature but only to what we know of nature. From God's perspective they could conform to certain laws unknown to us.

4.1222 *Contra Hume.* The Christian response to Hume's arguments was as variegated as the response to Spinoza's.

4.12221 *Thomas Sherlock.* Thomas Sherlock, the Bishop of London, wrote his immensely popular *Tryal of the Witnesses* (1729) against the Deist Thomas Woolston, but his arguments are relevant to Hume's critique of miracles. He presents a mock trial in which the apostles are accused of hoaxing the resurrection of Jesus. Woolston's attorney argues that because the resurrection violates the course

---

8. Ibid., 5:240.
9. Abbé Houtteville, *La religion chrétienne prouvée par les faits*, 1:33.

of nature, no human testimony could possibly establish it, since it has the whole witness of nature against it. Sherlock has a multifaceted reply.

First, on that principle many natural matters of fact would have to be pronounced false. If we admit testimony only when it accords with our prior conceptions, then a man living in a hot climate, for example, would never believe the testimony of others that water could exist in a solid state as ice. Second, the resurrection is simply a matter of sense perception. If we met a man who claimed to have been dead, we would be admittedly suspicious. But of what? Not that he is now alive, for that is evident to our senses, but that he was ever dead. But would we say it is impossible to prove by human testimony that his man died a year ago? Such evidence is admitted in any court of law. Conversely, if we saw a man executed and later heard he was alive again, we would be suspicious. But of what? Not that he had been dead, but that he was now alive. But again, could we say that it is impossible for human testimony to prove that a man is alive? The point is, we are suspicious in these cases not because the facts in question cannot be proved by evidence, but because we tend to believe our own senses rather than reports of others that go contrary to our preconceived opinions of what can and cannot happen. But as a historical fact, the resurrection requires no more ability in the witnesses than to be able to distinguish between a dead man and a living man. Sherlock is willing to grant that in miraculous cases we may require more evidence than usual; but it is absurd to say that such cases admit of no evidence.

Third and finally, the resurrection contradicts neither right reason nor the laws of nature. Similarly to Houtteville, Sherlock maintains that the so-called course of nature arises from the prejudices and imaginations of men. Our senses tell us what the usual course of things is, but we go beyond our senses when we conclude that it cannot be otherwise. The uniform course of things runs contrary to the resurrection, but that is no proof that it is absolutely impossible. The same Power that created life in the first place can give it to a dead body again—the latter feat is no greater than the former.

4.12222 *Gottfried Less.* Less, a German theologian at the University of Göttingen, discusses Hume's objections at length in his *Wahrheit der christlichen Religion* (1758). He defines a miracle as a work beyond the power of all creatures. There are two types of miracles: first degree miracles, which are performed directly by God; and second degree miracles, which are beyond human power but are done by finite spirit beings. Less admits that only second degree miracles can be proved, since one cannot be sure when God is acting directly. Miracles are both physically and morally possible: physically because God is the Lord of nature and morally because miracles constitute part of His plan to confirm divine teaching.

There are two steps in proving that a miracle has occurred. First, one must prove the historicity of the event itself. Second, one must prove that the event is a miracle. Less argues that the testimony of the disciples to Jesus' miracles meets even the stringent conditions laid down by Hume, and that therefore even he should accept the historicity of the gospel accounts. Although the apostles were unlearned men, all one needs in order to prove that something happened (say, a disease's being cured at a sheer verbal command) is five good senses and common sense. More specifically, Less argues that the miracles of Jesus were witnessed by hundreds of people, friends and enemies alike; that the apostles had the ability to testify accurately to what they saw; that the apostles were of such doubtless honesty and sincerity as to place them above suspicion of fraud; that the apostles, though of low estate, nevertheless had comfort and life itself to lose in proclaiming the gospel; and that the events to which they testified took place in the civilized part of the world under the Rome Empire, in Jerusalem, the capital city of the Jewish nation. Thus, there is no reason to doubt the apostles' testimony concerning the miracles and resurrection of Jesus.

But were these events miracles? Less maintains that they were and turns to a refutation of Hume's arguments. In response to the "in principle" argument, Less argues: first, because nature is the freely willed order of God, a miracle is just as possible as any other event. Therefore, it is just as believable as any other event. Second, testimony to an event cannot be refuted by prior experiences and observations. Otherwise we should never be justified in believing something outside our present experience; no new discoveries would be possible. Third, there is no contradiction between miracles and experience. Miracles are different events *(Contraria)* from experience in general, but not contradictory events *(Contradictoria)* to experience in general. For example, the contradiction to the testimony that Jesus raised certain people from the dead and Himself so rose three days after His death must necessarily be the exact opposite of this statement, namely, that Jesus never raised anyone from the dead and never Himself so rose. This latter statement would have to be proved in order to destroy the evidence for the gospels. But it would hardly be sufficient to assert that experience in general shows that dead men do not rise, for with this the Christian testimony is in full agreement. Only when the exact opposite is proved to be true could the Christian testimony be said to contradict experience.

As for Hume's "in fact" arguments, these are easily dismissed. First, it has already been shown that the witnesses to the gospel miracles were abundant and qualified. Second, the fact that people tend to believe miracle stories without proper scrutiny only shows that our scrutiny of such stories ought to be cautious and careful. Third, Jesus' miracles did not occur among a barbarous people, but in Jerusalem.

Fourth, Hume's allegation that all religions have their miracles is not in fact true, for no other religion claims to be able to prove its teachings through miracles. Less also examines in considerable detail the examples furnished by Hume and finds in each case that the evidence does not approach that for the gospel miracles.

4.12223 *William Paley.* Paley's two-volume *A View of the Evidences of Christianity* (1794) is undoubtedly the finest apologetic work of that era in English, and it exercised such considerable influence that it remainded compulsory reading for any applicant to Cambridge University right up until the twentieth century. Primarily a studious investigation of the historical evidence for Christianity from miracles, Paley's treatise constitutes an across-the-board refutation of Hume's arguments. It will be remembered that it was Paley who so masterfully expounded the teleological argument, and he makes clear that in this work he presupposes the existence of God as proved by that argument.

Given the existence of God, miracles are not incredible. For why should it be thought incredible that God should want to reveal Himself in the natural world to men, and how could this be done without involving a miraculous element? Further, any antecedent improbability in miracles is not so great that sound historical testimony cannot overcome it. Paley discerns the same fallacy in Hume's argument as did Less. A narrative of a fact can only be said to be contrary to experience if we, being at the time and place in question, observe that the alleged event did not in fact take place.

What Hume really means by "contrary to experience" is simply the lack of similar experience. (To say a miracle is contrary to universal experience is obviously question-begging, since it assumes in advance the miracle in question did not occur.) But in this case the improbability that results from our not having similar experiences is equal to the probability that we should have similar experiences. But what probability is there for that? Suppose God wished to inaugurate Christianity with miracles. What is the probability that we should also experience similar events today? Clearly, any such probability is negligible. Conversely then, any improbability resulting from our lack of such experiences is also negligible. According to Paley, Hume's argument assumes either that the course of nature is invariable or that if it is variable, these variations must be frequent and general. But what grounds are there for either of these assumptions? If the course of nature is the work of an intelligent Being, should we not expect that He would vary the course of nature only seldom at times of great importance?

As for determining whether a miracle has occurred, Paley considers Hume's account of the matter a fair one: which is more probable in any given case, that the miracle be true or the testimony be false? In answering this question, Paley reminds us, we must not remove the miracle from its theistic and historical context, nor can we ignore how the testimony and evidence arose. According to Paley, the real problem with Hume's skepticism becomes clear when we apply it to a test case: suppose twelve men, whom I know to be honest and reasonable people, were to assert that they saw personally a miraculous event in which it was impossible for them to have been tricked; furthermore, the governor called them before him for an inquiry and sentenced them all to death unless they were to admit the hoax; and they all went to their deaths rather than say they were lying. According to Hume, we should still not believe such men. But such incredulity, says Paley, would not be defended by any skeptic in the world.

Against Hume's "in fact" arguments, Paley maintains that no parallel to the gospel miracles exists in history. Like Less, he examines Hume's examples in considerable detail and concludes that it is idle to compare such cases with the miracles of the gospels. Even in cases not easily explained away, there is no evidence that the witnesses have passed their lives in labor and danger and have voluntarily suffered for the truth of what they reported. Thus, the circumstance of the gospel accounts is unparalleled.

4.12.3 *Summary.* Christian apologists thus contested Spinoza and Hume's objections to miracles from a variety of standpoints. It is noteworthy that virtually all the Christian thinkers presupposed the existence of God in their argument. It must be remembered that it was not a case of theism versus atheism but of Christian theism versus Deism. Moreover, God's existence was not always just assumed: Clarke and Paley formulated sophisticated arguments to justify belief in God. The Christians argued that given the existence of God, miracles are possible because of God's omnipotence (Clarke), because of His conservation of the world in being (Houtteville), and because of His sovereign freedom to act as He wills (Less).

Against the mechanistic Newtonian world-view, they argued variously that the course of nature is really only the regular pattern of the operation of God's will (Clarke), or that it is subject to God's freedom to alter it (Vernet, Houtteville, Less, Paley), or even that it may include within itself the capacity for miraculous events (Sherlock, Houtteville).

Against Spinoza's first objection, the apologists argued that miracles do not contradict God's nature because the laws of nature do not flow in necessitarian fashion from the being of God, but are freely willed and therefore alterable (Vernet); and miracles as well as the laws could be willed by God from eternity, so that their occurrence represents no change in God's decrees (Houtteville). Against his second objection, they maintained that miracles, while not proof of the existence of God, are proof of the *Christian* God. Hence, it is correct to say that the regular order of nature proves God's existence; but it is equally true to say that a miracle proves the action of God in the world (Clarke, Paley).

The Christian thinkers sometimes granted freely that one could not know whether God or a lesser being was at work in the miracle; but here they urged that it was the religious, doctrinal context that allowed one to determine if the miracle was divine (Clarke, Less).

As for Spinoza's charge that a supposed miracle may be caused by an unknown law of nature, they responded that it then becomes inexplicable why such events do not recur and why these mysterious laws operated coincidentally at the moment of Jesus' command (Le Clerc), and that this possibility is negligible when numerous and various miracles occur (Vernet); or they granted that such unknown laws might be God's means of acting within the course of nature (Sherlock, Houtteville).

In response to Hume's "in principle" argument they argued: Given God's existence, miracles are as possible as any other event (Less); and the probability that God would reveal Himself nullifies any inherent improbability in miracles (Paley). A miracle is a matter of sense perception like any other event and is therefore capable of being supported by historical testimony (Sherlock). A miracle is not contrary to experience as such, and therefore the testimony to a miracle cannot be nullified by the testimony to the regular order of other experiences (Less, Paley). The improbability that a miracle should occur in the past is equal to the probability that we should experience such events today, a probability that is slight or non-existent (Paley). Hume's argument, if equably applied, would eliminate not only miracles but many natural matters of fact as well (Sherlock, Less). Hume's argument leads to an indefensible skepticism regarding events amply established by reliable testimony (Paley).

In response to Hume's "in fact" argument, the Christian apologists simply sought to prove that in the case of Jesus' miracles and resurrection, the factual evidence was strong enough to establish the credibility of these events, in contrast to other stories of purported miracles (Less, Paley). In short, miracles are neither impossible nor unidentifiable.

4.13 ASSESSMENT

We have seen that the problem of miracles occupied a central place in the Deist controversy of the seventeenth and eighteenth centuries. Although the Christians argued vigorously on behalf of miracles, it was undoubtedly the arguments of Spinoza, Hume, and the Deists that posterity gave an eye to, for in the next century D. F. Strauss was able to proceed in his investigation of the life of Jesus on the a priori assumption that miracles are impossible. According to Strauss, this is not a presupposition requiring proof; on the contrary, to assume that miracles are possible is a presupposition requiring proof. Strauss asserts that God's interposition in the regular course of nature is "irreconcilable with enlightened ideas of the relation of God to the world."[10] Thus, any supposedly historical account of miraculous events must be dismissed out of hand; "indeed no just notion of the true nature of history is possible, without a perception of the inviolability of the chain of finite causes, and of the impossibility of miracles."[11] This presupposition governed the remainder of the nineteenth-century Life of Jesus movement. According to Albert Schweitzer, the historian of that movement, by the mid 1860s the question of miracles had lost all importance. He reports, "The exclusion of miracle from our view of history has been universally recognized as a principle of criticism, so that miracle no longer concerns the historian either positively or negatively."[12] This might lead one to think that the Deists had won the debate. But is this in fact the case?

4.131 THE NEWTONIAN WORLD-MACHINE VERSUS QUANTUM PHYSICS

It will be remembered that the backdrop for the Deist controversy was a view of the universe as a Newtonian world-machine that bound even the hands of God. With the advent of quantum physics, however, twentieth-century scientists have abandoned so iron-clad a view of natural law.

4.1311 *Prescriptive versus descriptive natural law.* Today natural law is understood as essentially *descriptive*, not *prescriptive*. This does not mean that it cannot serve as a basis for prediction, for it does; but this does mean that our formulation of a natural law can never be so certain as to be beyond reformulation under the force of observed facts. Thus, an event cannot be ruled out simply because it does not accord with the regular pattern of events. The advance of modern physics over Newtonian physics is not that natural law does not exist, but that our formulation of it is never final. After all, quantum physics does not mean to assert that matter and energy possess no properties, so that anything and everything can happen. Indeterminacy concerns only the sub-atomic level. On the macroscopic level, natural laws do hold. But the point is that our knowledge of these properties and laws is derived from and based on experience. The laws of nature are thus generalizations; they are not "laws" in the rigid, prescriptive sense, but observed patterns.

10. David Friedrich Strauss, *The Life of Jesus Critically Examined*, p. 737.
11. Ibid., p. 75.
12. Albert Schweitzer, *The Quest of the Historical Jesus*, 3d ed., trans. W. Montgomery (London: Adam & Charles Black, 1954), p. 111.

That would appear to bring some comfort to the modern defender of miracles, for he may now argue that it is illegitimate to exclude a priori a certain event that does not conform to known natural law, since our formulation of natural law is never final and so must take account of the event in question. It seems to me, however, that this does not settle the problem of miracles. It only shows that one cannot rule out in advance an event not conforming to known laws. So the defender of miracles has at least gained a hearing. But the operating assumption still seems to be that if the event really *did* run contrary to natural law, it would be impossible. Presumably if one had an accurate knowledge of genuinely descriptive natural laws, then he *could* know in advance whether the event was possible or not. The question still remains: is it possible for an event to occur that actually does not conform to natural laws that are genuinely descriptive of reality?

So although quantum physics has opened a crack in the door for the defender of miracles, it is not wide enough for him to put his whole case through. As one philosopher of science explains:

> There is no question that most events regarded as significantly 'miraculous' in religious contexts would, if they violate Newtonian laws, also be excessively improbable on well-established quantum laws, and therefore would be regarded as violations of these also. Thus, if we consider only the currently accepted theories of physics, the credibility of such miracles is no greater than in Newtonian theory.[13]

The resurrection of Jesus is a case in point. The fact that a man should be raised from the dead in a transformed existence is so disparate from the normal processes of decay that we may safely say that such an event actually lies outside the power of natural causes. The question therefore remains: can an event that actually does not conform to genuinely descriptive natural laws take place?

This, it seems to me, is the proper question concerning the problem of miracles: can an event occur that has neither physical nor human causes? Such an event need not be characterized as a "violation of the laws of nature," for that carries with it the connotations of breaking a civil law and smacks of the old prescriptivist view. It is psychologically less prejudicial to define a miracle as an event whose cause lies outside the system of natural causes. So although a psychological advantage has been gained, the twentieth-century defender of miracles still has to face the question of whether an event can occur that lies outside the productive capacity of natural causes.

Here it would seem to be of no avail to answer with Clarke that

13. Mary Hesse, "Miracles and the Laws of Nature," in *Miracles,* ed. C. F. D. Moule, p. 38.

matter has no properties and that the course of nature is simply God's regular action. For modern physics holds that matter does possess certain properties and that certain forces like gravitation and electro-magnetism are real forces operating in the world. Nor would it help to answer with Sherlock and Houtteville that nature may contain within itself the power to produce certain effects contrary to its normal operation. For this explanation is unconvincing in cases where the natural laws are sufficiently well-known so as to preclude with a high degree of probability the event's taking place. Moreover, this solution threatens to reduce the event in question to a freak of nature, the result of chance, not an act of God.

4.1312 *Logical and nomological possibility.* But granting that, what really has been proved? All the scientist conceivably has the right to say is that such a miraculous event is naturally impossible. But with that conclusion the defender of miracles may readily agree. Here we need to distinguish logical possibility from nomological possibility. Loosely speaking, something is logically possible if it is in accord with the law of contradiction. If it involves a contradiction, it is logically impossible. For example, a square circle is logically impossible. On the other hand something is nomologically (from *nomos*, "law") possible if it is in accord with natural laws. If it does not conform to natural laws, then it is nomologically impossible. For example, it is nomologically impossible for sound to travel through a vaccuum. Now is a miracle logically impossible? No, for it does not involve a logical contradiction. Is a miracle nomologically impossible? Yes, for it does not conform to natural laws; indeed, this is a tautology, since to lie outside the system of natural causes is to not conform with natural laws, or to be nomologically impossible.

Now the question is, what could conceivably transform an event that is logically possible but nomologically impossible into a real historical possibility? Clearly, the answer is the personal God of theism. For if a transcendent, personal God exists, then He could cause events in the universe that could not be produced by causes within the universe. It is precisely to such a God that the Christian apologists appealed. Given a God who is omnipotent, who conserves the world in being, and who is capable of acting freely, Christian thinkers seem to be entirely justified in maintaining that miracles are possible. Indeed, if the existence of such a God is even *possible*, then miracles are also possible. Only if atheism were proved to be true could one rationally deny the possibility of miracles. For if it is even possible that a transcendent, personal God exists, then it is equally possible that He has acted in the universe. Therefore, it seems to me that the Christian apologists argued in the main correctly against their Newtonian opponents, and that the advent of quantum physics had only strengthened their case.

4.132 SPINOZA'S OBJECTIONS

Turning to Spinoza's objections, again it seems to me that the Christian thinkers argued cogently.

4.1321 *Objection based on the immutability of nature.* With regard to the first objection, it must be kept in mind that Spinoza was a pantheist, so that "God" and "Nature" were interchangeable terms. With this understanding, it is no wonder that he argued for the immutable order of nature, for inasmuch as God and nature were to him the same, a violation of nature's laws would have been a violation of the very being of God.

But of course the question is not whether miracles are possible on a pantheistic worldview but on a theistic world view. If God is personal and distinct from the world, there seems to be no reason why even a total alteration of nature's laws should in any way affect God. Natural law ought not to be construed as logically necessary, as Spinoza thought, so there seems to be no reason God could not have chosen other laws or could not change existing ones. Vernet argued correctly that nature's laws depend on God's freely willed choice. Houtteville and Less also maintained correctly that the miracles, like the laws, could have been willed from eternity so that no change in God's will or decrees need come into question. Thus, Spinoza's first objection seems to presuppose his pantheism and need not trouble a modern defender of miracles.

4.1322 *Objection based on the insufficiency of miracles.* Spinoza's second objection was that miracles are insufficient to prove God's existence.

4.13221 *General remarks.*

4.132211 *The irrelevance of the objection.* As it is stated, the objection was simply irrelevant for most of the Christian apologists, for virtually all of them used miracles not as a proof for the existence of God but as a proof for His action in the world. Hence, Spinoza was really attacking a straw man.

4.132212 *Underlying assumptions.* Nevertheless, the supporting reasoning of the objection was relevant to the Christians' position. Spinoza's main point was that a proof for God must be absolutely certain. Since we infer God's existence from the immutable laws of nature, anything that casts doubt on those laws casts doubt on God's existence. Two assumptions seem to underlie this reasoning: first, that a proof for God's existence must be demonstratively certain; and second, that God's existence is inferred from natural laws. But Christian apologists denied both of these assumptions. The more empirically-minded of them held that a cogent argument for God's existence need not be demonstratively certain. Think, for example, of Paley's teleological argument: while not reaching absolute certainty, it claimed to make it more plausible to believe in God than not. Modern philosophers agree that if we were justified in accepting only those conclusions proved with demonstrative certainty, then we should know very, very little indeed. The second assumption fails to take account of the fact that there are other arguments for the existence of God not based on natural laws. For example, Clarke, while sharing Spinoza's concern for demonstrative certainty, nevertheless believed that the ontological and cosmological arguments provided rational grounds for accepting God's existence. So even if natural law were uncertain, that would not for Clarke call into question God's existence.

4.132213 *Exceptions to natural law.* But is Spinoza's objection in fact true? He seems to think that the admission of a genuine miracle would overthrow the natural law violated by the miracle. But Clarke and Paley argue more persuasively that a miracle need not overthrow the general regularity of nature; it only shows God's intervention at that particular point. As Richard Swinburne argues, a natural law is not abolished because of one exception; the exception must occur repeatedly whenever the conditions for it are present. If the event will not occur again under identical circumstances, then the law will not be abandoned. A natural law will not be reformulated unless a new version will yield better predictability of future events without being more complicated than the original law. But if the new version does no better in predicting the phenomena and explaining the event in question, then the event will simply remain an unexplained exception to the natural law. Thus, Spinoza's fear that miracles would destroy the fabric of natural law appears to be unjustified. Rather than leading us into the arms of atheism, exceptions to natural laws could lead us to discern the action of God in the world at that point.

4.13222 *Miracles and theism.* Spinoza's sub-point that miracles could not prove the existence of God, but only of a lesser being, did not strike against most of the Christian apologists because they were not trying to prove the existence of God. Having proved or presupposed God's existence, they used miracles chiefly to show that Christian theism was true. But they were very concerned about how to show in any particular case that a miracle was not demonic but divine.

4.132221 *Religio-historical context.* I think that their answer to this problem constitutes one of their most important and enduring contributions to the discussion of miracles. They held that the doctrinal context of the miracle makes it evident if the miracle is truly from God. In this way they drew attention to the religio-historical context in which the miracle occurred as the key to the interpretation of that miracle. That is very significant, for a miracle without a context is inherently ambiguous. This is the problem with Hume's example of the revivification of Queen Elizabeth: the event lacks any religious context and appears as a bald and unexplained anomaly. Hence, one feels a degree of sympathy for Hume's skepticism. But how different it is with the case of Jesus' resurrection! It occurs in the context of and as the climax to Jesus' own unparalleled life and teachings, and produced so profound an effect on His followers that they called Him Lord and proclaimed salvation for all men in His name. It ought, therefore, to give us serious pause, whereas the resuscitation of Queen Elizabeth would occasion only perplexity. The religio-historical context is crucial to the interpretation of a miraculous event.

4.132222 *Lesser divine beings.* Spinoza's concern with lesser spiritual beings like angels and demons would probably not trouble many twentieth-century minds. Such beings are part of the furniture, so to speak, of a wider theistic world view, so that no atheist today would seriously concede the gospel miracles and yet maintain they were performed by angels. It would not seem unwarranted to infer that if such events are genuine miracles, then they were wrought by God.

4.13223 *Identification of miracles.* Spinoza's final sub-point, that a supposed miracle may really be the effect of an unknown law of nature, is not really an object against the occurrence of miracles, but against the identification of miracles. Granted that miracles are possible, how can we know when one has occurred?

4.132231 *Anthony Flew's defense of Spinoza.* This problem has been persuasively formulated in our day by the English philosopher Antony Flew:

> We simply do not have, and could not have, any natural . . . criterion which enables us to say, when faced with something which is found to have actually happened, that here we have an achievement which nature, left to her own unaided devices, could never encompass. The natural scientist, confronted with some occurrence inconsistent with a proposition previously believed to express a law of nature, can find in this disturbing inconsistency no ground whatever for proclaiming that the particular law of nature has been supernaturally overridden![14]

4.132232 *Momentous, singular, various, and numerous occurrence of miracles.* The response of Sherlock and Houtteville to this objection, that an unknown law of nature is God's means of producing the event, is surely inadequate. For it could just as easily be the case that the event is no act of God at all, just a spontaneous accident of nature without religious significance. Rather I think Le Clerc and Vernet have taken a better tack: when the mircles occur at a momentous time (for example, a man's leprosy vanishing when Jesus

14. *Encyclopedia of Philosophy,* s.v. "Miracles," by Antony Flew.

spoke the words "Be clean") and do not recur regularly in history; and when the miracles in question are numerous and various; then the chance of their being the result of unknown natural causes is minimal. Since, as we shall see in 5.13223, most critics now acknowledge that Jesus did perform what we would call miracles, this answer to Spinoza and Flew seems to be a cogent defense of the supernatural origin of the gospel miracles.

4.132233 *Jesus' resurrection.* But even if we leave Jesus' miracles aside and focus our attention on His resurrection from the dead, I think the supernatural nature of that event alone may be successfully defended. We are not asking here whether the facts of the case, such as the empty tomb or resurrection appearances, might be explained in a natural manner. The question is, if Jesus actually did rise from the dead, would we then be justified in inferring a supernatural cause for that event? Here the overwhelming majority of people would say yes. Those who argue against the resurrection try to explain away the facts of the case without allowing that Jesus rose from the dead. I know of no critic who argues that the best explanation of the historical facts is that Jesus rose from the dead, but that His resurrection was no miracle but a perfectly natural occurrence. That would appear to be a somewhat desperate obstinacy. Two factors undergird this reasoning.

4.1322331 *Exceeds natural causes.* First, the resurrection so exceeds what we know of natural causes that it seems most reasonable to attribute it to a supernatural cause. Hume himself asserted that it has never in the history of the world been heard of that a truly dead man (in Jesus' case for a night, a day, and a night) has been raised from the dead. Given the length of time that Jesus had been dead, it would be idle to compare his resurrection with the resuscitation of persons pronounced clinically dead in hospitals. But more than that: it is very important to understand that the resurrection was more than the resuscitation of a corpse. It was not a return to the earthly, mortal life; rather it was the transformation of the body to a new mode of existence, which Paul described as powerful, glorious, imperishable, and Spirit-directed (1 Cor. 15:42-44). It is inconceivable that such an event could be the product of natural causes. Moreover, if it were the effect of purely natural causes, then its singularity in the history of mankind becomes very difficult to understand—why has it not happened again? In the nearly two thousand years since that event, no natural causes have been discovered that could explain it. On the contrary, the advance of science has only served to confirm that such an event is nomologically impossible.

4.1322332 *Occurs in significant context.* Second, the supernatural explanation is given immediately in the religio-historical context in which the event occurred. Jesus' resurrection was not merely an anomalous event, occurring without context; it came as the climax to Jesus' own life and teachings. As Wolfhart Pannenberg explains,

> The resurrection of Jesus acquires such decisive meaning, not merely because someone or anyone has been raised from the dead, but because it is Jesus of Nazareth, whose execution was instigated by the Jews because he had blasphemed against God.
>
> Jesus' claim to authority, through which he put himself in God's place, was . . . blasphemous for Jewish ears. Because of this Jesus was then also slandered before the Roman Governor as a rebel. If Jesus really has been raised, this claim has been visibly and unambiguously confirmed by the God of Israel, who was alleged blasphemed by Jesus.[15]

Thus the religio-historical context furnishes us with the key to the supernatural character of that event.

       4.132234 *Untenable skepticism.* One final remark on Spinoza's objection against the identification of a miracle: his argument, unlike Hume's, does not spring from the nature of historical investigation. Rather, the very eyewitnesses of the event could press Spinoza's objection. But in this case, the argument leads to an untenable skepticism. There comes a point when the back of skepticism is broken by the sheer reality of the miracle before us. I think, for example, of that delightful scene in Dickens's *Christmas Carol* in which Scrooge is confronted by Marley's ghost, all bound in chains:

> "You don't believe in me," observed the Ghost.
> "I don't," said Scrooge.
> "What evidence would you have of my reality beyond that of your senses?"
> "I don't know," said Scrooge.
> "Why do you doubt your senses?"
> "Because," said Scrooge, "a little thing affects them. A slight disorder of the stomach makes them cheats. You may be an undigested bit of beef, a blot of mustard, a crumb of cheese, a fragment of underdone potato. There's more gravy than grave about you, whatever you are. . . ."
> ". . . You see this toothpick?" said Scrooge.
> "I do," replied the Ghost.
> ". . . Well!" returned Scrooge, "I have but to swallow this, and be for the rest of my life persecuted by a legion of goblins, all of my own creation. Humbug, I tell you! Humbug!"
> At this the spirit raised a frightful cry, and shook its chain with such a dismal and appalling noise, that Scrooge held on tight to his chair, to save himself from falling into a swoon. But how much greater was his horror,

---

15. Wolfhart Pannenberg, *Jesus—God and Man*, p. 67.

when the phantom taking off the bandage round its head, . . . its lower jaw dropped down upon its breast!

Scrooge fell upon his knees, and clasped his hands before his face.

"Mercy!" he said. "Dreadful apparition, why do you trouble me?"

"Man of worldly mind!" replied the Ghost, "do you believe in me or not?"

"I do," said Scrooge. "I must.'"[16]

Such studied skepticism as Scrooge's becomes untenable when confronted with the evident reality of such a striking miracle. Can we imagine, for example, doubting Thomas, when confronted with the risen Jesus, studiously considering whether what he saw palpably before him might not be the effect of an unknown natural cause? Had Jesus Himself encountered such skepticism, would He not have attributed it to hardness of heart? In this light, such skepticism need not be demonstratively refuted but is self-condemned. Perhaps Pascal was right in saying that God has given evidence sufficiently clear for those with an open heart, but sufficiently vague so as not to compel those whose hearts are closed.

4.133 HUME'S OBJECTIONS
4.1331 *"In principle" argument.*
4.13311 *Either question-begging or confused.* The "in principle" argument, it seems to me, is either question-begging or confused. As Hume presents the argument, it appears to be clearly question-begging. To say that uniform experience is against miracles is to implicitly assume already that miracles have never occurred. It seems almost embarrassing to refute so sophisticated an objection by such a simple consideration, but nevertheless this answer seems to me to be entirely correct. The only way Hume can place uniform experience for the regularity of nature on one side of the scale is by assuming that the testimony for miracles on the other side of the scale is false. And that, quite simply, is begging the question.

But suppose we give Hume the benefit of the doubt and relax the meaning of the term "uniform experience" to mean merely "general experience." It seems to me that the argument so interpreted is still fallacious, because it embodies a fundamental confusion. Hume confuses the realms of science and history. In the realm of science the general experience of mankind has enabled us to formulate certain laws that describe the physical universe. That dead men do not rise is a generally observed pattern in our experience. But at most it only shows that a resurrection is nomologically impossible. That is a matter of science. But it does not show that such a nomologically impossible

16. Charles Dickens, "A Christmas Carol," pp. 18-19.

event has not in fact occurred. This is a matter of history. It is only by means of this category mistake that Hume is able to weigh evidence for a particular miracle in the same scale with evidence for natural laws. But as Less and Paley correctly pointed out, one cannot counterbalance the evidence for a particular miracle with evidence for the regularity of nature in general. If the historical evidence makes it reasonable to believe Jesus rose from the dead, then it is illegitimate to suppress this evidence because all other men have always remained in their graves.

Nor can it be objected that the evidence must be false because the event in question is nomologically impossible. It may well be the case that history proves that a nomologically impossible event has occurred. As Sherlock argued, a miraculous event is just as much a matter of sense perception as an ordinary event and can therefore be proved by historical testimony in the same way as a non-miraculous event. As history, they stand on the same par. As Paley further pointed out, Hume's principle could lead us into situations where we would be forced to deny the testimony of the most reliable witnesses because of general considerations; and this is an unrealistic skepticism. And that goes not only for miraculous events, but, as Sherlock and Less urged, for non-miraculous events as well. There are all sorts of events that make up the stuff of popular books and television shows on unexplained mysteries (such as levitations, disappearing persons, spontaneous human combustions, and so forth) that have not been scientifically explained, but—judging by their pointless nature, sporadic occurrence, and lack of any religious context—are not miracles. It would be folly for a historian to deny the occurrence of such events in the face of good eyewitness evidence to the contrary, simply because they do not fit in with known natural laws. Yet Hume's principle would require the historian to say that these events never occurred, which is indefensible.

4.13312 *Antony Flew's defense of Hume.* Flew has sought to redefend Hume's "in principle" argument. He writes:

> It is only and precisely by presuming that the laws that hold today held in the past and by employing as canons all our knowledge . . . of what is probable or improbable, possible or impossible, that we can rationally interpret the detritus of the past as evidence and from it construct our account of what actually happened. But in this context, what is impossible is what is physically, as opposed to logically impossible. And "physical possibility" is, and surely has to be, defined in terms of inconsistency with a true law of nature. . . .
>
> Our sole ground for characterizing a reported occurrence as miraculous is at the same time a sufficient reason for calling it physically impossible.[17]

17. *Encyclopedia of Philosophy,* s.v. "Miracles."

4.133121 *Inconsistency of Flew's position.* Now Flew's objection appears to be actually inconsistent with his defense of Spinoza's objection. There he asserted that our knowledge of nature is so incomplete that we can never regard any event as miraculous, since it could conform to an unknown law of nature. This would force us to take a totally open attitude toward the possibility of any event, for virtually anything could be possible in nature. But now he asserts precisely the opposite, namely, that our knowledge of natural law is so complete that not only can we determine which events are nomologically impossible, but we are also able to impose this standard over the past to expunge such events from the record. The two positions are incompatible. Flew thus seems to have worked himself into the following dilemma:

Either nomologically impossible events can be defined or not.

If they can be defined, then the occurrence of such events could be identified as miracles.

If they cannot be defined, then we must be open to anything's happening in history, including miracles.

4.133122 *Circularity of Flew's objection.* I have argued that nomologically impossible events can sometimes be defined and that Jesus' resurrection is such an event. Does this therefore mean, as Flew alleges, that I must regard this event as unhistorical? Not at all; Flew has made an unwarranted identification between nomological (or as he puts it, physical) possibility and real, historical possibility. The assumption hidden behind this identification is that nomologically impossible events cannot occur or, in other words, that miracles cannot happen, which is question-begging, as that is precisely the point to be proved. Thus, despite the apparent sophistication of his argument, Flew is actually arguing in a circle. If one wishes to talk about historical possibility or impossibility at all, these terms ought not to be defined in terms of scientific law, but in terms of historical evidence. Thus, for example, it is historically possible that Nietzsche's insanity resulted from venereal disease, it is historically impossible that Napoleon won the battle of Waterloo. On this basis only the evidence itself can tell us whether it is possible that Jesus rose from the dead.

4.13313 *Miracles and historical methodology.*

4.133131 *Ernst Troeltsch's principle of analogy.* Flew's real objection is that in order to study history, one must assume the impossibility of miracles. This viewpoint is simply a restatement of the nineteenth-century German theologian Ernst Troeltsch's principle of analogy. According to Troeltsch, one of the most basic historiographical principles is that the past does not differ essentially from the present. Though the events of the past are obviously not the same events as those of the present, they must be the same *kind* of events if historical investigation is to be possible. Troeltsch realized that this principle was incompatible with the miraculous events of the gospels and therefore held that they must be regarded as unhistorical.

4.133132 *Wolfhart Pannenberg's critique of Troeltsch's principle.* In our own day, however, Pannenberg has persuasively argued that Troeltsch's principle of analogy cannot be employed to banish all non-analogous events from history. According to Pannenberg, analogy, when properly defined, means that in an unclear historical situation we should interpret the facts in terms of known experience. Troeltsch, however, uses analogy to constrict all past events to purely natural events. But, Pannenberg maintains, the fact that an event bursts all analogies to the present cannot be used to dispute its historicity. When, for example, myths, legends, illusions, and the like are dismissed as unhistorical, it is not because they are unusual but because they are analogous to present forms of consciousness to which no historical reality corresponds. When an event is said to have occurred for which no present analogy exists, we cannot automatically dismiss its historicity; to do that we must have an analogy to some known form of consciousness to which no reality corresponds that would suffice to explain the situation. Pannenberg has thus converted Troeltsch's principle of analogy in such a way that it is not the lack of an analogy that shows an event to be unhistorical but the presence of a positive analogy to known thought forms that shows a purported miracle to be unhistorical. Hence, he has elsewhere affirmed that if the Easter narratives were shown to be essentially secondary constructions analogous to common comparative religious phonomena; if the Easter appearances were shown to correspond completely to the model of hallucinations; and if the empty tomb tradition were shown to be a late legend, then the resurrection should be evaluated as unhistorical. In this way, the lack of an analogy to present experience says nothing for or against the historicity of an event. Pannenberg's use of the principle preserves the analogous structure of the past to the present or to the known, thus making the investigation of history possible without thereby forcing the past into the mold of the present. It would therefore seem that Hume's "in principle" argument fares no better than Spinoza's objections.

4.1332 *"In fact" arguments.* If then there is no "in principle" objection to the identification of miracles, what may be said of Hume's "in fact" arguments? All of his points have force; but the fact remains that these general considerations cannot be used to decide the historicity of any particular miracle. They serve to make us cautious in the investigation of any miracle, but the only way the question of historicity can be solved is through such an investigation. Hume's fourth point (that miracles occur in all religions and thereby cancel each other out) does try to preclude an investigation; but it still remains an empirical question whether the evidence for any miracle supporting a counter-Christian claim is as well or better attested as the evidence for Jesus' miracles and resurrection. And if the latter should prove to be genuine, then we can forgo the investigation of every single counter-Christian miracle, for most of these pale into insignificance next to the gospel miracles.

4.134 CONCLUSION

Hence, I think that the Christian apologists argued correctly against their Deist opponents; and it is sad that the nineteenth century failed to discern this fact. The presupposition against miracles survives in theology only as a hangover from an earlier Deistic age and ought now to be once for all abandoned.

4.14 PRACTICAL APPLICATION

The material shared in both divisions of this *locus* do not, I must confess, admit of much practical application in evangelism. I have never encountered a non-Christian who rejected the gospel because of an overt objection to miracles. Nevertheless, this section is extremely important because the presupposition of modern biblical criticism has been the impossibility of miracles in history, so that a conservative approach to the Scriptures necessitates a prior defense of the possibility of miracles. Thus, the material in this section is critical to a reform of biblical scholarship, without which we evangelicals cannot win in the theological community.

In addition, however, I do think people with whom we discuss Christ do sometimes have covert problems with miracles. They do not formulate their misgivings into an argument; they just find it hard to believe that the miraculous events of the gospel really occurred. Insofar as we sense this is the case, we need to bring this presupposition out into the open and explain why there are no good grounds for it. Show the unbeliever that he has no reasons for rejecting the possibility of miracles and challenge him that the universe may be a much more wonderful place than he believes. In my own case, the virgin birth was a stumbling block to my coming to faith—I simply could not believe such a thing. But when I reflected on the fact that God had created the entire universe, it occurred to me that it would not be too difficult for Him to make a woman become pregnant. Once the non-Christian understands who God is, then the problem of miracles should cease to be a problem for him.

4.2 THE PROBLEM OF HISTORICAL KNOWLEDGE

"The uniqueness and the scandal of the Christian religion," writes George Ladd, rest in the mediation of revelation through historical events." Christianity is not a code for living or a philosophy of religion; rather it is rooted in real events of history. To some this is scandalous, because it means that the truth of Christianity is bound up with the truth of certain historical facts, such that if those facts should be disproved, so would Christianity. But at the same time, this makes Christianity unique because, unlike most other world religions, we now have a means of verifying its truth by historical evidence.

This, however, brings us face to face with the problem of historical knowledge; that is to say, How is it possible to learn anything about the human past with any degree of assurance? On the popular level, this expresses itself in the attitude that history is uncertain and irrelevant to us today. It has been said that history is a series of lies that everyone has decided to agree on. On the scholarly level, the problem finds expression in the outlook of historical relativism, which denies the objectivity of historical facts. This outlook has profound implications for Christian theology in the areas of apologetics, hermeneutics, and doctrine of revelation, to name a few. It would make it impossible to demonstrate historically the accuracy of the biblical narratives, since the past cannot be objectively established. One would be free to impose whatever meaning one chose upon the narratives, since facts have no meaning. And one could leave aside the doctrine of the inerrancy of Scripture, since it would be meaningless to speak of "errors" if historical relativism were true. Therefore, it is imperative that the Christian scholar handle certain critical issues in the philosophy of history as a prelude to an examination of the biblical documents themselves.

4.21 LITERATURE CITED OR RECOMMENDED

4.211 HISTORICAL BACKGROUND

Anselm *Cur Deus Homo.* In *Basic Writings.* 2d ed. Translated by S. N. Deane. Introduction by C. Hartshorne. Open Court Library of Philosophy. LaSalle, Ill.: Open Court, 1968. Pp. 171-288.

De la Chaise, Filleau. "Discours sur les livres de Moise." In *Discours sur les "Pensées" de M. Pascal.* Edited with an introduction by V. Giraud. Collections des chefs-d'oeuvre méconnues. Paris: Editions Bossard, 1922.

Grotius, Hugo. *The Truth of the Christian Religion.* Notes by J. Le Clerc. Translated by J. Clarke. London: 1709.

Kümmel, Werner Georg. *The New Testament: The History of the Investigation of its Problems.* Translated by S. McL. Gilmour and H. C. Kee. Nashville: Abingdon, 1972.

Ladd, George. "The Knowledge of God: The Saving Acts of God." In *Basic Christian Doctrines.* Edited by Carl F. H. Henry. New York: Holt, Rinehart, and Winston, 1962. Pp. 7-13.

Leslie, Charles. *A Short and Easie Method with the Deists.* 2d ed. London: C. Brome, E. Pode, & Geo. Strahan, 1699.

Mornay, Philippe de. *De la verité de la religion chrestienne.* Anvers: Imprimerie de Christofle Plantin, 1581. Translated as *A Work Concerning the Trueness of the Christian Religion,* by P. Sidney and A. Goldring. London: 1617.

Thomas Aquinas. *Summa theologiae.* 60 vols. London: Eyre & Spottiswoode for Blackfriars, 1964.

Thompson, J. Westfall, and Holm, Bernard J. *A History of Historical Writing.* 2 vols. New York: Macmillan, 1942.

Vives, Juan Luis. *De veritate fidei christianae.* Reprint. London: Gregg International, 1964.

4.212 ASSESSMENT

Aron, Raymond. "Relativism in History." In *The Philosophy of History in Our Time.* Edited by H. Meyerhoff. Garden City, N.Y.: Doubleday, 1959. Pp. 153-62.

Beard, Charles. "That Noble Dream." In *The Varieties of History.* Edited by F. Stern. Cleveland: World, Meridian, 1956. Pp. 314-28.

Becker, Carl. "What Are Historical Facts?" In *The Philosophy of History in Our Time.* Edited by H. Meyerhoff. Garden City, N.Y.: Doubleday, 1959. Pp. 120-39.

Berlin, Isaiah. "The Concept of Scientific History." In *Philosophical Analysis and History.* Edited by W. H. Dray. Sources in Contemporary Philosophy. New York: Harper & Row, 1966.

Blake, Christopher. "Can History Be Objective?" In *Theories of History.* Edited by P. Gardiner. Glencoe, Ill.: Free Press, 1959. Pp. 329-43.

Carr, E. H. *What Is History?* New York: Random House, Vintage, 1953.

Collingwood, R. G. "Are History and Science Different Kinds of Knowledge?" In *Essays in the Philosophy of History.* Edited by W. Debbins. Austin, Tex.: U. of Texas, 1965. Pp. 23-33.

———. *An Autobiography.* London: Oxford U., 1939.

———. "Croce's Philosophy of History." In *Essays in the Philosophy of History.* Edited by William Debbins. Austin, Tex.: U. of Texas, 1965. Pp. 3-22.

———. *Essays in the Philosophy of History.* Edited by W. Debbins. Austin, Tex.: U. of Texas, 1965.

———. *The Idea of History.* Edited by T. M. Know. Oxford: Oxford U., Galaxy, 1956.

Debbins, William. "Introduction." In *Essays in the Philosophy of History,* by R. G. Collingwood. Edited by W. Debbins. Austin, Tex.: U. of Texas, 1965.

Donagan, Alan. "Introduction." In *Philosophy of History.* Edited by A. Donagan and B. Donagan. Sources in Philosophy. New York: Macmillan, 1965. Pp. 1-22.

Gardiner, Patrick. *The Nature of Historical Explanation.* London: Oxford U., Galaxy, 1961.

Harrison, R. K. *Introduction the Old Testament.* Grand Rapids: Eerdmans, 1969.

Mandelbaum, Maurice. *The Problem of Historical Knowledge.* New York: Harper & Row, Harper Torchbooks, 1967.

Orwell, George. *1984: A Novel.* London: Secker & Warburg, 1949.

Pirenne, Henri. "What Are Historians Trying to Do?" In *The Philosophy of History in Our Time.* Edited by H. Meyerhoff. Garden City, N.Y.: Doubleday, 1959. Pp. 87-100.

Popper, Karl. "Has History Any Meaning?" In *The Philosophy of History in Our Time.* Edited by H. Meyerhoff. Garden City, N.Y.: Doubleday, 1959. Pp. 300-312.

———. *The Poverty of Historicism.* London: Routledge & Kegan Paul, 1957. Reprint. New York: Harper & Row, Harper Torchbooks, 1964.

Walsh, W. H. *Philosophy of History: An Introduction.* New York: Harper & Row, Harper Torchbooks, 1965.

White, Morton. "Can History Be Objective?" In *The Philosophy of History in Our Time.* Edited by H. Meyerhoff. Garden City, N.Y.: Doubleday, 1959. Pp. 188-202.

———. *Foundations of Historical Knowledge.* New York: Harper & Row, Harper Torchbooks, 1965.

Yamauchi, Edwin. "Immanuel Velikovsky's Catastrophic History." *Journal of the American Scientific Affiliation* 25 (1973):134-39.

4.22 HISTORICAL BACKGROUND

Though men have written histories from earliest times, historiography as a science is a product of the modern age.

4.221 MEDIEVAL PERIOD

To understand the development of this science and its impact upon apologetics, let us turn back to the Middle Ages.

4.2211 *Medieval dearth of historiography.* After the Patristic age, the West, in contrast to the Byzantine lands, lapsed into a period of intellectual and cultural decline that lasted from the fifth to the eleventh centuries. Only in ecclesiastical circles were literacy and learning retained, for the masses were to a great extent illiterate. Most of the medieval histories of this time consisted of chronicles that simply listed events and their dates. Around A.D. 900 historiography almost completely disappeared. For the medieval historians, the biblical writers, and the church Fathers on the one hand, together with the classical writers and poets on the other, were considered "authors" (cf. 1.211), or authorities, whose testimony was not questioned. Their successors counted as mere "writers" or "compilers," who adduced the testimony of authorities. Thus, verbatim reiteration became a virtue, and a writer describing the history of the recent past, for which no authorities could be adduced, often felt obliged to apologize to his readers for writing in his own words.

The character of medieval historical writing as reiteration of authorities was largely determined by Isidore Bishop of Seville (d. 636), who argued in his *Etymologies* that since history, as contrasted to both fable and myth, narrates what truly took place, it must be an eyewitness account. Therefore, the narration of past events is simply a matter of compilation of the testimonies of authorities, who were taken to be eyewitnesses. Writing history consisted of copying one's sources. This historiographical method has been called the "scissors and paste" method by modern historians such as R. G. Collingwood, who emphasize the historian's liberty to criticize his sources.

Although the eleventh and twelfth centuries experienced a revival of culture and learning, this had little effect on historiography. With important exceptions, history continued in the main to be a recapitulation of authorities; and by the thirteenth century history as a literary form had collapsed back into chronicle. It is instructive to note that when in 1286 the administration of the University of Paris drew up a booklist of all the texts necessary for basic reading at the university, only three out of 140 were historical in nature. It was not until the fifteenth century that modern historiography was born, and not until even later that history became a widely read literary genre.

Given this circumstance, it would be unrealistic to expect a historical apologetic for the Christian faith from medieval thinkers.

4.2212 *Impact on apologetics.* What then could be done to commend rationally the Christian faith to unbelievers? Some thinkers, epitomized by Anselm, sought to prove the deity and incarnation of Christ (and hence the truth of the biblical books authorized by him) by a priori reasoning alone. At the conclusion of *Cur Deus homo* Anselm's dialogue partner confesses:

> All things you have said seem to me reasonable and incontrovertible. And by the solution of the single question proposed, do I see the truth of all that is contained in the Old and New Testament. For, in proving that God became man by necessity, leaving out what was taken from the Bible . . . you convince both Jews and Pagans by the mere force of reason. And the God-man himself originates the New Testament and approves the Old. And, as we must acknowledge him to be true, so no one can dissent from anything contained in these books.[1]

Anselm's deductive approach circumvented the need for any historical investigation of the facts, because everything was proved by a rational necessity.

On the other hand, we find very early on, and then with increasing sophistication in the thirteenth century, the development of a philosophical framework well-suited for historical argumentation, even if it was itself devoid of such argumentation. According to this approach, one supported the authority of Scripture by the empirical signs of credibility, mainly miracle and prophecy. Those were the chief signs employed by Augustine to justify belief in the authority of Scripture. Although early scholasticism tended to follow Anselm's a priori approach, during the thirteenth century this approach became less convincing, and increasing weight was given instead to the external signs.

According to Thomas Aquinas, the truths of faith, while unprovable directly, can nevertheless be confirmed or proved indirectly by means of miracle and prophecy. For Aquinas, miracle is the most important sign of credibility. It confirms the truths of faith in two ways: it confirms the truth of what the miracle worker teaches, and it makes known God's presence in the miracle worker. Hence he says with regard to Christ's miracles: "Christ wrought miracles in order to confirm his teaching, and in order to demonstrate the divine power that was his."[2] I have argued that this analysis of miracle is essentially correct

---

1. Anselm *Cur Deus homo* 2.22.
2. Thomas Aquinas *Summa theologia* 3a.43.3.

(4.132221; 4.132233). For Aquinas, therefore, the crucial problem is *historical:* How do I know that the miracles in question ever occurred? Here there is danger of reasoning in a circle: miracles confirm that the Scripture is from God; therefore what it teaches is authoritatively true; therefore the miracles recorded in Scripture really occurred. Now Aquinas himself never so reasons—he just leaves the historical question unanswered. But the philosophical framework he constructs is well-suited to historical argumentation for the events in question, thus filling the gap and avoiding circularity.

Because the medievals lacked the historical method, they could not argue in any substantial way for the historicity of the events recorded in the gospels. About the only proof they offered for the historicity of the miracles and fulfilled prophecies was the origin and growth of the Christian church. But with the rise of historical consciousness, that deficit could be remedied and the medieval framework could be filled out with historical evidences.

4.222 MODERN PERIOD

Modern apologetics has been to a great extent historical apologetics. Let us examine briefly how this came to pass.

4.2221 *Rise of historical consciousness.* It is probably no coincidence that the rise of historical apologetics paralleled the rise of modern historiography. The modern science of historical study was born in the Italian Renaissance. The first stirrings of the Renaissance spirit in Italy found expression in the search for ancient manuscripts. The humanists cultivated the use of classical Latin and Greek and found their greatest delight in the discovery of documents of antiquity in those languages. They developed the skills of historical criticism; on the basis of internal criteria alone Lorenzo Valla was able to expose the famous Donation of Constantine, on the basis of which the Catholic church claimed secular authority over Italy, as a forgery. Despite this embarrassment, for nearly a century the papacy supported the humanist writers, and learning and the arts flourished in Rome. In search of ancient manuscripts, Italian humanists visited the monasteries of Northern Europe, and the new learning spread, eventually making its way into the university chairs of Germany and into cultivated circles elsewhere. France, after its invasion of Italy in 1494, thoroughly imbibed the spirit of the Italian Renaissance. Before the end of the fifteenth century, Oxford University was already offering courses in classical Greek and Latin, and Cambridge University soon followed suit. The embodiment of the ideal Renaissance humanist was Erasmus, who occupied much of his life translating classical works into Latin and editing the Greek New Testament. Lorenzo Valla sought to restore the original Greek text of the New Testament through the use of ancient manuscripts. Erasmus published Valla's corrections as annotations on the New Testament in 1505, and they provided the model for Erasmus's edition of the Greek New Testament in 1516.

The Protestant Reformation spurred the development of the science of history by turning attention to the Patristic age in order to accentuate the Roman Catholic church's departures from the faith of the Fathers. In their effort to demonstrate that Catholic doctrines and institutions were not of divine origin, but were human accretions not present in the early church, the Reformers stimulated historical research. And, of course, the Catholic Counter-reformers had a tremendous stake in the study of history, because for the Catholic church a defense of a historical tradition was a defense of the Catholic faith. By the end of the seventeenth century, the most successful practitioners of the science of history were Catholics of the scholarly orders. Historical writing also became popular literature. Every class in European society took interest in the new historical scholarship and sought to use it to support their own points of view. During the sixteenth and seventeenth centuries, historical writing became one of the most popular literary forms, avidly sought by a growing reading public. Between 1460 and 1700 it has been estimated that more than 2.5 million copies of seventeen of the most prominent ancient historians were published in Europe. During the eighteenth century this interest intensified. According to J. Westfall Thompson, "No other age had such a voracious interest in historical literature as the eighteenth century. Everyone read and talked history."[3]

4.2222 *Impact on apologetics.* Without the rise of modern historical consciousness the development of historical apologetics would have been impossible. Protestant apologists were especially effective during the seventeenth and eighteenth centuries in their use of historical arguments for the faith. The course of this development is quite interesting. Although Hugo Grotius may rightly be called the father of modern apologetics, he had important precursors in Juan Luis Vives and Philippe de Mornay.

4.22221 *Juan Luis Vives.* Vives was a Spanish humanist educated in Paris. He lived very much in the mainstream of European life and traveled so frequently to England and throughout the Continent that Erasmus called him an amphibious animal! After his fifth stay in England, he left for the Netherlands, never to return to Spain. From 1538-40 he worked on his apology *De veritate fidei christianae.* He died in 1540, and the book was published in 1543. In Vives we find a blend of medieval theology with humanist methodology. That is to say, Vives was a Thomist who accepted the framework of the signs of

3. J. Westfall Thompson and Bernard J. Holm, *A History of Historical Writing,* 2:94.

credibility, but as a humanist he began to provide historical reasons for the credibility of Scripture.

His work tries to deal critically with the question of why Christ is mentioned primarily in Christian sources. He speaks of the true history of Christ and provides a list of historical facts about Jesus. He provides both internal and external evidence for the authenticity of the gospels. His arguments are primitive and amount to little more than assertion, but they are the first glimmerings of a historical approach to the credibility of Scripture. Vives is significant because in him we see the links between modern historical apologetics and the Renaissance rise of historical consciousness on the one hand and the medieval framework of the signs of credibility on the other.

4.22222 *Philippe de Mornay.* Mornay, one of the most important Reformed leaders of the late sixteenth century, was a veteran of the Huguenot persecution in France and founder of the Protestant Academie de Saumur. In 1581, writing in French instead of Latin, Mornay penned his treatise *De la verité de la religion chrestienne.* Although never quoting Vives, Mornay nonetheless appears to have been influenced by him, judging by parallel structure and passages between their works.

Mornay makes explicit his appeal to history: he claims that one can prove the divinity of Christ by means of philosophy and history. He says, "The philosopher thinks only of nature; the historian only of his documents. And from the two we have concluded the deity of Christ and the truth of our Scriptures."[4] Hence, his case is based on what he calls arguments and testimonies. The historical material is brought to bear in the final chapter, demonstrating that "the Gospel truly contains the history and doctrine of Jesus, Son of God."[5] Here he argues for the reliability of the gospel accounts on the basis of the disciples' unwavering witness even unto death. He appeals to the great number of witnesses, to the changed lives of the disciples, and to the conversion of Paul as evidence for the historicity of the resurrection. Again, his arguments are not sophisticated by modern standards; but they represent an important advance over his predecessors in the development of historical apologetics.

4.22223 *Hugo Grotius.* A renowned expert in international law and himself a historical writer, Hugo Grotius was the first to provide a developed historical argument for Christianity in his *De veritate religionis christiannae* (1627). He openly expressed his appreciation of the works of his predecessors, Vives and Mornay. *De veritate* is divided into six books: book one defends a cosmological argument

4. Philippe de Mornay, *De la vérité de la religion chrestienne,* preface.
5. Ibid., p. 835.

and demonstrates God's revelation in Israel's history; book two contains historical proofs for Jesus' miracles and resurrection; book three treats the authority of Scripture; book four demonstrates Christianity's superiority to paganism; book five contains the proof from prophecy to show Christianity's superiority to Judaism; and book six refutes the Islamic religion.

Grotius clearly understood the importance of the science of history for the truth of the Christian faith. He discriminates between the methods employed in mathematics, physics, ethics, and history. In historical proofs we must rely on testimony free from all suspicion of falsity—otherwise the whole structure and use of history collapses. He notes that many historical narrations are commonly accepted as true on no other ground than authority; but the history of Christ is attested by strong proofs that declare it to be true.

Grotius begins by pointing out that it is certain that Jesus of Nazareth was an actual historical person living in Judea under the reign of Tiberius. This fact is acknowledged in historical writings from Christians, Jews, and pagans alike. Further, He was put to death and thereafter worshiped by men. The reason for this worship was that He had performed various miracles during his life. Many of the early Christians such as Polycarp, Irenaus, Athenagorus, Origen, Tertullian, Clement of Alexandria, and so forth were raised in other religions, yet came to worship this man Jesus as God because they had made a diligent inquiry and discovered that He had wrought many miraculous deeds. Moreover, none of their opponents—neither Celsus nor Julian nor the Rabbinic doctors—could deny that Jesus had done these miracles. It is not possible to explain away Jesus' miracles as either wrought by nature or by the devil. With regard to the first of these possibilities, it is not naturally possible that terrible diseases and infirmities should be cured by the sound of a man's voice or his mere touch. As to the second, Christ's teaching was diametrically opposed to Satan, so that His miracles could hardly be attributed to demonic power.

Grotius then argues that Christ's resurrection can also be proved by credible reasons. He points out that the apostles claimed to be eyewitnesses of the risen Christ. They even appealed to the testimony of five hundred brethren who had seen Jesus after His resurrection. Now it would have been impossible for so many to conspire together to perpetrate such a hoax. And what was there to gain by lying? They could expect neither honor, nor wealth, nor worldly profit, nor fame, nor even the successful propagation of their doctrine. If they lied, says Grotius, it had to be for the defense of their religion. But in this case, they either sincerely believed that this religion was true or they did not. If not, then they would never have chosen it for their own and rejected the safer, more customary religions. But if they believed it to be true, then the resurrection of Jesus cannot be avoided. For had He not risen, contrary to His prediction, that would have destroyed the very foundation of any faith the disciples had. Moreover, their own religion prohibited lying and any bearing of false witness. And besides this, no one, and especially so many, would be willing to die for a lie that they themselves had made up, a lie that would bring them absolutely no worldly good. And it is clear from their writings that the apostles were not madmen. Finally, the conversion of the apostle Paul bore witness to the reality of the resurrection.

Grotius concludes by handling two theoretical problems. First, to those who object that the resurrection is impossible, Grotius simply replies that it involves no logical contradiction to say that a dead man has been restored to life. Second, the significance of the resurrection Grotius finds in its confirming the new doctrine taught by Jesus, especially in light of Jesus' prediction that He would rise from the dead.

In his argument for Jesus' resurrection, Grotius presents his opponents with a dilemma. Given the authenticity of the gospels and 1 Corinthians, the apostolic testimony to the event of the resurrection can only be denied if the apostles were either lying or sincerely mistaken. But neither of these are reasonable. Therefore, the resurrection must be a historical event. We find here in rudimentary form the dilemma that would be sharpened and pressed by subsequent generations of Christian apologists against their Deist opponents.

4.22224 *Filleau de la Chaise.* The period between Blaise Pascal (d. 1662) and Pierre Bayle's skeptical *Dictionnaire historique et critique* (1695) has been called the golden age of classical French apologetics. This period included thinkers such as Malebranche, Huet, Bossuet, and Abbadie. The tone for this era—and indeed for that of the next century—was set by Pascal's disciple Filleau de la Chaise in his *Discours sur les preuves des livres de Moyse* (1672). He was important because he inaugurated as a self-conscious methodology in apologetics the method of proof *par les faits* (by the facts).

Filleau held that the proper method of persuading people of the truth of the Christian religion does not consist in trying to make its theological mysteries comprehensible or reasonable, but in showing that the mysteries are entailed in the truth of certain indisputable historical facts. He states:

> If men know anything with assurance, it is the facts; and of everything that falls within their knowledge, there is nothing in which it would be more difficult to deceive them and over which there would be less occasion for dispute. And thus, when one will have made them see that the Christian

religion is inseparably attached to facts whose truth cannot be sincerely contested, they must submit to all that it teaches or else renounce sincerity and reason.[6]

This method of proving Christianity by the facts was in French apologetics a logical extension of the function of the signs of credibility in attesting the truths of faith coupled with the historical method. Because truths of faith are above reason, they cannot be directly proved, but can nevertheless be indirectly confirmed by miracle and prophecy. Similarly, Filleau contended that we may prove the mysteries of the faith, not directly, but indirectly by the historical facts that entail their truth.

Thus, French apologists began to make a bifurcation between the *contenant* and the *contenu* of the faith. Roughly rendered, the distinction contrasted the "container" of the faith to the "content" of the faith. Though the content of the Christian religion, that is, the body of theological doctrines, may be above reason, nonetheless the container of this religion, that is, the historical events of the gospel story, is demonstrable by the facts; hence, the *contenu* is indirectly proved by historical verification of the *contenant*. Under the influence of this conception, there was during the seventeenth and eighteenth centuries a marked swing in French apologetics toward historical apologies.

4.22225 *Charles Leslie.* In eighteenth-century England there was a similar turn toward empirical, historical proofs of Christianity. Although John Locke set the pattern for English thought in this century by his defense of the reasonableness of Christianity on the basis of Jesus' miracles, it was Charles Leslie who enunciated clearly the method of proving Christianity by the facts in his *Short and Easie Method with the Deists* (1697).

The short and easy method recommended by Leslie is the historical proof of the matters of fact on which Christianity is founded. He argues that when one examines the biblical narratives as one would any matter of fact, one will find them to be historically reliable. Hence, he maintains that one must either reject all the historical works of classical antiquity or else admit the gospel accounts along with them. Following in Locke's footsteps, Leslie helped to set the tone for the hundreds of historical apologies published in England during the next century.

There was a subtle, yet decisive, difference between French and English historical apologetics. Both agreed that revelation may be discerned by what the medievals called the signs of credibility, miracle and

6. Filleau de la Chaise, "Discours sur les livres de Moise," pp. 104-5.

prophecy, but they differed in the following way. By making a distinction between the *contenant* and the *contenu*, the French thinkers underscored the bifurcation between truths of reason and truths of faith, the latter being in themselves rationally imcomprehensible and only indirectly verifiable; the English apologists tended to dissolve the distinction between truths of reason and truths of faith, the upper story collapsing down into the lower, so that all truths became in a sense truths of reason, demonstrable by philosophy, science, history, and so forth. When English writers spoke of truths above reason, they did not generally mean mysterious or incomprehensible truths, as did their French counterparts; rather they meant simply truths that we lack the necessary facts to prove. But in both cases, it was the methodology of history that they counted on to carry the weight of the case for the truth of the Christian faith.

4.223 NINETEENTH AND TWENTIETH CENTURIES

During the nineteenth and twentieth centuries the parallel development of historiography and historical apologetics was disrupted.

4.2231 *Historicism and relativism.* The nineteenth century saw the greatest advances in the science of history that had theretofore occurred. The climax of this development came in the school of historicism, shaped by the prodigious influence of the German historian Leopold von Ranke. Von Ranke, through his doctoral students and in turn through their students, was responsible for shaping a whole generation of great historians. The earmark of nineteenth-century historicism was objectivity. The task of the historian was to uncover the objective facts, and let those facts speak for themselves. The subjective element—the historian's own personality, biases, outlook, milieu, and so forth—did not enter the historical equation. Von Ranke's goal in doing history, to use his famous phrase, was to describe the past "*wie es eigentlich gewesen ist*" (as it actually was). He apparently saw no reason, given the enormous industry that he brought to his research and that he instilled in his students, that this goal could not be achieved.

During the twentieth century there came a sharp reaction to von Ranke's naive objectivism. The school of historical relativism emphasized the inextricable subjective element in the writing of history. In the United States, relativism was associated particularly with the historians Charles Beard and Carl Becker. Against von Ranke, they denied that historical facts are "out there," waiting to be discovered. Facts do not bear their own meaning piggy-back; it is the historian who must ascribe meaning to the facts. And the historian, who is himself a product of his time and place in history, cannot assume the point of a neutral observer in writing history. The personal element is always in the equation. Von Ranke's goal of describing the past as it really was is illusory; rather, the historian must himself reconstruct the past on the basis of the present. Ironically, the viewpoint of historical relativism is often referred to today as historicism, so that this term now means exactly the opposite of what it meant in the nineteenth century.

4.22.32 *Impact on apologetics.* One might expect that during the nineteenth century the historical apologetic for Christianity would flower. Seeing instead that it withered away, we might suspect that the historical method had simply got too big for its theological britches and had exposed the gospels as historically unreliable documents. That would, however, be misleading. The chief obstacle to a historical case for the gospels, as we have seen, was the nineteenth century's conviction that miracles had no place in a historical narrative. Because this presupposition was accepted into biblical criticism, the historical method assumed great importance there, whereas it did not take hold in apologetics. The nineteenth century's enthusiasm for the historical may be seen in the old quest for the historical Jesus. One after another life of Jesus appeared during this century, each trying to rediscover the nonmiraculous Jesus behind the supernatural figure of the gospels. Indeed, in that movement one may see the greatest weakness of von Ranke's method exemplified: apparently unaware of the personal element they all brought to their research, each writer reconstructed a historical Jesus after his own image. There was Strauss's Hegelian Jesus, Reman's sentimental Jesus, Bauer's non-existent Jesus, Ritschl's liberal Jesus, and so forth. As one observer remarked, each one looked down the long well of history and saw his own face reflected at the bottom. The movement finally ground to a halt in skepticism, since no nonmiraculous Jesus could be uncovered in the gospel traditions. Rather than accept the supernatural Jesus as historical, however, biblical critics ascribed that belief to the theology of the early church, which they said so overlaid the traditions about the historical Jesus that He was no longer recoverable.

During the twentieth century, the historical method—usually called the historical-critical method—has continued to play the decisive role in biblical exegesis. But both dialectical and existential theology severed the theological truth of the gospel from the facts concerning the historical Jesus. Hence, any historical apologetic was conceived to be worse than useless, since it focused on the historical Jesus instead of the Christ of faith—a distinction introduced by the German theologian Martin Kähler at the close of the nineteenth century and subsequently taken up into dialectical and existential theology. It is only since the second half of this century that a new quest of the historical Jesus has begun, this time more cautious and chastened; and once more historical apologetics is beginning to reassert itself.

4.23 ASSESSMENT

4.231 RELATIVIST OBJECTIONS TO THE OBJECTIVITY OF HISTORY

If a historical apologetic is to be possible, the objections of historical relativism need to be overcome. This does not mean a return to naive von Rankian historicism. Of course the subjective element cannot be eliminated. But the question is whether this subjective element need be so predominant that the study of history is vitiated. In order to answer this question, let us examine more closely the objections of historical relativism. They may be summarized under two main points: first, we cannot know anything for sure about the past because we cannot directly observe the past; and second, we cannot reconstruct the past objectively because we are not neutral observers, but rather products of our time, place, culture, circumstances, and so forth. Let me explain each of these objections in turn.

4.2311 *The problem of lack of direct access.* Here historical relativists often point out the difference between the scientist and the historian. The scientist, they say, has the objects of his research right in front of him as he experiments; but the historian's objects of research no longer exist for him to observe or experiment with. This position has two important implications.

4.23111 *Historical facts exist only in the mind.* First, it affects how one views historical facts. According to one famous relativist, Carl Becker, it means that historical facts are only in the mind. The event itself is gone, so all we have are the historian's statements about the event. It is those statements that are historical facts. If one were to reply that the event itself is a historical fact because it had an enduring impact on the course of history, Becker would say it had an impact only because people had "long memories"; if everyone forgot the event, it would no longer be a historical fact. Thus, historical events really only exist in your mind, not in the past. Two notions are in turn implied by this implication; I shall call them sub-implications.

4.231111 *Facts have no meaning.* The first sub-implication is that facts have no meaning and that the historian must put his own meaning onto the facts. Because the event itself is gone and the facts are only in the historian's mind, this means, in Becker's words, that "even if you could present all the facts, the miserable things wouldn't say anything, would say nothing at all." Therefore, the historian must put his own meaning on the facts. As Becker further says, "the event itself, the facts, do not say anything, do not impose any meaning. It is the historian who speaks, who imposes a meaning."[7]

4.231112 *History is the product of the historian.*

7. Carl Becker, "What Are Historical Facts?" pp. 130-31.

The second sub-implication is that history is largely a result of the historian's own biases, personality, interest, and so forth. Because the historian determines the meaning of the facts himself, the history he writes will be just a reflection of himself. In this way, the past is really the product of the present.

4.23112 *There is no way to test for truth in history.* There is a second important implication of the historian's not having direct access to the past. It means that there is no way to test the truth of historical facts. A scientist has the method of experimentation to test his hypotheses. But the historian cannot do that, because the events are gone. The scientist has the advantage of predictability and repeatability, which the historian lacks. So how can the historian test his hypotheses? As historian Patrick Gardiner asks,

> In what sense can I be said to know an event which is in principle unobservable, having vanished behind the mysterious frontier which divides the present from the past? And how can we be sure that anything really happened in the past at all, that the whole story is not an elaborate fabrication, as untrustworthy as a dream or a work of fiction?[8]

So because the historian cannot directly observe the facts, there is the unsolved problem of how to test for truth in history.

Thus, the problem of the lack of direct access to the past raises two challenges to those who want to learn something from history: first, What is the nature of historical facts? and second, How can one test the truth of historical facts?

4.2312 *The problem of lack of neutrality.* The second objection of historical relativists to knowledge of the past as it actually happened is that we cannot reconstruct the past objectively because we are not neutral observers, but are the products of our time, place, culture, and so forth. The historian cannot "stand back" and observe what has happened from a neutral perspective because the historian, too, is caught up in the historical flow of events. Henri Pirenne makes the point:

> Historical syntheses depend to a very large degree not only upon the personality of their authors, but upon all the social, religious, or national environments which surround them. It follows, therefore, that each historian will establish between the facts relationships determined by the convictions, the movements, and the prejudices that have molded his own point of view.[9]

Because of this, each new generation must rewrite history in its own way. The history written today will be judged inferior and obsolete by

---

8. Patrick Gardiner, *The Nature of Historical Explanation*, p. 35.
9. Henri Pirenne, "What Are Historians Trying to Do?" p. 97.

the historians of the next generation. But their work will also be shaped by their culture and so forth. Thus, in the words of philosopher Karl Popper, "There can be no history of the past as it actually did happen; there can only be historical interpretations; and none of them final; and every generation has a right to frame its own."[10] Therefore, history can never be objectively written; the historian always looks at the past through the colored glasses of the present, as determined by his society and environment.

4.232 CRITIQUE OF HISTORICAL RELATIVISM

These two basic objections, then, need to be answered before we examine the historical evidence for Christianity: first, the problem of the lack of direct access to the past; and second, the problem of the lack of neutrality.
   4.2321 *The problem of lack of direct access.* We saw that relativists argue that the historian cannot directly observe the objects of his investigation as a scientist can.
   4.23211 *Denial of the objection.* In actuality that is simply not true. It is just patently false that the historian always works with indirect data and the scientist with direct.
   4.232111 *Scientist often lacks direct access.* In the first place, the scientist does not always have direct access to his objects of study. In the modern natural sciences, especially the theoretical sciences like physics, the scientist's research is characterized by the very inaccessibility of the objects of his study. Such theoretical entities as black holes, quarks, and neutrinos are postulated as the best explanations for the observable data, but they themselves cannot be directly observed. So the scientist has very often only indirect access to his objects of research.
   4.232112 *Historian often has direct access.* Secondly, the historian often does have direct access to his data. He is not simply dependent on the reports of earlier historians. For example, archaeological data furnishes direct access to the objects of the historian's investigation. The renowned English historian R. G. Collingwood states,

> scissors and paste (is) not the only foundation of historical method. Archaeology has provided a wonderfully sensitive method for answering questions to which not only do literary sources give no direct answer, but which cannot be answered even by the most ingenious interpretation of them.[11]

10. Karl Popper, "Has History Any Meaning?" p. 303.
11. R. G. Collingwood, *An Autobiography,* p. 135.

Thus, the historian, like the scientist, often has direct access to evidence. Now, I am not confusing the evidence with the events themselves, which are admittedly past; but I am saying, in Gardiner's words, that much of our historical knowledge "is constructed out of evidence which is present here and now to our senses."[12] And archaeology is only one of the means to secure such evidence. As Old Testament scholar R. K. Harrison explains, modern historians are not so heavily dependent on subjective literary sources as before, because the sciences of linguistics, sociology, anthropology, numismatics, and archaeology have become so developed.[13]

In fact, we can at this point draw a very instructive analogy: what history is to the humanities, geology is to the sciences. The major difference between history and geology is the human factor, not the accessibility of the data. Whereas the subject matter of the geologist is the earth's history, the subject matter of the historian is human history. Basically their task is the same. As Collingwood states, "The historian's real work is the reconstruction in thought of a particular historical event; the geologist's, the reconstruction in thought of a particular geological epoch at a particular place."[14] If this is the case, then the relativists' argument based on the inaccessibility of the past loses all its punch. For the subject matter of the geologist is every bit as indirect as that of the historian, and yet geology is part of science, which is the model of objectivity to the relativist. Since lack of direct access cannot preclude geological knowledge, neither can it preclude historical knowledge. Therefore, I categorically reject the relativists' argument based on the lack of direct access to the past.

4.23212 *Nature of historical facts.* Now remember there are two implications of this objection. First, there is the problem of the nature of historical facts.

4.232121 *Objectivity of historical facts.* Becker says that facts exist only in the mind. He says that the facts are merely the historian's statements about events. Now this does not make sense. For Becker also says the facts have no meaning. Now surely he does not want to say that the historian's statements have no meaning! His position is self-contradictory. May I suggest a better definition for a historical fact? A historical fact is either the historical event itself or a piece of accurate information about that event. Thus a historian makes statements about the facts.

Seen in this light, Becker's statement that facts exist only in the mind is somewhat silly. His belief forces him to the bizarre conclusion that Lincoln's assassination made a difference in history only because people

12. Gardiner, *Historical Explanation,* p. 39.
13. R. K. Harrison, *Introduction to the Old Testament,* p. 292.
14. R. G. Collingwood, "Croce's Philosophy of History," p. 19.

have long memories, but that if everyone had forgotten Lincoln's death within 48 hours, then it would have made no difference at all and would have ceased to be a historical fact! It is difficult to take such an idea seriously. For clearly, Lincoln's death would have made an immense impact on U.S. history whether *anyone* remembered it or not. It was primarily Lincoln's *absence*, not memories of Lincoln, that made such a difference in U.S. history. Even if everyone had forgotten that there even was a Lincoln, the absence created by the death of that great man would still have had its devastating results. In other words, the facts exist independently of our minds and still have their impact even long after they are forgotten. So I think it is clear that relativists have misconstrued the nature of historical facts.

4.232122 *Meaning and historical facts.* There were two sub-implications arising from the idea that historical facts are just in one's mind.

4.2321221 *Meaning inherent to the concept of "fact."* A little reflection will reveal that the first sub-implication, that historical facts have no meaning, is a preposterous notion. For what do we mean by the phrase *facts without meaning?* What in the world is a "meaningless" fact? It is a notion trembling on the brink of self-contradiction. Meaning is inherent in the very concept of *fact.* To describe a fact *is* to give its meaning. Thus, if I say, "It is a fact that Garfield was the twentieth President of the United States," the meaning of the fact, if not obvious enough, is given by simply defining its terms: It is a fact that a man named Garfield was the twentieth man to be the head of the executive branch of the government of the country named the United States. What the fact is *is* its meaning. The notion of a meaningless fact is absurd; there can be no such thing. Insofar as a thing is a fact, it has meaning, because meaning is inherent in the concept of fact.

4.2321222 *Relativists' implicit concession.* In reality, relativists recognize that facts have meaning. For although they say facts have no meaning, they do not really treat history in so roughshod a manner. This is evident in three ways:

4.23212221 *A common core of indisputable historical facts exists.* Thus, one relativist confesses that "there are basic facts which are the same for all historians," facts which it is "the duty" of the historian to present accurately.[15] Even Becker, while saying that facts have no meaning, admits that "some things, some 'facts' can be established and agreed upon"—examples include the date of the Declaration of Independence, Caesar's crossing the Rubicon, the sale of indulgences in 1517, Lincoln's assassination, and so forth.[16] Not even

15. E. H. Carr, *What Is History?* p. 8.
16. Becker, "Historical Facts," p. 132.

the most radical relativist is prepared to abandon history as a hopeless bog of subjectivism. As historian Isaiah Berlin puts it, if someone were to tell us that *Hamlet* was written at the court of Genghis Khan in outer Mongolia, we would not think he was merely wrong, but out of his mind![17] But if there is a common, incontrovertible core of historical facts, then the relativist has surrendered his point that the facts do not speak for themselves or have meaning. It is a simple truth that, in historian Christopher Blake's words, there "is a very considerable part" of history that is "acceptable to the community of professional historians beyond all question," be they Marxists or Liberals, Catholics or Protestants, nineteenth-century Germans or twentieth-century Englishmen.[18] If one were to ask me what facts make up this backbone of history, I think few historians would disagree with very much of what has been catalogued in a book such as Langer's *Encyclopedia of World History.* Thus, the existence of a common core of historical facts shows that even relativists believe facts do have meaning.

4.23212222 *It is possible to distinguish between history and propaganda.* "All reputable historians," states W. H. Walsh, make a distinction between history and propaganda. The latter may serve some purpose, says Walsh, but, he insists, it is "emphatically not history."[19] A good example of such propaganda is the Soviets' practice of "rewriting" history to serve their purposes. According to Morton White, when Stalin came to power, he had Russian history rewritten so that it was he and Lenin who lead the Bolshevik Revolution instead of Lenin and Trotsky. According to White,

> It has been shown by students of the Russian Revolution that mountains of books, newspapers, pamphlets, decrees, and documents had to be consigned to the "memory hole," mashed to pulp, or brought out in corrected editions in order to substitute for Lenin-Trotsky a new duality-unity, Lenin-Stalin.[20]

White charges that the most dangerous thing about historical relativism is the way it can be used to justify historical distortions. The ultimate result of this totalitarian fiddling with the past is envisioned by George Orwell in *1984:*

> "There is a Party slogan dealing with control of the past," he said. Repeat it, if you please."
> "Who controls the past controls the future; who controls the present controls the past," repeated Winston obediently.

17. Isaiah Berlin, "The Concept of Scientific History," p. 11.
18. Christopher Blake, "Can History Be Objective?" p. 331.
19. W. H. Walsh, *Philosophy of History: An Introduction,* p. 111.
20. Morton White, *Foundations of Historical Knowledge,* p. 268.

"Who controls the present controls the past," said O'Brien, nodding his head with slow approval . . .

"I tell you Winston that reality is not external. Reality exists in the human mind, and nowhere else. Not in the individual mind, which can make mistakes, and in any case soon perishes; only in the mind of the Party, which is collective and immortal. Whatever the party holds to be truth *is* truth."[21]

If the facts have no meaning and say nothing, then there is no way to protest this propagandizing of history. On relativist grounds, there is no way to distinguish history from propaganda. But again, no relativist could countenance such a notion. They want to say that the facts *do* make a difference and that propagandists cannot distort them at will. But the only way to do that is to acknowledge that facts do have meaning.

4.23212223 *It is possible to criticize poor history.* All historians distinguish good history from poor. A good example is Immanuel Velikovsky's attempt to rewrite ancient history on the basis of world-wide catastrophes caused by extra-terrestrial forces in the fifteenth, eighth, and seventh centuries B.C. Velikovsky completely reconstructs ancient history, dismissing entire ancient kingdoms and languages as fictional. In a meticulously documented essay on Velikovsky's theories, archaeologist Edwin Yamauchi incisively criticizes the proposed reconstruction, relentlessly plucking out one support after another by a detailed analysis of ancient documents, archaeology, and philology until the whole structure tumbles down in ruin. His conclusion is succinct: "Velikovsky's reconstruction is a catastrophic history in a double sense. It is a history based on catastrophe, and it is a disastrous catastrophe of history." Now no relativist could make such a statement. If facts have no meaning, then Velikovsky's views are as good as anybody's. Yet, as Yamauchi observes, the reaction of historians to Velikovsky's proposals was "quite hostile."[22] In saying that such a rewrite is poor history or biased or inaccurate, historians implicitly admit that the facts themselves do say something and are not like a wax nose that can be pulled and twisted about to suit any historian's whim. So in criticizing poor history, the relativist acknowledges that the facts have meaning.

To summarize, then, the relativists' contention that facts have no meaning is shown to be false by three considerations: First, a common core of indisputable historical events exists; second, it is possible to distinguish between history and propaganda; and third, it is possible to

21. George Orwell, *1984: A Novel*, pt. 3, chap. 2.
22. Edwin Yamauchi, "Immanuel Velikovsky's Catastrophic History," pp. 138, 134.

criticize poor history. So the supposed lack of direct access to the data does not imply that the facts are just in your mind and without meaning.

4.232123 *The historian and historical facts.* The second sub-implication of the relativists' argument that facts are just in the mind is that history is the product of the historian himself. I plan to deal with this argument when I discuss whether the historian can reconstruct the past objectively, or whether what he writes is determined by his society and so forth. I shall argue that because the facts are not just in his mind but are, as it were, out there, the past is not just the product of the historian's mind, but is determined by the external facts themselves.

4.23213 *Testing for truth in history.* The second major implication of the lack of direct access to the data concerns the testability of historical hypotheses. Since the historian cannot perform experiments like a scientist, how can he test the truth of his theories?

4.232131 *Systematic consistency.* May I suggest that the test for truth is *systematic consistency*? As explained earlier (1.1321), by consistency I mean obedience to the laws of logic. Nothing can be true if it is contradictory or otherwise illogical. By systematic, I mean fitting all the facts of experience. One may have a nice, airtight, logical system, but if it does not explain the facts, there is no reason to regard it as true. But if something is logical and fits all the facts of experience, then it passes the test for truth and deserves to be regarded as true.

4.232132 *Hypothetico-deductive method.* The problem arises as to how to apply this test in history. May I suggest that the historian applies this test in exactly the same way as the scientist? The modern scientist invents a hypothesis to provide a systematically consistent explanation of the facts, and then he deduces from the hypothesis specific conditions that would either confirm or disprove his hypothesis. Then he performs certain experiments to see which conditions obtain.

The historian follows the same procedure. He reconstructs a picture of the past. This is his hypothesis. Then he deduces certain conditions from it that will confirm or disprove his hypothesis. He then checks to see which conditions exist. He does this not by experiments, as the scientist does, but by historical evidence. As Collingwood says, "The historian's picture of the past stands in a peculiar relation to something called evidence. The only way in which the historian can judge of its truth is by considering this relation."[23] Collingwood is saying that the historian's hypothesis must be corroborated by the evidence, for exam-

23. R. G. Collingwood, *The Idea of History,* p. 246.

ple, archaeological evidence. "By treating coins, pottery, weapons, and other artifacts as evidence," one historian writes, "the historian raises his study to the level of a science. What happened in the past is what the evidence indicates as having happened."[24]

In his hypothetical-deductive process of testing, the historian is very much like the scientist, especially the geologist, who also lacks direct access to his data and the opportunity of lab experiments. Collingwood gives the conclusion: "The analysis of science in epistemological terms is identical with the analysis of history, and the distinction between them as separate kinds of knowledge is an illusion."[25]

4.232133 *Nature of historical knowledge.* One final point needs to be made. The goal of historical knowledge is to obtain probability, not mathematical certainty. An item can be said to be a piece of historical knowledge when it is related to the evidence in such a way that any reasonable man ought to accept it. This is the situation with most all of our knowledge: we accept what has sufficient evidence to render it probable. The knowledge that the earth is round, that there are mountains out there, even that there are other people in the same room, is based on probability. Similarly, in a court of law, the verdict is awarded to the case that is made most probable by the evidence. The jury is asked to decide if the accused is guilty—not beyond all doubt, which is impossible—but beyond all reasonable doubt. It is exactly the same in history: we should accept the hypothesis that provides the most plausible explanation of the evidence.

To summarize, then, we test for truth by systematic consistency, and the method of applying this test is the same in history as it is in science. The historian should accept the hypothesis that most reasonably explains all the evidence. Thus, the supposed lack of direct access to the data is no stumbling block to testing for truth in history and so gaining an accurate knowledge of the past.

So we can conclude: First, the historian's access to his data is often as direct as the scientist's, particularly the geologists; second, meaning is inherent in the description of historical facts themselves; and third, we can test for truth in history by systematic consistency as applied in the hypothetical-deductive model, which is the same as the scientist's.

4.2322 *Problem of lack of neutrality.* Let us move now to the second major objection to our gaining knowledge from the past: the lack of neutrality. Remember, relativists argue that because we all are shaped by personality and environment, no historian can objectively reconstruct the past. In what I have said already, we have begun to expose the fallacies of this objection:

24. William Debbins, "Introduction," p. xiv.
25. R. G. Collingwood, "Are History and Science Different Kinds of Knowledge?" p. 32.

4.23221 *Confusion of act of knowledge with content of knowledge.* When we judge the truth of a historical work, it is not so important *how* the knowledge of the past was learned, as *what* the content of that knowledge is. As the historian Maurice Mandelbaum explains, if we say a historical work is false, we say it is false because it does not accord with the facts, not because of sociological factors surrounding the historian.[26] As long as historical facts have meaning and are not just in the mind, then the cultural conditioning of the historian is secondary. As long as the content of the historian's knowledge accords with the facts, then how he got that knowledge is unimportant.

4.23222 *Confusion of formulation of a hypothesis with testing of a hypothesis.* It is not so important how the historian comes to arrive at his hypothesis as how his hypothesis is tested. So long as it is tested by the objective facts, it is of secondary importance what factors influenced the historian to come up with his hypothesis in the first place. Thus, Morton White emphasizes that although a number of psychological and social factors may influence the formulation of a hypothesis, the historian still has to submit to objective tests that have nothing to do with personality, milieu, or general world view.[27] This is just the same as in science. The scientist who discovered the chemical structure of the Benzin molecule got the idea from a dream he had of a snake holding its own tail, thus forming a circular structure. I do not mean to say that there is not a "logic of discovery" that the scientist (or historian) follows in framing fruitful hypotheses. The point is that so far as the *truth* of the hypothesis is concerned, it does not matter how the historian or scientist comes up with his hypothesis—he could have learned it at his mother's knee, for all that it matters. So long as the hypothesis is tested by the facts, there is no danger of sacrificing objectivity.

4.23223 *Historian can make plain his point of view.* And third, the objection fails to realize that the historian can make it plain what his point of view is. Karl Popper says that the best way out of the problem of having unconscious points of view is to state clearly one's view and to recognize that there are also other points of view.[28] Raymond Aron states that "relativism is transcended as soon as the historian ceases to claim a detachment which is impossible, recognizes what his point of view is, and consequently puts himself in a position to recognize the points of view of others."[29] Thus, there is simply the need to be honest in writing history.

To summarize, the problem of a lack of neutrality cannot prevent us

26. Maurice Mandelbaum, *The Problem of Historical Knowledge*, p. 184.
27. Morton White, "Can History Be Objective?" p. 199.
28. Karl Popper, *The Poverty of Historicism*, p. 152.
29. Raymond Aron, "Relativism in History," p. 160.

from learning the truth about the past because: First, the objection commits the fallacy of confusing the act of knowledge with the content of knowledge; second, the objection confuses the formulation of a hypothesis with the testing of the hypothesis; and third, the objection fails to realize that the historian can make it plain just what his point of view is.

Why, then, are histories rewritten each generation? In his classic book *The Problem of Historical Knowledge*, Maurice Mandelbaum provides seven reasons.[30] None of these count against historical objectivity. Some of the reasons are: new sources and evidence are discovered; recent history always needs to be reworked as we gain perspective on what has happened; new appreciation of a certain form of art, music, literature, and so forth may arise in one generation after another. Far from eliminating knowledge of the past as it actually was, the rewriting of history serves to advance our knowledge of the past as new discoveries are made.

4.233 CONCLUSION

Therefore, we can conclude that neither the supposed problem of lack of direct access to the past nor the supposed problem of the lack of neutrality can prevent us from learning something from history. And if Christianity's claims to be a religion rooted in history are true, then history may lead us to a knowledge of God Himself.

4.24 PRACTICAL APPLICATION

Like the material in the previous section, the content of this section has little direct applicability to evangelism. I have never met a non-Christian who overtly objected to the gospel message because of historical relativism. But again, this material is very important to a broader defense of the conservative approach to the Scriptures and to the gospel. Non-conservatives sometimes appeal to relativistic reasoning in order to justify an approach to the Scriptures that admits of inconsistencies in the historical narratives, because there is no such thing as "error" if the past cannot be objectively described. Because the historical aspect of the narrative can have no objective content, they say, the true import of Scripture lies in its spiritual message. The Bible is thus infallible in faith and morals, but not in matters of history. Such historical relativism can only lead further to a depreciation of the importance of the historical for faith. For then the events of the life, death, and resurrection of Jesus cannot be said to be part of the objective past, because the gospels do not represent objective history. It is

---

30. Mandelbaum, *Problem of Historical Knowledge*, pp. 298-304.

critical if we are not to lapse into mere mythology that we defend the objectivity of history and, thus, of the gospels.

Moreover, one does occasionally encounter non-Christians in evangelism who seem very skeptical about history. With such persons I think it would be especially effective to share the three ways in which relativists implicitly concede the objectivity of history (4.23212221-3). If they insist on a complete historical skepticism, then we should explain to them the utter unliveability of such a view. If we are to get along in this world, we need a method of sorting out to the best of our ability what has and has not happened. The results of this procedure will allow for the possibility that the historical foundations of the Christian faith will be as well established as many other purely natural events. Therefore, it would be hypocrisy to admit the one but not the other. Insist on this fundamental dilemma in dealing with the non-Christian.

5.0 DE CHRISTO

5.1 THE CLAIMS OF CHRIST

The Christian religion stands or falls with the person of Jesus Christ. Judaism could survive without Moses, Buddhism without Buddha, Islam without Mohammad; but Christianity could not survive without Christ. This is because unlike most other world religions, Christianity is belief in a person, a genuine historical individual—but at the same time a special individual, whom the church regards as not only human, but divine. At the center of any Christian apologetic therefore must stand the person of Christ; and very important for the doctrine of Christ's person are the personal claims of the historical Jesus. Did He claim to be God? Or did He regard himself as a prophet? Or was He the exemplification of some highest human quality, such as love or faith? Who did Jesus of Nazareth claim to be?

5.11 LITERATURE CITED OR RECOMMENDED

5.111 HISTORICAL BACKGROUND

Bartsch, Hans-Werner. ed. *Kerygma and Myth*. 2 vols. Translated by R. H. Fuller. London: SPCK, 1953.

Marshall, I. Howard. *I Believe in the Historical Jesus*. Grand Rapids: Eerdmans, 1977.

Paulus, Heinrich Eberh. Gottlob. *Das Leben Jesu, als Grundlage einer reinen Geschichte des Urchristentums*. 2 vols. Heidelberg: C. F. Winter, 1828.

Robinson, James. *A New Quest of the Historical Jesus*. Studies in Biblical Theology 25. London: SCM, 1959.

Schweitzer, Albert. *The Quest of the Historical Jesus*. 3d ed. Translated by W. Montgomery. London: Adam & Charles Black, 1954.

Strauss, David Friedrich. *The Life of Jesus Critically Examined*. Translated by G. Eliot. Edited with an Introduction by P. C. Hodgson. Lives of Jesus Series. London: SCM, 1973.

Wrede, Wilhelm. *The Messianic Secret*. Translated by J. O. G. Greig. Cambridge: James Clarke, 1971.

5.112 ASSESSMENT

Dunn, James D. G. *Jesus and the Spirit*. London: SCM, 1975.

Ellis, E. E. "Dating the New Testament." *New Testament Studies* 26 (1980):487-502.

Green, Michael. "Jesus and Historical Skepticism," In *The Truth of God Incarnate*. Edited by M. Green. Grand Rapids: Eerdmans, 1977. Pp. 107-39.

———. "Jesus in the New Testament." In *The Truth of God Incarnate*, Edited by M. Green. Grand Rapids: Eerdmans, 1977. Pp. 17-57.

Gruenler, Royce Gordon. *New Approaches to Jesus and the Gospels*. Grand Rapids: Baker, 1982.

Hengel, Martin. *The Son of God: The Origin of Christology and the History of Jewish-Hellenistic Religion*. Translated by John Bowden. Philadelphia: Fortress, 1976.

Hick, John, ed. *The Myth of God Incarnate*. London: SCM, 1977.

Marshall, I. Howard. *The Origins of New Testament Christology*. Downers Grove, Ill.: Inter-Varsity, 1976.

Moule, C. F. D. *The Origin of Christology*. Cambridge: Cambridge U., 1977.

Pelikan, Jaroslav. *The Christian Tradition: A History of the Development of Doctrine*. Vol. 1, *The Emergence of the Catholic Tradition (100-600)*. Chicago: U. of Chicago, 1971.

Pöhlmann, Horst Georg. *Abriss der Dogmatik*. 3d revised edition. Gütersloh: Gerd Mohn, 1980.

Trilling, Wolfgang. *Fragen zur Geschichtlichkeit Jesu*. Düsseldorf: Patmos Verlag, 1966.

5.12 HISTORICAL BACKGROUND

Before we can explore this problem, let us take a brief look at the recent historical background of Jesus research.

5.121 LIFE OF JESUS MOVEMENT

During the late eighteenth and nineteenth centuries, European theology strove to find the historical Jesus behind the figure portrayed in the gospels. The chief effort of this quest was to write a biography of Jesus as it supposedly really was, without the supernatural accretions found in the gospels. One after another these lives of Jesus appeared, each author thinking to have uncovered the real man behind the mask.

Early lives of Jesus tended to portray Him as spiritual man who was forced to make claims about Himself that He knew were false in order to get the people to listen to His message. For example, Karl Bahrdt in his *Ausführung des Plans und Zwecks Jesu* (1784-92) maintained that Jesus belonged to a secret order of Essenes, dedicated to weaning Israel of her worldly messianic expectations in favor of spiritual, religious truths. In order to gain a hearing from the Jews, Jesus claimed to be the Messiah, planning to spiritualize the concept of Messiah by hoaxing His death and resurrection. To bring this about, Jesus provoked His arrest and trial by His triumphal entry into Jerusalem. Other members of the order, who secretly sat on the Sanhedrin, ensured his condemnation. Luke the physician prepared Jesus' body by means of drugs to withstand the rigors of crucifixion for an indefinite time. By crying loudly and slumping His head Jesus feigned His death on the cross, and a bribe to the centurion guaranteed that His legs would not be broken. Joseph of Arimathea, another member of the order, took Jesus to a cave, where he resuscitated Jesus by his ministrations. On the third day, they pushed aside the stone over the mouth of the cave, and Jesus went forth, frightening away the guards and appearing to Mary and subsequently to His other disciples. Thereafter, He lived in seclusion among the members of the order.

Similar to Bahrdt's theory was Karl Venturini's life of Jesus in his *Natürliche Geschichte des grossen Propheten von Nazareth* (1800-1802). As a member of a secret society, Jesus sought to persuade the Jewish nation to substitute the idea of a spiritual Messiah for their conception of a worldly Messiah. But His attempt backfired: He was arrested, condemned, and crucified. However, He was taken down from the cross and placed in the tomb alive, where He revived. A member of the secret society, dressed in white, frightened away the guards at the tomb, and other members took Jesus from the tomb. During forty days thereafter He appeared to various disciples, always to return to the secret place of the society. Finally, His energy spent, He retired permanently.

Much of the early Life of Jesus movement was spent in trying to provide natural explanations for Jesus' miracles and resurrection. The high water-mark of the natural explanation school came in H. E. G. Paulus's *Das Leben Jesu* (1828), in which Paulus devised all sorts of clever explanations to explain away the substance of the gospel miracles while still accepting the form of the factual accounts.

But with his *Das Leben Jesu, kritisch bearbeitet* (1835), D. F. Strauss sounded the death knell for this school. According to Strauss, the miraculous events in the gospels never happened; rather they are myths, legends, and editorial additions. Jesus was a purely human teacher who made such an impression on His disciples that after His death they applied to Him the myths about the Messiah that had evolved in Judaism. Thus, out of the Jesus of history evolved the Christ of the gospels—the Messiah, the Lord, the incarnate Son of God. Though such a mythological Jesus never actually existed, nevertheless the myth embodies a profound truth, namely, the Hegelian truth of the unity of the infinite and the finite, of God and man, not, indeed, of God and the individual man Jesus, but of God and mankind as a whole. Strauss was a self-confessed pantheist, and it was this truth that the myth of the God-man embodied.

The reaction in Germany against Strauss was virulent, but the Life of Jesus movement did not return to a supernatural view of Jesus. The question of miracles was dead, and the chief issue that remained was the interpretation of the man behind the myth. With the rise of liberal theology in the second half of the nineteenth century, Jesus became a great moral teacher. The kingdom of God was interpreted by Albrecht Ritschl and Wilhelm Herrmann as an ethical community of love among men. Although Jesus employed apocalyptic language, His real meaning, according to Ritschl, was ethical. He lived in complete devotion to His vocation of founding this kingdom and therefore serves as the model of the ethical life for all men. According to Herrmann, Jesus completely identified with the moral ideal of the kingdom of God and is thus God's unique representative among men.

Up until this point all of the researchers shared the optimistic view that a purely human Jesus was discoverable behind the gospel traditions, that indeed a life of Jesus was possible. By this time New Testament criticism had evolved the two-source theory, that is, that the synoptic problem was to be solved by postulating Matthew and Luke's use of Mark and another source of sayings of Jesus, arbitrarily designated Q. It was believed that in these two most primitive sources the true, historical Jesus was to be found.

This optimism received a crushing blow at the hands of Wilhelm Wrede in his theory of the "Messianic secret." Wrede was exercised by the problem, why does Jesus in Mark always seek to conceal His identity as the Messiah, commanding people to tell no one who He really is? Wrede's ingenious answer was that since Jesus never made such divine claims about Himself, Mark had to come up with some reason why people are unaware of Jesus' messianic claims, which the Christian church had written back into the gospel traditions and had asserted Jesus had made. To get around this problem Mark invented the "Messianic secret" motif, that is, that Jesus tried to conceal His identity: and he wrote his gospel from the perspective of this motif. The consequence of Wrede's theory was that it now became clear that even the most primitive sources about Jesus were theologically colored and that therefore a biography of the historical Jesus was impossible.

5.122 ALBERT SCHWEITZER AND THE END OF THE OLD QUEST

Thus, according to Albert Schweitzer, the historian of this intriguing movement, the old Life of Jesus movement ground to a halt in nearly complete skepticism. The liberal Jesus who went forth proclaiming the ethical kingdom of God and the brotherhood of man never existed, but is a projection of modern theology. We do not know who Jesus really was, says Schweitzer; He comes to us as a man unknown. What we do know about Him is that He actually believed the end of the world was near and that He died in His fruitless attempt to usher in the eschatological kingdom of God. Schweitzer intimates that Jesus may have been psychologically deranged; hence His eschatological expectation and suicidal course of action. Schweitzer thus not only pronounced the final rites over the liberal Jesus, but he was instrumental in the rediscovery of the eschatological element in Jesus' preaching.

The net result of the old quest of the historical Jesus was the discovery of theology in even the earliest sources of the gospels. This meant that a biography of the human Jesus could not be written. The theology of the early church had, they felt, so colored the documents that it was no longer possible to extract the Jesus of history from the Christ of faith.

5.123 DIALECTICAL AND EXISTENTIAL THEOLOGY

This conviction characterized theology during the first half of the present century. For dialectical and existential theology, the Jesus of history receded into obscurity behind the Christ of faith. Karl Barth took almost no cognizance of New Testament criticism regarding Jesus. It is the Christ proclaimed by the church that encounters us today. The events of the gospels are *geschichtlich*, but not *historisch*, a distinction that could be rendered as *historic*, but not *historical*. That is to say, those events are of great importance for history and mankind, but they are not accessible to ordinary historical research like other events. Even though the later Barth wanted to place more emphasis on the historicity of the events of the gospels, he never succeeded in placing them in the ordinary world of space and time. What really mattered to him was not the historical Jesus, but the Christ of faith.

Similarly, Bultmann held that all that could be known about the historical Jesus could be written on a 4" x 6" index card, but that this lack of information was inconsequential. Like Strauss, he held the gospel narratives to be mythologically colored throughout; and he, too, sought by demythologizing to find the central truth expressed in the

myth. He turned, not to Hegel, but to Heidegger for the proper interpretation of the Christ-myth in terms of authentic existence in the face
of death. It was this Christ-idea that was significant for human existence; as for the historical Jesus, the mere *"dass* seines Gekommen-
seins"—the *that* of His coming—that is to say, the mere fact of His
existence, is enough.

5.124 THE NEW QUEST OF THE HISTORICAL JESUS

Some of Bultmann's disciples, however, such as Ernst Käsemann,
could not agree with their master that the mere fact of Jesus's existence
was enough to warrant our acceptance of the meaning of the Christ-
idea as constitutive for our lives today. Unless there is some connection
between the historical Jesus and the Christ of faith, then the latter
reduces to pure myth, and the question remains why this myth should
be thought to embody a truth that supplies the key to my existence.
Thus, New Testament criticism has heralded a "new quest for the historical Jesus," but this time considerably more cautious and modest
than the old quest.

Those pursuing the new quest are painfully conscious of the presence
of theology in the gospel narratives and are reluctant to ascribe to the
historical Jesus any element that may be found in the theology of the
early church. Indeed, James Robinson actually differentiates between
the historical Jesus and the Jesus of history. The latter is the Jesus who
really lived; the former is the Jesus that can be *proved* as a result of
historical research. Robinson says the new quest concerns only the
historical Jesus, not the Jesus of history. Moreover, Robinson believes
that because of the presence of theology in the gospels, the burden of
proof rests on the scholar who would ascribe some fact to the historical
Jesus, not on the scholar who would deny that fact. In other words, we
ought to presuppose that any feature common to both Jesus in the
gospels and to early church theology should not characterize the historical Jesus but is properly regarded as a product of Christian theology.
This attitude seems to underlie a great deal of New Testament criticism, although it has been sharply criticized. It has been pointed out
that such a procedure would require that Jesus should have had absolutely no effect on the early church, since any elements common to
both are regarded as products of the church alone. Robinson's procedure threatens to construct a theoretical and historical Jesus that is in
fact very unlike the Jesus of history—in which case the whole enter-
prise becomes rather pointless.

Sharp-sighted critics have recognized that the commonality of some
feature shared by the Jesus of the gospels and the early church does not
constitute sufficient grounds for rejecting it as an authentic feature of
the teaching of Jesus of history; therefore, to distinguish between the
historical Jesus and the Jesus of history may be positively misleading.

Most scholars are really after the Jesus of history and want to know what He claimed and taught. But in that case, it would be wrong to lay the burden of proof solely on the scholar who sees some authentic element in the Jesus of the gospels; at the very least, one ought to say that scholars claiming to prove *either* authenticity or inauthenticity must bear the burden of proof for their assertions.

5.13 ASSESSMENT

Let us turn now to an assessment of Christ's personal claims in light of contemporary research.

5.131 DENIAL OF CHRIST'S DIVINE CLAIMS

As our departure point, let us take a look at a recent controversy surrounding the problem of the person of Christ.

5.1311 *John Hick and* The Myth of God Incarnate. In the late 1970's a group of seven British theologians, headed by John Hick of the University of Birmingham, caused a great stir in the press and among laymen by publishing a book provocatively entitled *The Myth of God Incarnate*. In it they asserted that today the majority of New Testament scholars agree that the historical Jesus of Nazareth never claimed to be the Son of God or the Lord or the Messiah or indeed any of the divine titles that are attributed to Christ in the gospels. Rather, these titles developed later in the Christian church and were written back into the traditions handed down about Jesus, so that in the gospels He appears to claim these divine titles for Himself. But in fact, the real Jesus never said any such things at all. The idea of Jesus as divine was developed by the Christian church decades after Jesus Himself was dead and buried. Thus, the divine Christ of the gospels who appears as God incarnate is a myth, and ought to be rejected.

5.1312 *Dissolution of the traditional Christian apologetic.* Now as I say, the book caused quite a stir. As the authors of the book pointed out, the average layman is almost entirely unaware of what the professional theologians believe or say, and it was quite a shock for many people to learn that the majority of scholars no longer thought that Jesus claimed to be the Son of God, and so forth. So quite naturally, many church-going laymen were quite upset. In particular, the view expounded by the seven theologians plays havoc with the popular apologetic based on the claims of Christ. According to popular apologetics, Jesus claimed to be God, and His claims were either true or false. If they were false, then either He was intentionally lying or else He was deluded. But neither of these alternatives is plausible. Therefore, His claims cannot be false; He must be who He claimed to be, God incarnate, and we must decide whether we shall give our lives to

Him or not. Now certainly the majority of scholars today would agree that Jesus was neither a liar nor a lunatic; but that does not mean they acknowledge Him as Lord. Rather, as we have seen, most would say that the Jesus who claimed to be the Son of God is a legend, a mythological product of the Christian church. Thus, the dilemma posed by the traditional apologetics is undercut, for Jesus Himself never claimed to be God.

5.132 DEFENSE OF CHRIST'S DIVINE CLAIMS

What can be said in response to this critique? In assessing the viewpoint expressed by the seven authors, one will have to admit that what they have said is, indeed, partly true: namely, it is true that the majority of New Testament scholars today do not believe that the historical Jesus ever claimed to be the Son of God, Lord, and so forth. Whether or not they have good reasons for their skepticism is another question.

5.1321 *The Christological titles.*

5.13211 *In general.* Those who deny that Jesus made any extraordinary personal claims face the very severe problem of explaining how it is that the worship of Jesus as Lord and God came about at all in the early church. It does little good to say the early church wrote their beliefs about Jesus back into the gospels, for the problem is the very origin of those beliefs themselves. Studies by New Testament scholars such as Martin Hengel of Tübingen University, C. F. D. Moule of Cambridge, and others have proved that within twenty years of the crucifixion a full-blown Christology proclaiming Jesus as God incarnate existed. How does one explain this worship by monotheistic Jews of one of their countrymen as God incarnate, apart from the claims of Jesus Himself? The great church historian Jaroslav Pelikan points out that all the early Christians shared the conviction that salvation was the work of a being no less than Lord of heaven and earth and that the redeemer was God Himself. He observes that the oldest Christian sermon, the oldest account of a Christian martyr, the oldest pagan report of the church, and the oldest liturgical prayer (1 Cor. 16:22) all refer to Christ as Lord and God. He concludes, "Clearly it was the message of what the church believed and taught that 'God' was an appropriate name for Jesus Christ."[1] But if Jesus never made any such claims, then the belief of the earliest Christians in this regard becomes inexplicable.

5.13212 *In particular.* For example, it seems to me very likely that Jesus did claim to be the Son of Man. Most laymen think this title refers to Jesus' humanity, just as the title *Son of God*

---

1. Jaroslav Pelikan, *The Christian Tradition: A History of the Development of Doctrine,* vol. 1: *The Emergence of the Catholic Tradition (100-600),* p. 173.

refers to His deity. But this fails to take into account the Jewish background of the term. In the book of Daniel, the Son of Man is a divine figure who will come at the end of the world to establish the kingdom of God and judge mankind. This was Jesus' favorite self-description and is the title found most frequently in the gospels (80 times). Yet remarkably, this title is found only once outside the gospels in the rest of the New Testament. That shows that the designation of Jesus as "Son of Man" was not a title that arose in later Christian usage and was then read back into the gospels. There seems to be no good reason to deny that Jesus regarded Himself and called Himself "the Son of Man."

Now some critics are willing to allow this, but they maintain that in calling Himself "Son of Man" Jesus merely meant "a human person," just as the Old Testament prophet Ezekiel referred to himself as "a son of man." But as C. F. D. Moule of Cambridge University points out, with Jesus there is a crucial difference. For Jesus did not refer to himself as "a son of man," like Ezekiel, but as "the Son of Man." Most critics have overlooked Jesus' constant use of the definite article with the title. By calling himself "the Son of Man," Jesus was directing attention to the divine end-time figure of Daniel 7. During the intertestamental period, this title—"the Son of Man"— was used of the divine person who would come to usher in the kingdom of God. It was this title that Jesus seized upon and used to describe who He was. It may well be that Jesus preferred this title to "Messiah" because the latter title had become so overlaid with political and temporal considerations in Jewish thinking that to claim to be the Messiah would obscure rather than elucidate the true nature of His mission.

5.1322 *Implicit Christology.* So, as I said, one might well question the skepticism of most critics with regard to the titles used by Christ in the gospels. But we may actually leave that aside for now. For the main point I want to make is that although it is true that most critics agree that Jesus did not use the christological titles found in the gospels, that is only part of the story. What the seven British theologians failed to tell their audience is that most New Testament critics also agree that Jesus also made other claims about Himself, claims that imply virtually the same thing as the titles. In other words, the titles only serve to express *explicitly* what Jesus had already said about Himself *implicitly.*

That puts an entirely different face on the matter! To read the British theologians, one would come away with the impression that Jesus thought of Himself as a mere man, perhaps a prophet or teacher. But such an impression would be far from the truth. In fact, New Testament scholarship is agreed that Jesus regarded Himself as much more than a mere man, a prophet, or a teacher. But the authors of the *Myth of God Incarnate* are either ignorant of this fact or have chosen to remain deliberately silent about it, thereby creating a thoroughly false impression. Let us therefore review some of the personal claims of Jesus widely accepted in New Testament scholarship, wholly apart from the question of christological titles.

5.13221 *Jesus thought of Himself as being the Son of God in a unique sense.*

5.132211 *His prayer life.* Jesus *always* prayed to God as "Abba," the word a Jewish child used for "Papa." For a Jew the very name of God was sacred, and no one would dare to pray to God in so familiar a manner. But Jesus always talked to his Father in such a way. It might be said that early Christians also prayed to God as "Abba," for example in Romans 8:15. But such a usage was derived from Jesus' own practice. And notice that although Jesus taught His disciples to pray to God as "Abba," He never joined with them in praying "*Our* Father . . ." On the contrary he always prayed to God as "*My* Father." Jesus' prayer life thus shows that He thought of himself as God's Son in a unique sense that set Him apart from the rest of the disciples.

5.132212 *Matthew 11:27.* This fact is clearly expressed in the words of Jesus in Matthew 11:27: "All things have been handed over to Me by my Father; and no one knows the Son, except the Father; nor does anyone know the Father, except the Son, and anyone to whom the Son wills to reveal Him." There is good evidence to show that this is indeed a genuine word of Jesus: (a) it comes from an old source that is shared by Matthew and Luke; (b) the idea of the mutual knowledge of Father and Son is a Jewish idea, indicating its origin in a Semitic-speaking milieu; (c) early church theology did not work out the Father-Son relationship, indicating that this verse is not the later product of Christian theology; and (d) the verse says the Son is unknowable, which is not true for the post-Easter church. We *can* know the Son. This strongly implies a pre-Easter origin of the saying. Thus, there is good evidence that this verse records a genuine word of Jesus. But what does the saying tell us about Jesus' self-consciousness? It tells us that Jesus claimed to be the Son of God in an *exclusive* and *absolute* sense. Jesus says here that His relationship of sonship to God is unique. And He also claims to be the *only one* who can reveal the Father to men. In other words, Jesus claims to be the absolute revelation of God. Think of it! The historical Jesus of Nazareth claimed to be the absolute revelation of God Himself. Hence, I think it is clear that Jesus thought of Himself as the Son of God in a unique sense.

5.13222 *Jesus claimed to act and speak with divine authority.* His sense of divine authority is evident in several ways.

5.132221 *His style of teaching.* His sense of authority is especially evident in the Sermon on the Mount. The typical rabbinic style of teaching was to quote extensively from learned teachers, who provided the basis of authority for one's own teaching. But Jesus did exactly the opposite. He began, "You have heard that it was said to the men of old . . ." and then quoted some interpretation of the law of Moses. Then he continued, "But I say to you . . ." and gave His own teaching. No wonder that Matthew comments, "When Jesus had finished these words, the multitudes were amazed at His teaching; for He was teaching them as one having authority, and not as their scribes" (Matt. 7:28-29).

    5.132222 *His use of amēn.* The expression frequently attributed to Jesus, "Truly, truly I say to you," is unique and was used by Jesus to preface His teaching. It served to mark off His authoritative word on some subject.

    5.132223 *His role as an exorcist.* It is an embarrassment to many modern theologians, but it is historically certain that Jesus believed He had the power to cast out demons. This was a sign to people of His divine authority. He declared, "If I cast out demons by the finger of God, then the kingdom of God has come upon you" (Luke 11:20). This saying, which is recognized by New Testament scholarship as genuine, is remarkable for two reasons. First, it shows that Jesus claimed divine authority over the spiritual forces of evil. Second, it shows that Jesus believed that in Himself the kingdom of God had come. According to Jewish thinking, the kingdom of God would come at the end of history when the Messiah would reign over Israel and the nations. But Jesus was saying, "My ability to rule the spiritual forces of darkness shows that in me the kingdom of God is already present among you."

Thus, most New Testament critics acknowledge that the historical Jesus acted and spoke with a self-consciousness of divine authority, and that furthermore, He saw in his own Person the coming of the long-awaited kingdom of God.

    5.13223 *Jesus believed Himself able to perform miracles.* Jesus said to the disciples of John the Baptist, "Go and report to John what you hear and see: the blind receive sight and the lame walk, the lepers are cleansed and the deaf hear, and the dead are raised up, and the poor have the gospel preached to them (Matt. 11:4-5). James D. G. Dunn, a British New Testament scholar, comments: "Whatever the 'facts' were, Jesus evidently believed that he had cured cases of blindness, lameness, and deafness—indeed there is no reason to doubt that he believed lepers had been cured under his ministry and dead restored to life."[2]

One might well go on to argue that Jesus could surely not have been

2. James D. G. Dunn, *Jesus and the Spirit*, p. 60.

mistaken about such palpable facts as these, and that therefore Jesus of Nazareth must have had the power to work miracles. Indeed, Wolfgang Trilling, an East German New Testament scholar, reports that the consensus of New Testament scholarship agrees that Jesus did perform "miracles"—however one might want to interpret or explain these. According to Trilling, there is no doubt that Jesus performed the sort of miraculous acts ascribed to Him in the gospels. But for our purposes, we need not go so far. The point remains that it is certain that Jesus at least thought He had the power to perform miracles; and in that the majority of New Testament critics agree.

5.13224 *Jesus claimed to determine men's eternal destiny before God.* Jesus held that men's attitudes toward Himself would be the determining factor in God's judgment on the judgment day. He proclaimed, "I say to you, everyone who confesses Me before men, the Son of Man shall confess him also before the angels of God; but he who denies Me before men shall be denied before the angels of God" (Luke 12:8-9). I have no doubt that in this passage Jesus is referring to Himself as the Son of Man, not referring to some third figure besides Himself. But be that as it may, the point is that whoever the Son of Man may be, Jesus is claiming that men will be judged before Him on the basis of their response to Jesus. Think of it: men's eternal destiny is fixed on their response to Jesus. Make no mistake: if Jesus were not the divine Son of God, then this claim could only be regarded as the most narrow and objectionable dogmatism. For Jesus is saying that men's salvation depends on their confession to Jesus Himself.

5.133 CONCLUSION

A discussion of Jesus' personal claims could go on and on, but I think this is sufficient to indicate the radical self-concept of Jesus. Here is a man who thought of Himself as the Son of God in a unique sense, who claimed to act and speak with divine authority, who held Himself to be a worker of miracles, and who believed that men's eternal destiny hinged on whether or not they believed in Him. Royce Gruenler sums it up: "It is a striking fact of modern New Testament research that the essential clues for correctly reading the implicit christological self-understanding of Jesus are abundantly clear." There is, he concludes, "absolutely convincing evidence" that Jesus did intend to stand in the very place of God Himself.[3] So extraordinary was the person who Jesus thought Himself to be that Dunn at the end of his study of the self-consciousness of Jesus feels compelled to remark, "One last question cannot be ignored: Was Jesus mad?"[4] Dunn rejects the hypothesis that

3. Royce Gordon Gruenler, *New Approaches to Jesus and the Gospels,* p. 74.
4. Dunn, *Jesus,* p. 86.

Jesus was insane because it cannot account for the full portrait of Jesus that we have in the gospels. The balance and soundness of Jesus' whole life and teachings make it evident that He was no lunatic. But notice that by means of these claims of Jesus, wholly apart from the disputed question of christological titles, we are brought back around again to the same dilemma posed by the traditional apologetic: if Jesus was not who He claimed to be, then He was either a charlatan or a madman, neither of which are plausible. Therefore, why not accept Him as the divine Son of God, just as the earliest Christians did?

Horst Georg Pöhlmann in his *Abriss der Dogmatik* reports, "In summary, one could say that today there is virtually a consensus concerning that wherein the historical in Jesus is to be seen. It consists in the fact that Jesus came on the scene with an *unheard of authority*, namely with the authority of God, with the *claim of the authority to stand in God's place and speak to us and bring us to salvation.*"[5] This involves, says Pöhlmann, an implicit Christology. He concludes:

> This unheard of claim to authority, as it comes to expression in the antitheses of the Sermon on the Mount, for example, is *implicit* Christology, since it presupposes a unity of Jesus with God that is deeper than that of all men, namely a unity of essence. This . . . claim to authority is explicable only from the side of his deity. This authority only God himself can claim. With regard to Jesus there are only two possible modes of behavior: either to believe that in him God encounters us or to nail him to the cross as a blasphemer. *Tertium non datur.*[6]

There is no third way.

5.14 PRACTICAL APPLICATION

It is to me intellectually gratifying to see how modern New Testament criticism has actually served to support rather than undermine a high view of Christ. The refusal of radical critics to draw the obvious Christological implications of unquestionably authentic sayings of Jesus is due not to lack of historical evidence but to their personal anti-metaphysical and, quite frankly, anti-Chalcedonian prejudices. The evidence thus vindicates the approach of the traditional apologetic.

But here a word of caution would be in order. Often one hears it said, "I don't understand all those philosophical arguments for God's existence and so forth. I prefer historical apologetics." I suspect those who say this think that historical apologetics are easy and will enable them to avoid the hard thinking involved in the philosophical arguments.

5. Horst Georg Pöhlmann, *Abriss der Dogmatik*, p. 230.
6. Ibid.

But this section ought to teach us clearly that this is not so. It is naive and outdated to simply trot out the dilemma "Liar, Lunatic, or Lord" and adduce several proof texts where Jesus claims to be the Son of God, the Messiah, and so forth. Rather, if this apologetic is to work, we must do the requisite spadework of sorting out those claims of Jesus that can be established as authentic, and then draw out their implications. This will involve not only mastering Greek but also the methods of modern criticism and the criteria of authenticity. Far from being easy, historical apologetics, if done right, is every bit as difficult as philosophical apologetics. The only reason most people think historical apologetics to be easier is because they do it superficially. But, of course, one can do philosophical apologetics superficially, too! My point is that if we are to do a credible job in our apologetics, we need to do the hard thinking and the hard work required, or at least to rely on those who have.

Now in applying this material in evangelism, I think it is often more effective when used defensively than offensively. That is to say, if the unbeliever says Jesus was just a good man or religious teacher, then confront him with Christ's claims. Used offensively to convince someone that Jesus was divine, this apologetic can be derouted on the popular level. Many people will say Jesus was a man from outer space, and the more you argue with them the more they become entrenched in this position. Of course, such a view is hopelessly insane, so that, oddly enough, this apologetic is probably more effective on the scholarly level than on the popular. I think that it is more effective to argue that Jesus' claims provide the religio-historical context in which the resurrection becomes significant, as it confirms those claims. Of course, the non-Christian might still say Jesus was from outer space and came back to life like E.T., in which case the most effective strategy is not to argue with him at all, but just point out that no scholar believes such a thing. If you argue with him, this gives the impression that his view is worth refuting and therefore has some credibility, which it does not. So simply brush it aside, and it is to be hoped that the unbeliever, not wishing to feel intellectually isolated, will not take it too seriously either. Taken in conjunction with evidence for the resurrection—and one might add, with the evidence for Jesus' miracles and with fulfilled prophecy, which I have not discussed—, the radical claims of Jesus become a powerful apologetic for the Christian faith.

5.2 THE RESURRECTION OF JESUS

God and immortality: those were the two conditions we saw to be necessary if man is to have a meaningful existence. I have argued that God exists, and now we have come at length to the second consideration, immortality. Against the dark background of modern man's despair, the Christian proclamation of the resurrection is a bright light of hope. The earliest Christians saw Jesus' resurrection as both the vindication of His personal claims and as the harbinger of our own resurrection to eternal life. If Jesus rose from the dead, then His claims are vindicated and our Christian hope is sure; if Jesus did not rise, our faith is futile and we fall back into despair. How credible is then the New Testament witness to the resurrection of Jesus?

5.21 Literature Cited or Recommended

5.211 HISTORICAL BACKGROUND

Craig, William Lane. *The Historical Argument for the Resurrection of Jesus.* Toronto: Edwin Mellen, forthcoming.

Ditton, Humphrey. *A Discourse Concerning the Resurrection of Jesus Christ.* London: J. Darby, 1712.

Fuller, Daniel P. *Easter Faith and History.* London: Tyndale, 1968.

Houttevile, Abbé. *La religion chrétienne prouvée par les faits.* 3 vols. Paris: Mercier & Boudet, 1740.

Less, Gottfried. *Wahrheit der christlichen Religion.* Göttingen: G. L. Förster, 1776.

Paley, William. *A View of the Evidences of Christianity.* 2 vols. 5th ed. London: R. Faulder, 1796. Reprint. Westmead, England: Gregg, 1970.

Reimarus, Hermann Samuel. *Fragments.* Translated by R. S. Fraser. Edited by C. H. Talbert. Lives of Jesus Series. London: SCM, 1971.

Semler, Johann Salomo. *Abhandlung von freier Untersuchung des Canon.* Texte zur Kirchen- und Theologiegeschichte 5. Gütersloh: G. Mohn, 1967.

————. *Beantwortung der Fragmente eines Ungennanten insbesondere vom Zweck Jesu and seiner Jünger.* 2d ed. Halle: Verlag des Erziehungsinstituts, 1780.

Sherlock, Thomas. *The Tryal of the Witnesses of the Resurrection of Jesus.* London: J. Roberts, 1729.

Strauss, David Friedrich. "Hermann Samuel Reimarus and His 'Apology.'" In *Fragments,* by H. S. Reimarus. Translated by R. S. Fraser. Edited by C. H. Talbert. Lives of Jesus Series. London: SCM Press, 1971. Pp. 44-57.

————. *The Life of Jesus Christ Critically Examined.* Translated by G. Eliot. Edited with an Introduction by P. C. Hodgson. Lives of Jesus Series. London: SCM, 1973.

Tholuck, Friedrich August. "Abriss einer Geschichte der Umwälzung, welche seit 1750 auf dem Gebiete der Theologie in Deutschland statt gefunden." In *Vermischte Schriften grösstentheils Apologetischen Inhalts.* 2 vols. Hamburg: Friedrich Perthes, 1859.

Turrettin, J. Alph. *Traité de la verité de la religion chrétienne.* Translated by J. Vernet. 2d ed. 7 vols. Geneva: Henri Albert Gosse, 1745-55.

5.212 ASSESSMENT

Alsup, John. *The Post-Resurrection Appearances of the Gospel Tradition.* Stuttgart: Calwer Verlag, 1975. This is the most important work on the post-resurrection appearances.

Blinzler, Josef. "Die Grablegung Jesu in historischer Sicht." In *Resurrexit.* Edited by Edouard Dhanis. Rome: Editrice Libreria Vaticana, 1974. The best piece on the burial.

Bode, Edward Lynn. *The First Easter Morning.* Analecta Biblica 45. Rome: Biblical Institute Press, 1970. The best work on the empty tomb.

Craig, William Lane. "The Bodily Resurrection of Jesus." In *Gospel Perspectives I.* Edited by R. T. France and D. Wenham. Sheffield, England: JSOT, 1980. Pp. 47-74.

————. "The Empty Tomb." In *Gospel Perspectives II.* Edited by R. T. France and D. Wenham. Sheffield, England: JSOT, 1981. Pp. 173-200.

Dodd, C. H. "The Appearances of the Risen Christ: A study in the form criticism of the Gospels." In *More New Testament Studies.* Manchester: U. of Manchester, 1968. Pp. 102-33.

Ellis, E. Earle, ed. *The Gospel of Luke*. New Century Bible: London: Nelson, 1966.

Fuller, R. H. *The Formation of the Resurrection Narratives*. London: SPCK, 1972.

Grass, Hans. *Ostergeschehen und Osterberichte*. 4th ed. Göttingen: Vandenhock & Ruprecht, 1974. This influential work is the most important over-all treatment of the historicity of the resurrection.

Gundry, Robert. *Sōma in Biblical Theology*. Cambridge: Cambridge U., 1976. The best work on the second part of 1 Corinthians 15.

Jeremias, Joachim. "Die älteste Schicht der Osterüberlieferung." In *Resurrexit*. Edited by Edouard Dhanis. Rome: Editrice Libreria Vaticana, 1974.

Klappert, Berthold. "Einleitung." In *Diskussion um Kreuz und Auferstehung*. Edited by B. Klappert, Wuppertal: Aussaat Verlag, 1971. Pp. 9-52.

Kremer, Jacob. *Die Osterevangelien—Geschichten um Geschichte*. Stuttgart: Katholisches Bibelwerk, 1977.

Lehmann, Karl. *Auferweckt am dritten Tag nach der Schrift*. Quaestiones disputatae 38. Freiburg: Herder, 1968. The most important work on the first part of 1 Corinthians 15.

Moule, C. F. D. *The Phenomenon of the New Testament*. Studies in Biblical Theology 2/1. London: SCM, 1967.

Müller, Julius. *The Theory of Myths, in Its Application to the Gospel History Examined and Confuted*. London: John Chapman, 1844.

Perrin, Norman. *The Resurrection According to Matthew, Mark, and Luke*. Philadelphia: Fortress, 1977.

Sherwin-White, A. N. *Roman Society and Roman Law in the New Testament*. Oxford: Clarendon, 1963.

Van Daalen, D. H. *The Real Resurrection*. London: Collins, 1972.

Von Campenhausen, Hans Freiherr. *Der Ablauf der Osterereignisse und das leere Grab*. 3d rev. ed. Sitzungsberichte der Heidelberger Akademie der Wissenschaften. Heidelberg: Carl Winter, 1966.

Wilckens, Ulrich. *Auferstehung*. Themen der Theologie 4. Stuttgart: Kreuz Verlag, 1970.

5.22 HISTORICAL BACKGROUND

The historical apologetic for the resurrection played a central role in the case of the Christian apologists during the Deist controversy. A review of their arguments and of the reasons for the decline of this form of apologetics will be useful in preparing the way for a modern assessment of the resurrection. Too often Christians today employ an apologetic for the resurrection that was suitable for use against eighteenth-century opponents but is today ineffective in dealing with the objections raised by modern biblical criticism.

5.221 THE CASE FOR THE RESURRECTION IN THE
TRADITIONAL APOLOGETIC

The traditional apologetic may be summarized in three steps.

5.2211 *The gospels are authentic.* The point of this step
in the argument was to defend the apostolic authorship of the gospels.
The reasoning was that if the gospels were actually written by the
disciples, then quite simply they were either true accounts or they were
lies. Since the Deists granted the apostolic authorship of the gospels,
they were reduced to defending the implausible position that the gospels were a tissue of deliberate falsehoods. In order to demonstrate the
authenticity of the gospels, Vernet (cf. 4.12213) appeals to both internal and external evidence.

5.22111 *Internal evidence.* Under internal evidence,
Vernet notes that the style of writing in the gospels is simple and alive,
what we would expect from their traditionally accepted authors. Moreover, since Luke was written before Acts, and since Acts was written
prior to the death of Paul, Luke must have an early date, which speaks
for its authenticity. The gospels also show an intimate knowledge of
Jerusalem prior to its destruction in A.D. 70. Jesus' prophecies of that
event must have been written prior to Jerusalem's fall, for otherwise
the church would have separated out the apocalyptic element in the
prophecies, which makes them appear to concern the end of the world.
Since the end of the world did not come about when Jerusalem was
destroyed, so-called prophecies of its destruction that were really written after the city was destroyed would not have made that event appear
so closely connected with the end of the world. Hence, the gospels
must have been written prior to A.D. 70. Further, the gospels are full of
proper names, dates, cultural details, historical events, and customs
and opinions of that time. The stories of Jesus' human weaknesses and
of the disciples' faults also bespeak the gospels' accuracy. Furthermore,
it would have been impossible for forgers to put together so consistent
a narrative as that which we find in the gospels. The gospels do not try
to suppress apparent discrepancies, which indicates their originality.
There is no attempt at harmonization between the gospels, such as we
might expect from forgers. Finally, the style of each particular gospel is
appropriate to what we know of the personality of the traditional authors. Less (cf. 4.12222) adds to Vernet's case the further point that the
gospels do not contain anachronisms; the authors appear to have been
first-century Jews who were witnesses of the events. Paley (cf. 4.12223)
adds a final consideration: the Hebraic and Syriac idioms that mark the
gospels are appropriate to the traditional authors. He concludes that
there is no more reason to doubt that the gospels come from the traditional authors than there is to doubt that the works of Philo or Josephus are authentic, *except* that the gospels contain supernatural events.

5.22112 *External evidence.* Turning next to the external evidence for the gospels' authenticity, Vernet argues that the disciples must have left *some* writings, engaged as they were in giving lessons to and counseling believers who were geographically distant; and what could these writings be if not the gospels and epistles themselves? Similarly, Paley reasons that eventually the apostles would have needed to publish accurate narratives of Jesus' history, so that any spurious attempts would be discredited and the genuine gospels preserved. Moreover, Vernet continues, there were many eyewitnesses who were still alive when the books were written who could testify whether they came from their purported authors or not. Most importantly, the extrabiblical testimony unanimously attributes the gospels to their traditional authors. No finer presentation of this point can be found than Paley's extensive eleven-point argument.

First, the gospels and Acts are cited by a series of authors, beginning with those contemporary with the apostles and continuing in regular and close succession. This is the strongest form of historical testimony, regularly employed to establish authorship of secular works; and when this test is applied to the gospels, their authenticity is unquestionably established. Paley traces this chain of testimony from the Epistle of Barnabas, the Epistle of Clement, and the Shepherd of Hermas all the way up to Eusebius in A.D. 315. Less presents similar evidence and concludes that there is better testimony for the authenticity of the New Testament books than for *any* classical work of antiquity.

Second, the Scriptures were quoted as authoritative and as one-of-a-kind. As proof Paley cites Theophilus, the writer against Artemon; Hippolitus, Origen, and many others.

Third, the Scriptures were collected very early into a distinct volume. Ignatius refers to collections known as the Gospel and the Apostles, what we today call the gospels and the epistles. According to Eusebius, about sixty years after the appearance of the gospels Quadratus distributed them to converts during his travels. Irenaeus and Melito refer to the collection of writings we call the New Testament.

Fourth, these writings were given titles of respect. Polycarp, Justin Martyr, Dionysius, Irenaeus, and others refer to them as Scriptures, divine writings, and so forth.

Fifth, these writings were publicly read and expounded. Citations from Justin Martyr, Tertullian, Origen, and Cyprian go to prove the point.

Sixth, copies, commentaries, and harmonies were written on these books. Noteworthy in this connection is Tatian's *Diatessaron*, a harmony of the four gospels, from about A.D. 170. With the single exception of Clement's commentary on the Revelation of Peter, Paley emphasizes, no commentary was ever written during the first 300 years after

Christ on any book outside the New Testament.

Seventh, the Scriptures were accepted by all heretical groups as well as by orthodox Christians. Examples include the Valentinians, the Carpocratians, and many others.

Eighth, the gospels, Acts, thirteen letters of Paul, 1 John, and 1 Peter were received without doubt as authentic even by those who doubted the authenticity of other books now in the canon. Caius about A.D. 200 reckoned up about 13 of Paul's letters but insisted that Hebrews was not written by Paul. About twenty years later Origen cites Hebrews to prove a particular point, but noting that some might dispute the authority of Hebrews, he states that his point may be proved from the *undisputed* books of Scripture and quotes Matthew and Acts. Though he expresses doubt about some books, Origen reports that the four gospels alone were received without dispute by the whole church of God under heaven.

Ninth, the early opponents of Christianity regarded the gospels as containing the accounts upon which the religion was founded. Celsus admitted that the gospels were written by the disciples. Porphyry attacked Christianity as found in the gospels. The Emperor Julian followed the same procedure.

Tenth, catalogues of authentic Scriptures were published, which always contained the gospels and Acts. Paley supports the point with quotations from Origen, Athanasius, Cyril, and others.

Eleventh, the so-called apocryphal books of the New Testament were never so treated. It is a simple fact, asserts Paley, that with a single exception, no apocryphal gospel is ever even quoted by any known author during the first three hundred years after Christ. In fact there is no evidence that any inauthentic gospel whatever existed in the first century, in which all four gospels and Acts were written. The apocryphal gospels were never quoted, were not read in Christian assemblies, were not collected into a volume, were not listed in the catalogues, were not noticed by Christianity's adversaries, were not appealed to by heretics, and were not the subject of commentaries or collations, but were nearly universally rejected by Christian writers of succeeding ages.

Therefore, Paley concludes, the external evidence strongly confirms the authenticity of the gospels. Even if it should be the case that the names of the authors traditionally ascribed to the gospels are mistaken, it still could not be denied that the gospels do contain the story that the original apostles proclaimed and for which they labored and suffered.

Taken together, then, the internal and external evidence adduced by the Christian apologists served to establish the first step of their case, that the gospels are authentic.

5.2212 *The text of the gospels is pure.* The second step

often taken by the Christian thinkers was to argue that the text of the gospels is pure. This step was important to ensure that the gospels we have today are the same gospels as originally written.

Vernet, in support of the textual purity of the gospels, points out that because of the need for instruction and personal devotion, these writings must have been copied many times, which increases the chances of preserving the original text. In fact, no other ancient work is available in so many copies and languages, and yet all these various versions agree in content. The text has also remained unmarred by heretical additions. The abundance of manuscripts over a wide geographical distribution demonstrates that the text has been transmitted with only trifling discrepancies. The differences that do exist are quite minor and are the result of unintentional mistakes. The text of the New Testament is every bit as good as the text of the classical works of antiquity.

To these considerations, Less adds that the quotations of the New Testament books in the early church Fathers all coincide. Moreover, the gospels could not have been corrupted without a great outcry on the part of orthodox Christians. Against the idea that there could have been a deliberate falsifying of the text Houtteville (cf. 4.12214) argues that no one could have corrupted all the manuscripts. Moreover, there is no precise time when the falsification could have occurred, since, as we have seen, the New Testament books are cited by the church Fathers in regular and close succession. The text could not have been falsified before all external testimony, since then the apostles were still alive and could repudiate any such tampering with the gospels. In conclusion, Vernet charges that to repudiate the textual purity of the gospels would be to reverse all the rules of criticism and to reject all the works of antiquity, since the text of those works is less certain than that of the gospels.

5.2213 *The gospels are reliable.* Having demonstrated that the gospels are authentic and that the text of the gospels is pure, the Christian thinkers were now in a position to argue that the gospels are historically reliable.

5.22131 *The apostles were neither deceivers nor deceived.* Their argument basically boiled down to a dilemma: if the gospel accounts of Jesus' miracles and resurrection are false, then the apostles were either deceivers or deceived. Since both of these alternatives are implausible, it follows that the gospel accounts must be true.

5.221311 *The apostles were not deceived.* Let us turn first to the arguments presented against the second horn of the dilemma: that the apostles were deceived. This alternative embraces any hypothesis holding that Jesus did not rise from the dead but that the disciples sincerely believed He had.

Humphrey Ditton in his *Discourse Concerning the Resurrection of*

Jesus Christ (1712) argues that the apostles could not have been mistaken about the resurrection. In the first place, the witnesses to the appearances were well qualified. There were a great many witnesses, and they had personal knowledge of the facts over an extended period of forty days. It is unreasonable, therefore, to ascribe their experience to imagination or dreaming. Moreover, the disciples were not religious enthusiasts, as is evident from their cool and balanced behavior even in extreme situations. Sherlock (cf. 4.12221) responds to the charge that the evidence for the resurrection consists of the testimony of silly women by pointing out that they, too, had eyes and ears to report accurately what they experienced; and far from being gullible, they were actually disbelieving. He observes also that the women were never in fact used as witnesses to the resurrection in the apostolic preaching. Finally, he adds, the testimony of the men is none the worse off for having the testimony of the women as well. (This exchange obviously took place before the days of feminist consciousness!)

Paley answers the allegation that the resurrection appearances were the result of "religious enthusiasm" (that is, were hallucinations) by arguing that the theory fails on several counts. First, not just one person but many saw Christ appear. Second, they saw Him not individually, but together. Third, they saw Him appear not just once, but several times. Fourth, they not only saw Him but touched Him, conversed with Him, and ate with Him. Fifth and decisively, the religious enthusiasm hypothesis fails to explain the nonproduction of the body. It would have been impossible for Jesus' disciples to have believed in their master's resurrection if His corpse still lay in the tomb. But it is equally incredible to suppose that the disciples could have stolen the body and perpetrated a hoax. Furthermore, it would have been impossible for Christianity to come into being in Jerusalem if Jesus' body were still in the grave. The Jewish authorities would certainly have produced it as the shortest and completest answer to the whole affair. But all they could do was claim that the disciples had stolen the body. Thus, the hypothesis of religious enthusiasm, in failing to explain the absence of Jesus' corpse, ultimately collapses back into the hypothesis of conspiracy and deceit, which, Paley remarks, has pretty much been given up in view of the evident sincerity of the apostles, as well as their character and the dangers they underwent in proclaiming the truth of Jesus' resurrection.

5.221312 *The apostles were not deceivers.* With Paley's last remark, we return to the first horn of the dilemma: that the disciples were deceivers. This alternative encompasses any hypothesis holding that the disciples knew that the miracles and resurrection of Jesus did not take place, but that they nevertheless claimed that they did.

One of the most popular arguments against this theory is the obvious sincerity of the disciples as attested by their suffering and death. No more eloquent statement of the argument can be found than Paley's: he seeks to show that the original witnesses of the miraculous events of the gospels passed their lives in labors, dangers, and sufferings, voluntarily undertaken in attestation to and as a consequence of the accounts which they delivered.

Paley argues first from the general nature of the case. We know that the Christian religion exists. Either it was founded by Jesus and the apostles or by others, the first being silent. The second alternative is quite incredible. If the disciples had not zealously followed up what Jesus had started, Christianity would have died at its birth. If this is so, then a life of missionary sacrifice must have been necessary for those first apostles. Such a life is not without its own enjoyments, but they are only such as spring from sincerity. With a consciousness at bottom of hollowness and falsehood, the fatigue and strain would have become unbearable.

There was probably difficulty and danger involved in the propagation of a new religion. With regard to the Jews, the notion of Jesus' being the Messiah was contrary to Jewish hopes and expectations; Christianity lowered the esteem of Jewish law; and the disciples would have had to reproach the Jewish leaders as guilty of an execution that could only be represented as an unjust and cruel murder. As to the Romans, they could have understood the kingdom of God only in terms of an earthly kingdom—thus, a rival. And concerning the heathen, Christianity admitted no other god or worship. Although the philosophers allowed and even enjoined worship of state deities, Christianity could countenance no such accommodation. Thus, even in the absence of a general program of persecution, there were probably random outbursts of violence against Christians. The heathen religions were old and established and not easily overthrown. Those religions were generally regarded by the common people as equally true, by the philosophers as equally false, and by the magistrates as equally useful. From none of these sides could the Christians expect protection. Finally, the nature of the case requires that these early apostles must have experienced a great change in their lives, now involved as they were in preaching, prayer, religous meetings, and so forth.

What the nature of the case would seem to require is in fact confirmed by history. Writing seventy years after Jesus' death, Tacitus narrates Nero's persecution about thirty years after Christ, how the Christians were clothed in the skins of wild beasts and thrown to dogs, how others were smeared with pitch and used as human torches to illuminate the night while Nero rode about Rome in the dress of a charioteer, viewing the spectacle. The testimonies of Suetonius and

Juvenal confirm the fact that within thirty-one years after Jesus' death, Christians were dying for their faith. From the writings of Pliny the Younger, Martial, Epictetus, and Marcus Aurelius, it is clear that believers were voluntarily submitting to torture and death rather than renounce their religion. This suffering is abundantly attested in Christian writings as well. Christ had been killed for what He said; the apostles could expect the same treatment. Jesus' predictions in the gospels of sufferings for His followers were either real predictions come true or were put into His mouth because persecution had in fact come about. In Acts, the sufferings of Christians are soberly reported without extravagance. The epistles abound with references to persecutions and exhortations to steadfastness. In the early writings of Clement, Hermas, Polycarp, and Ignatius, we find the sufferings of the early believers historically confirmed.

It is equally clear that it was for a *miraculous* story that these Christians were suffering. After all, the only thing that could convince these early Christians that Jesus was the Messiah was that they *thought* there was something supernatural about Him. The gospels are a miraculous story, and we have no other story handed down to us than that contained in the gospels. Josephus's much disputed testimony can only confirm, not contradict, the gospel accounts. The letters of Barnabas and Clement refers to Jesus' miracles and resurrection. Polycarp mentions the resurrection of Christ, and Irenaeus relates that he had heard Polycarp tell of Jesus' miracles. Ignatius speaks of the resurrection. Quadratus reports that persons were still living who had been healed by Jesus. Justin Martyr mentions the miracles of Christ. No relic of a nonmiraculous story exists. That the original story should be lost and replaced by another goes beyond any known example of corruption of even oral tradition, not to speak of the experience of written transmissions. These facts show that the story in the gospels was in substance the same story that Christians had at the beginning. That means, for example, that the resurrection of Jesus was always a part of this story. Were we to stop here, remarks Paley, we have a circumstance unparalleled in history: that in the reign of Tiberius Caesar a certain number of persons set about establishing a new religion, in the propagation of which they voluntarily submitted to great dangers, sufferings, and labors, all for a miraculous story which they proclaimed wherever they went, and that the resurrection of a dead man, whom they had accompanied during His lifetime, was an integral part of this story.

Since it has been already abundantly proved that the accounts of the gospels do stem from their apostolic authors, Paley concludes, then the story must be true. For the apostles could not be deceivers. He asks:

Would men in such circumstances pretend to have seen what they never saw; assert facts which they had not knowledge of; go about lying to teach virtue; and, though not only convinced of Christ's being an imposter, but having seen the success of his imposture in his crucifixion, yet persist in carrying on; and so persist, as to bring upon themselves, for nothing, and with full knowledge of the consequence, enmity and hatred, danger and death?[1]

The question is merely rhetorical, for the absurdity of the hypothesis of deceit is all too clear.

A second popular argument against the disciples' being deceivers was that their character precludes their being liars. Humphrey Ditton observes that the apostles were simple, common men, not cunning deceivers. They were men of unquestioned moral integrity, and their proclamation of the resurrection was solemn and devout. They had absolutely nothing to gain in worldly terms in preaching this doctrine. Moreover, they had been raised in a religion that was vastly different from the one they preached. Especially foreign to them was the idea of the death and resurrection of the Jewish Messiah. That mitigates against their concocting this idea. The Jewish laws against deceit and false testimony were very severe, which would act as a deterrent to fraud. Finally, they were evidently sincere in what they proclaimed. In light of their character so described, asks Ditton bluntly, *why not believe the testimony of these men?*

A third argument pressed by the apologists was that the notion of a conspiracy is ridiculous. Vernet thinks it inconceivable that one of the disciples should suggest to the others that they say Jesus was risen when both he and they knew the precise opposite to be true. How could he possibly rally his bewildered colleagues into so detestable a project? And are we then to believe that those men would stand before judges declaring the truth of this product of their imaginations? Houtteville asserts that a conspiracy to fake the resurrection would have had to have been of such unmanageable proportions that the disciples could never have carried it off. Ditton points out that had there been a conspiracy, it would certainly have been unearthed by the disciples' adversaries, who had both the interest and the power to expose any fraud. Common experience shows that such intrigues are inevitably exposed even in cases where the chances of discovery are much less than in the case of the resurrection.

Yet a fourth argument, urged by Less, was that the gospels were written in such temporal and geographical proximity to the events they record that it would have been almost impossible to fabricate events. Anyone who cared to could have checked out the accuracy of what they reported. The fact that the disciples were able to proclaim the resurrection in Jerusalem in the face of their enemies a few weeks after the

1. William Paley, *A View of the Evidences of Christianity,* 1:327-8.

crucifixion shows that what they proclaimed was true, for they could never have proclaimed the resurrection under such circumstances had it not occurred.

Fifth, the theft of the body from the tomb by the disciples would have been impossible. Ditton argues that the story of the guard at the tomb is plausible, since the Jews had the ability and motivation to guard the tomb. But in this case, the disciples could not have stolen the body on account of the armed guard. The allegation that the guards had fallen asleep is ridiculous, because in that case they could not have known that it was the disciples who had taken the corpse. Besides, adds Houtteville, no one could have broken into the tomb without waking the guard.

Sixth, even the enemies of Christianity acknowledged Jesus' resurrection. The Jews did not publicly deny the disciples' charge that the authorities had bribed the guard to keep silent. Had the charge been false, they would have openly denounced it. Thus, the enemies of Christianity themselves bore witness to the resurrection.

Seventh and finally, the dramatic change in the disciples shows that they were absolutely convinced Jesus had risen from the dead. They went from the depths of despair and doubt to a joyful certainty of such height that they preached the resurrection openly and boldly and suffered bravely for it.

Thus, the hypothesis of deceit is just as implausible as the hypothesis that the apostles had been deceived. But since neither of these alternatives is reasonable, the conclusion can only be that they were telling the truth and that Jesus rose from the dead.

5.22132 *The origin of Christianity proves the resurrection.* In addition to this fundamental dilemma, the Christian apologists also refurbished the old argument from the origin of the church. Suppose, Vernet suggests, that no resurrection or miracles occurred: how then could a dozen men, poor, coarse, and apprehensive, turn the world upside down? If Jesus did not rise from the dead, declares Ditton, then either we must believe that a small, unlearned band of deceivers overcame the powers of the world and preached an incredible doctrine over the face of the whole earth, which in turn received this fiction as the sacred truth of God; or else, if they were not deceivers, but enthusiasts, we must believe that these extremists, carried along by the impetus of extravagant fancy, managed to spread a falsity that not only common folk, but statesmen and philosophers as well, embraced as the sober truth. Because such a scenario is simply unbelievable, the message of the apostles, which gave birth to Christianity, must be true.

5.222 THE DECLINE OF HISTORICAL APOLOGETICS

Paley's *View of the Evidences* (1794) constituted the high-water mark of the historical apologetic for the resurrection. During the nineteenth century this approach dramatically receded; indeed, it would be difficult to find a significant and influential thinker defending the Christian faith on the basis of the evidence for the resurrection. It seems to me that there were two factors that served to undermine the traditional apologetic.

5.2221 *The advance of biblical criticism.* The first of those was the advance of biblical criticism. In England the Deist controversy subsided; in France it was cut short by the Revolution; but in Germany it was taken up into a higher plane. There is a direct link between Deism and the advance in biblical criticism that began in Germany in the late eighteenth century.

5.22211 *The late eighteenth-century crisis in German theology.* The flood of Deist thought and literature that poured into eighteenth-century Germany from England and France wrought a crisis in German orthodox theology. That theology had been characterized by an extremely rigid doctrine of biblical inspiration and infallibility and by a devotional pietism. The critique of the Deists undermined the faith of many in the inerrancy of Scripture, but their piety would not allow them to join themselves to the Deist camp and reject Christianity. This group of scholars, generally called Rationalists, therefore sought to resolve the crisis by forging a new way between orthodoxy and Deism, namely, they loosed the religious meaning of a text from the historicity of the events described therein. The historical events were only the form, the husk, in which some spiritual, trans-historical truth was embodied. What was of importance was the substance, the kernel, not the mere external trappings. In this way, the Rationalists could accept the Deist critique of miracles but at the same time retain the spiritual truth expressed in these stories. With regard to the resurrection we have seen that many Rationalists adopted some form of the apparent death theory to explain away the resurrection; but for most it still retained its spiritual significance and truth. The Rationalists thus sought a middle ground between the Deists and the supernaturalists. The Deists and supernaturalists agreed that if the events of the gospels did not in fact occur, then Christianity was false. But the Rationalists, while holding with the Deists that the events never occurred, nevertheless held with the supernaturalists that Christianity was true. Let us take a look at two of the principal figures in this radical new direction.

5.222111 *Herrmann Samuel Reimarus.* Reimarus, a professor of oriental languages at Hamburg, struggled privately with gnawing doubts about the truth of the biblical revelation. From 1730-1768 he wrote them down, and his writing evolved into an enormous 4,000-page critique of the Bible. He was troubled by the many contradictions he found in the Bible and could not accept the stories of the Flood, the crossing of the Red Sea, and the resurrection of Jesus. He denied miracles and came to accept a Deistic natural religion. Nevertheless, he never published his opinions but only showed his manuscript to a few close friends and two of his children. After his death, Reimarus's daughter gave the manuscript to Gottfried Lessing, who became librarian in Wolfenbüttel. In 1774 Lessing began to publish excerpts from the manuscript, passing them off as anonymous fragments found in the library's archives. In 1777 he published Reimarus's attack on the historicity of Jesus' resurrection, which set German orthodoxy in an uproar.

According to Reimarus, Jesus only claimed to have been an earthly Messiah, and having tried to establish His reign and failed, He was executed. But the disciples stole Jesus' corpse and spread the story of Jesus' resurrection, touting Him as a spiritual Messiah so that they could continue the easy life of preaching that they had enjoyed with Jesus while He was alive. Reimarus realized that to maintain this position he must refute the evidence for the historicity of the resurrection. In his mind, this consisted of the witness of the guard at the tomb, the witness of the apostles, and the fulfillment of Old Testament prophecies. Against the testimony of the guard, Reimarus employed the arguments of the English Deists. He argued that the story is improbable in itself and is full of contradictions. He held it to be an invention of Matthew that the other evangelists rejected. In order to undermine the testimony of the apostles, Reimarus capitalized on the inconsistencies and contradictions in the resurrection narratives. If those were not enough, there is the overriding problem of the privacy of Jesus' appearances. The apostles' testimony is suspect because they are the only ones who supposedly saw Christ. Finally, Reimarus made short shrift of the proof from prophecy. The interpretations of the Old Testament passages in question are so strained as to be unconvincing. Besides, the whole procedure begs the question anyway, since it assumes Jesus was in fact raised from the dead, and thus the prophecies apply to Him! In conclusion, Reimarus summarized his case:

> (1) the guard story is very doubtful and unconfirmed, and it is very probable the disciples came by night, stole the corpse, and said afterward Jesus had arisen; (2) the disciples' testimony is both inconsistent and contradictory; and (3) the prophecies appealed to are irrelevant, falsely interpreted, and question-begging.[2]

Thus, Christianity is quite simply a fraud.

      5.222112 *Johann Salomo Semler.* Among the

---

2. Hermann Samuel Reimarus, *Fragments*, p. 104.

many who undertook to refute Reimarus was Johann Semler, a conservative Rationalist. In his earlier *Abhandlung von freier Untersuchung des Canon* (1771) Semler had broken the ground for the new Rationalist approach to the Scriptures. Semler had been the assistant at the University of Halle to S. J. Baumgarten, who chronicled the course of Deism in his *Nachrichten von einer Hallischen Bibliothek* (1748-51), reviewing almost every English Deist and apologetic work. Semler actually assisted Baumgarten in the reading and translation of Deist literature and thus became open to Deist influences.

At the same time, Semler had a background in Pietism and had no desire to undermine Christianity. Therefore, he made a distinction between the timeless, spiritual truths in Scripture and the merely local truths. It was his conviction that only the spiritual truths may properly be called the Word of God. He thus introduced into theology the decisive distinction between the Scriptures and the Word of God. Since only the spiritual truths are the Word of God, it is no longer possible to regard the Scriptures as a whole as divinely inspired. Rather, the Word of God is clothed in fallible, human forms, which have only local importance. These fallible forms represent God and Jesus' accommodation to human weakness. Included among these accommodations is the miraculous element in Scripture. No Christian can be obligated to believe that such events literally happened, for they are not part of the Word of God. Thus, we are free to examine the historical narratives as we would any other ordinary narrative, since inspiration concerns only the timeless truths they embody. Should the narrative be shown to be unhistorical, that is of little consequence, for that cannot have any effect on the Word of God. The proof that certain events are unhistorical is irrelevant to divine truths.

Given his views of Scripture, it seems somewhat surprising to find Semler writing a refutation of Reimarus in his *Beantwortung der Fragmente eines Ungenannten* (1779). Reimarus's bitter attack seems to have forced him back to the orthodox end of the spectrum. But in the way he defends the resurrection, we can see the beginning of the end for the historical apologetic for the resurrection. He emphatically subordinates the resurrection to the teachings of Jesus and removes from it any apologetic significance. According to Semler, Christianity consists of the spiritual doctrines taught by Christ. Reimarus mistakenly thinks that in refuting the three purported grounds for belief in the resurrection, he has thereby struck down the essential truths of Christianity. But this is far from true, asserts Semler. In the first place, one may be a Christian without believing in the resurrection of Jesus. In the second place, the true ground for belief in the resurrection is the self-evident truth of Christ's teachings. For Semler, belief in Christ's teaching entails belief in Christ's resurrection: "The resurrection of Jesus hangs together with Jesus' life and goal; whoever has experienced his teachings will also believe that God has raised him from the dead."[3] The proof of the resurrection is not the three points mentioned by Reimarus; the proof is the spiritual teachings of Christ. In specific response to Reimarus's refutation of the three purported grounds, Semler grants all three to Reimarus—but for Semler they are simply irrelevant and present no problem once one has abandoned the doctrine of verbal inspiration.

Thus, Semler undercut the traditional apologetic in various ways: while affirming the truth of the resurrection, he nonetheless admitted that belief in the resurrection was not essential to being a Christian; he provided no historical reason to accept the reliability of the gospel accounts with regard to this event; he denied that the resurrection has any power to confirm Christ's teaching; and he instead subordinated the resurrection to the teachings of Christ, the self-evident Word of God, making the latter the proof of the former.

5.22212 *The hermeneutic of mythological interpretation.* By loosing the Word of God from the Scriptures and making its truth self-attesting, Semler enabled Rational theology to adhere to the doctrines of Christianity while denying their historical basis. During the time between Semler and Strauss, the natural explanation school predominated. The old conspiracy theory of Reimarus was rejected as an explanation for the resurrection of Jesus, and instead the apparent death theory enjoyed popularity among Rationalists. Even F. D. E. Schleiermacher, known as the father of modern theology, accepted this explanation. But the roof really caved in on the traditional apologetic with the advent of David Friedrich Strauss and his hermeneutic of mythological explanation.

5.222121 *David Friedrich Strauss.* Strauss's *Leben Jesu* (1835) marks a watershed in the history of biblical criticism, to which modern form and redaction criticism may be traced. The year 1835 marks a turning point in the history of the Christian faith.

Strauss's approach to the gospels, and to the resurrection in particular, may be seen as an attempt to forge a third way between the horns of the dilemma posed by the traditional apologetic; which says that if the miracles and resurrection of Jesus are not historical facts, then the apostles were either deceivers or deceived, both of which are impossible. Reimarus had chosen to defend the first horn, arguing that the disciples had hoaxed the resurrection. Paulus had chosen to defend the second horn, arguing that the disciples had been mistaken about Jesus' return from the dead. What Strauss saw clearly was that neither of

---

3. Johann Salomo Semler, *Beantwortung der Fragmente eines Ungennanten insbesondere vom Zweck Jesu and seiner Jünger,* p. 266.

these alternatives was plausible, and so he sought a third alternative in the mythological explanation. According to this view, the miraculous events of the gospels never happened, and the gospel accounts of them are the result of a long process of legend and religious imagination:

> In the view of the church, Jesus was miraculously revived; according to the deistic view of Reimarus, his corpse was stolen by the disciples; in the rationalistic view, he only appeared to be dead and revived; according to our view the imagination of his followers aroused in their deepest spirit, presented their Master revived, for they could not possibly think of him as dead. What for a long time was valid as an external fact, first miraculous, then deceptive, finally simply natural, is hereby reduced completely to the state of mind and made into an inner event.[4]

Strauss thus denied that there was any external fact to be explained. The gospel accounts of the resurrection were unreliable legends colored by myth. Hence, the dilemma of "deceivers or deceived" did not arise. The fact that the resurrection was unhistorical did not rob it of its religious significance (here we see the change wrought by Semler), for a spiritual truth may be revealed within the husk of a delusion.

Strauss believed that the chief problem in applying the mythical interpretation to the New Testament is that the first century was no longer an age of myths. But although it was a time of writing, if there was a long period of oral transmission during which no written record existed then marvelous elements could begin to creep in and grow into historical myths. Strauss recognized as well that adherence to this theory necessitated denying the contemporary authorship of the gospels and the influence of eyewitnesses. Hence, Strauss regarded it as "the sole object" of his book to examine the internal evidence in order to test the probability of the authors' being eyewitnesses or competently informed writers.[5] Strauss gave short shrift to the external testimony to the gospels: he believed Mark to be compiled from Matthew and Luke and hence not based on Peter's preaching; the Matthew mentioned by Papias is not our Matthew; Acts so contradicts Paul that its author could not be his companion; the earliest reference to John is in A.D. 172, and the gospel's authenticity was disputed by the Alogoi. Nor could living eyewitnesses prevent the accrual of legend: first, the legends could have originated in areas where Jesus was not well known; second, the apostles could not be everywhere at once to correct or suppress unhistorical stories; and third, eyewitnesses themselves would be tempted to fill up the gaps in their own knowledge with stories. Strauss argued that the Jews lagged behind the Romans and Greeks in their

---

4. David Friedrich Strauss, "Herrmann Samuel Reimarus and His 'Apology,'" pp. 280-81.
5. David Friedrich Strauss, The Life of Jesus Critically Examined, p. 70.

historical consciousness; even Josephus's work is filled with marvelous tales. Myths about the Messiah had already arisen between the exile and Christ's day. All that was wanting was the application of these myths with some modification to Jesus by the Christian community.

With regard to the resurrection accounts, Strauss used arguments similar to Reimarus's to demonstrate their unreliability. For example, if the body was embalmed and wrapped, why do the women return for this purpose? Was the body placed in the tomb because it was Joseph's or because it was near? The story of the guard is improbable, and the inconsistencies in the empty tomb narrative are irreconcilable. As for the appearances, why should Jesus command the disciples to go to Galilee when He was going to appear to them in Jerusalem? And why did He command them to stay in Jerusalem when he was going to Galilee? For such reasons, no credence can be given to the gospel stories of the empty tomb or resurrection appearances.

Despite this, Strauss admitted that Paul's challenge in 1 Corinthians 15 concerning living witnesses to an appearance of Jesus before 500 brethren makes it certain that people were alive at that time who believed they had seen the risen Christ. How is that to be explained? Certainly not by supernatural intervention, for that is unenlightened. "Hence, the cultivated intellect of the present day has very decidedly stated the following dilemma: either Jesus was not really dead, or he did not really rise again."[6] But that Jesus did not die on the cross is the defunct theory of Rationalism; therefore, Jesus did not rise. The correct explanation of the appearances is to be found in the appearance to Paul. His experience makes clear that the appearances were not external to the mind. What happened is that the disciples, convinced that Jesus was the Messiah, began to search the Scriptures after His death. There they found the dying and glorified Messiah of Isaiah 53. So Jesus must be alive! Soon they would see him, especially the women. Having hallucinated appearances of Christ, they would naturally infer His grave was empty, and by the time they returned from Galilee to Jerusalem, which was certainly not as soon as Pentecost, there was no closed tomb to refute them. In this way belief in Jesus' resurrection originated, and eventually the legendary gospel accounts arose.

5.222122 *Impact on the traditional apologetic.* Strauss's work completely altered the tone and course of German theology. Gone forever was the central dilemma of the eighteenth-century apologetic for the resurrection. Now the evangelists were neither deceivers nor deceived but stood at the end of a long process in which the original events were completely reshaped through mythological and

6. Ibid., p. 736.

legendary influences. The dissolution of the apologists' dilemma did not itself entail that the supernaturalist view was false. But for Strauss the supernaturalist view was not only disproved by the inconsistencies and contradictions noted by Reimarus but was *a priori* ruled out of court because of the presupposition of the impossibility of miracles. Any event that stood outside the inviolable chain of finite causes was *by definition* mythological. Therefore the resurrection could not possibly be a miraculous and historical event.

This is the challenge that Strauss has left to Christian apologetics. The position of Bultmann in this century with regard to the resurrection is virtually the same as Strauss's. It is no longer effective to argue for the resurrection today by refuting theories as to who stole the body or that Jesus did not really die. They are no longer the issue. The issue is whether the gospel narratives are historically credible accounts or unhistorical legends.

5.2222 *The tide of subjectivism.* The other reason, it seems to me, for the decline in historical apologetics during the nineteenth century is the tide of subjectivism that swept away an objective approach to matters of religious belief. We do not have time to develop this here, but let me say in passing that during the nineteenth century there came a backlash to the Age of Reason, and Romanticism swept Europe. This was spurred on in England by the Great Awakening, which emphasized the subjective, personal experience of faith. In France, the very emotive, subjective side of thinkers such as Rousseau emerged as a widespread reaction to the prior age of the *philosophes,* which ended in Revolution and the Reign of Terror. In Germany the effect of the philosophy of Kant and surging German Romanticism combined to color religious faith with a strong subjectivism. The net result of this tide of subjectivism was that apologetics moved from objective evidences for faith to emphasizing the moral grounds for faith or the beauties of faith itself. This subjective turn also enabled one to live with the destruction that was increasingly being wrought on the biblical narrative by the hammers of biblical criticism.

5.23 ASSESSMENT

The case for the historicity of the resurrection of Jesus seems to me to rest upon the evidence for three great, independently established facts: the empty tomb, the resurrection appearances, and the origin of the Christian faith. If these three facts can be established and no plausible natural explanation can account for them, then one is justified in inferring Jesus' resurrection as the most plausible explanation of the data. Accordingly, let us examine the evidence for each of these facts.

5.231 THE EMPTY TOMB

Here we wish to look first at the fact of the empty tomb and then at attempts to explain the empty tomb.

5.2311 *The fact of the empty tomb.* Here I want to summarize briefly eight lines of evidence supporting the fact that Jesus' tomb was found empty.

5.23111 *Historical reliability of the story of Jesus' burial supports the empty tomb.*

5.231111 *Why the reliability of the burial story supports the empty tomb.* Now you might ask, how does the fact of Jesus' burial prove that His tomb was found empty? The answer is this: if the burial story is true, then people would have known where the tomb was. But in that case, the tomb must have been empty when the disciples began to preach that Jesus was risen. Why? First, the disciples could not have believed in Jesus' resurrection if His corpse still lay in the tomb. It would have been complete idiocy to believe that a man was raised from the dead when his body was still in the grave. Second, even if the disciples had preached this, no one else would have believed them. So long as the people of Jerusalem thought that Jesus' body was in the tomb, they would never have believed such foolishness as that He had been raised from the dead. And third, even if they had, the Jews would have exposed the whole affair simply by pointing to Jesus' tomb or perhaps even exhuming the body as decisive proof that Jesus had not been raised. Thus, you see, if the story of Jesus' burial is true, then the story of the empty tomb must be true as well.

5.231112 *Evidence for the burial story.* And, unfortunately for those who deny the empty tomb, nearly all New Testament scholars agree that Jesus' burial is one of the best-established facts about Jesus. Now time does not permit me to go into all the details of the evidence for the burial. But let me just mention a couple points: First, Jesus was probably buried by Joseph of Arimathea. According to the gospels, Joseph of Arimathea laid Jesus' body in the tomb. Joseph is described as a rich man, a member of the Jewish Sanhedrin. The Sanhedrin was a sort of Jewish Supreme Court made up of seventy men, which presided in Jerusalem. Its members were the leading men of Judaism. It seems very unlikely that Christian tradition could invent Joseph of Arimathea, give him a name, place him on the Sanhedrin, and say he was responsible for Jesus' burial if this were not true. The members of the Sanhedrin were too well-known to allow either fictitious persons to be placed on it or false stories to be spread about one of its actual members' being responsible for Jesus' burial. Therefore, it seems very likely that Joseph was the actual, historical person who buried Jesus in the tomb.

Second, Paul's testimony provides early evidence of Jesus' burial. In

1 Corinthians 15:3-5 Paul quotes an old Christian saying that he had received from the earliest disciples. The saying is a summary of the early Christian preaching and may have been used in what we might call "discipleship classes." Its form would have made it suitable for memorization. Here is what it says:

> For I delivered to you as of first importance what I also received, that Christ died for our sins according to the Scriptures, and that He was buried, and that He was raised on the third day according to the Scriptures, and that He appeared to Cephas, then to the twelve.

Now notice the second part of this saying refers to Jesus' burial. When one matches the events of this Christian saying with the events described in the apostle's preaching in Acts and in the gospels, it is clear that the second line of the saying is a summary of the story of Jesus' burial in the tomb. Thus, we have here very early evidence for Jesus' burial, evidence that is so early it can not be explained away as legend. For these and many other reasons, the vast majority of scholars accept the historical reliability of Jesus' burial. But if we accept this, then, as I have explained, it is nearly obligatory that we also accept the historicity of the empty tomb.

5.23112 *Paul's testimony implies the fact of the empty tomb.* Although Paul does not explicitly mention the empty tomb, two phrases in the old Christian saying that he cites in 1 Corinthians 15 seem to me to imply it.

5.231121 *"He was buried."* First, the expression "He was buried," followed by the expression "He was raised" implies the empty tomb. The idea that a man could be buried and then be raised from the dead and yet his body still remain in the grave is a peculiarly modern notion. For the Jews there would have been no question but that the tomb of Jesus would have been empty. As E. E. Ellis remarks, "It is very unlikely that the earliest Palestinian Christians could conceive of any distinction between resurrection and physical, 'grave-emptying' resurrection. To them an *anastasis* (resurrection) without an empty grave would have been about as meaningful as a square circle."[7] Therefore, when Paul says that Jesus was buried and then was raised, he automatically assumes that an empty tomb was left behind.

5.231122 *"On the third day."* Second, the expression "on the third day" implies the empty tomb. Since no one actually saw Jesus rise from the dead, why did the early disciples proclaim that He had been raised "on the third day"? The most likely answer is that it

---

7. E. Earle Ellis, ed., *The Gospel of Luke*, p. 273.

was on the third day that the women discovered the tomb of Jesus empty; and so naturally the resurrection itself came to be dated on that day. In this case, the expression "on the third day" is a time-indicator pointing to the discovery of the empty tomb.

These two expressions in the early Christian saying quoted by Paul thus indicate that the early Christian fellowship out of which the saying sprung adhered to the fact of Jesus' empty tomb. Hence, such belief cannot be written off as a late legendary development.

5.23113 *The empty tomb story is part of Mark's source material and is therefore very old.* In writing the story of Jesus' passion, Mark apparently employed a source of information that is accordingly very early.

5.231131 *Source included the empty tomb story.* This pre-Markan passion source in all probability included the empty tomb story. The burial story and empty tomb story form one smooth, continuous narrative. They are linked by grammatical and linguistic ties. It seems unlikely that the early Christians would have circulated a story of Jesus' passion ending in His burial. The passion story is incomplete without victory at the end. Hence, the pre-Markan source probably included and may have ended with the discovery of the empty tomb.

5.231132 *Source is very old.* But that means that the empty tomb story is very old. The German commentator on Mark, Rudolf Pesch, argues that since Paul's traditions concerning the Last Supper (1 Cor. 11) presuppose the Markan account, that implies that the Markan source goes right back to the early years of the Jerusalem fellowship. Pesch also draws attention to the fact that the pre-Markan passion source never refers to high priest by name. It is as if I were to refer to something "the President" had done, and I and my listeners both knew whom I was referring to, namely, the man currently in power. Pesch believes that this is the case as well in the pre-Markan passion source. Since Caiaphas held office from A.D. 18-37, this means that at the latest Mark's source dates from within seven years of Jesus's crucifixion. This is incredibly early, and makes the hypothesis of legend with regard to the empty tomb an idle theory.

5.23114 *The phrase "the first day of the week" is very ancient.* This goes to confirm the point made in 5.23113. According to the Markan account, the empty tomb was discovered by the women "on the first day of the week."

5.231141 *Predates "on the third day."* We have already learned from the Christian saying quoted by Paul that the earliest Christians proclaimed the resurrection of Jesus "on the third day." As E. L. Bode explains, if the empty tomb story were a late legend it would almost certainly have been formulated in terms of the accepted and widespread third day motif. The fact that Mark uses "on the first day of the week" confirms that his tradition is very old, even antedating the third day reckoning.

       5.231142 *Is awkward Greek, but good Aramaic.* This fact is confirmed by the linguistic character of the phrase in question. For although "the first day of the week" is very awkward in the Greek, when translated back into Aramaic it is perfectly smooth and normal. This suggests that the empty tomb tradition reaches all the way back to the original language spoken by the first disciples themselves. Once again, this makes the legend hypothesis virtually impossible.

       5.23115 *The story is simple and lacks legendary development.* The Markan account is straightforward and shows no signs of legendary embellishment. To appreciate this fact, it would be a good idea to compare Marks' account of the empty tomb with the account found in the so-called Gospel of Peter, a forgery from around A.D. 125. In this account, the tomb is not only surrounded by Roman guards but also by all the Jewish Pharisees and elders as well as a great multitude from all the surrounding countryside who have come to watch the resurrection. Suddenly in the night there rings out a loud voice in heaven, and two men descend from heaven to the tomb. The stone over the door rolls back by itself, and they go into the tomb. Then three men come out of the tomb, two of them holding up the third man. The heads of the two men reach up into the clouds, but the head of the third man reaches up beyond the clouds. Then a cross comes out of the tomb, and a voice from heaven asks, "Have you preached to them that sleep?" And the cross answers, "Yes." In another forgery called the Ascension of Isaiah, Jesus comes out of the tomb sitting on the shoulders of the angels Michael and Gabriel! This is how legends look: they are colored by theological and other developments. By contrast, the gospel account is simple and seems to be pretty much a straight report of what happened.

       5.23116 *The tomb was probably discovered empty by women.* In order to see why this is so, we need to understand two things about the place of women in Jewish society. First, women were not qualified to serve as legal witnesses. The testimony of a woman was regarded as so worthless that they could not even serve as witnesses in a court of law. If a man committed a crime and was observed in the very act by some women, he could not be convicted because their testimony was regarded as so worthless that it could not even be admitted into court. Second, women occupied a low rung on the Jewish social ladder. Compared to men, women were second-class citizens. Consider these Jewish texts: "Sooner let the words of the Law be burnt than delivered to women!" and again: "Happy is he whose children are male, but unhappy is he whose children are female!" Now, given their low social status and inability to serve as witnesses, it is quite amazing that it is women who are the discoverers and principal witnesses of the empty tomb. If the empty tomb story were a legend, then certainly it would have been the male disciples who would have been made to discover the empty tomb. The fact that despised women, whose testimony was worthless, were the chief witnesses to the fact of the empty tomb can only be plausibly explained if, like it or not, they actually were the discoverers of the empty tomb. Hence, the gospels are accurate in this respect.

5.23117 *The disciples could not have preached the resurrection in Jerusalem had the tomb not been empty.* One of the most amazing facts about the early Christian belief in Jesus' resurrection was that it originated in the very city where Jesus was crucified. The Christian faith did not come to exist in some distant city, far from eyewitnesses who knew of Jesus' death and burial. No, it came into being in the very city where Jesus had been publicly crucified, under the very eyes of its enemies. If the proclamation of Jesus' resurrection were false, all the Jews would have had to do to nip the Christian heresy in the bud would have been to exhume the corpse of Jesus and parade it through the streets of the city for all to see. Had the tomb not been empty, then it would have been impossible for the disciples to proclaim the resurrection in Jerusalem as they did.

5.23118 *The earliest Jewish propaganda against the Christians presupposes the empty tomb.* In Matthew 28:11-15 we have the earliest Christian attempt to refute the Jewish propaganda against the Christian proclamation of the resurrection:

> While they were on their way, behold, some of the guard came into the city and reported to the chief priests all that had happened. And when they had assembled with the elders and counseled together they gave a large sum of money to the soldiers, and said, "You are to say, 'His disciples came by night and stole Him away while we were asleep.' And if this comes to the governor's ears, we will win him over and keep you out of trouble." And they took the money and did as they had been instructed; and this story was widely spread among the Jews, and is to this day.

Now, our interest is not so much in Matthew's story of the guard at the tomb as in his incidental remark at the end, "This story was widely spread among the Jews, and is to this day." This remark reveals that Matthew was concerned to refute a widespread Jewish explanation of the resurrection. Now what were the Jews saying in response to the disciples' proclamation that Jesus was risen? That these men are full of new wine? That Jesus' body still lay in the tomb in the hillside? No.

They were saying, "The disciples stole away his body." Think about that. "The disciples stole away his body." The Jewish propaganda did not deny the empty tomb but instead entangled itself in a hopeless series of absurdities trying to explain it away. In other words, the Jewish propaganda that the disciples stole the body presupposes that the body was missing. Thus, the Jewish propaganda itself shows that the tomb was empty. This is historical evidence of the highest quality, since it comes not from the Christians but from the very enemies of the early Christian faith.

5.23119 *Conclusion.* Taken together these eight considerations constitute a powerful case that Jesus' tomb was indeed found empty on the first day of the week by a group of His women followers. As a historical fact, this seems to be well-established. According to D. H. Van Daalen, "It is extremely difficult to object to the empty tomb on historical grounds; those who deny it do so on the basis of theological or philosophical assumptions."[8] But those assumptions cannot alter the facts themselves. New Testament scholars seem to be increasingly aware of this. According to Jacob Kremer, a New Testament critic who has specialized in the study of the resurrection: "By far most exegetes hold firmly to the reliability of the biblical statements about the empty tomb," and he furnishes the list of twenty-eight scholars to which his own name may be added: Blank, Blinzler, Bode, von Campenhausen, Delorme, Dhanis, Grundmann, Hengel, Lehmann, Léon-Dufour, Lichtenstein, Mánek, Martini, Mussner, Nauck, Rengstorff, Ruckstuhl, Schenke, Schmitt, Schubert, Schwank, Schweizer, Seidensticker, Strobel, Stuhlmacher, Trilling, Vögtle, and Wilckens.[9] I can think of at least sixteen more that he failed to mention: Benoit, Brown, Clark, Dunn, Ellis, Gundry, Hooke, Jeremias, Klappert, Ladd, Lane, Marshall, Moule, Perry, Robinson, and Schnackenburg. Perhaps most amazing of all is that even two Jewish scholars, Lapide and Vermes, have declared themselves convinced on the basis of the evidence that Jesus' tomb was empty.

5.2312 *Explaining the empty tomb.* Now if this is the case, that leads us to our second main point: explaining the empty tomb. Down through history, those who denied the resurrection of Jesus have been obligated to come up with a convincing alternative explanation. In fact, they have come up with only about two:

5.23121 *Conspiracy theory.* According to this explanation, the disciples stole the body of Jesus, thus faking the resurrection. This was, as we say, the first counter-explanation for the empty tomb, and it was revived by the Deists during the eighteenth century.

8. D. H. Van Daalen, *The Real Resurrection*, p. 41.
9. Jacob Kremer, *Die Osterevangelien—Geschichten um Geschichte*, pp. 49-50.

Today, however, this explanation has been completely given up by modern scholarship. At least three considerations undergird this consensus:

5.231211 *Is morally impossible.* Whatever the disciples were, they were not charlatans and hoaxers. They were genuinely devout men who tried to pursue the righteousness that Jesus had taught them. But this theory forces us to regard them as cheap frauds.

5.231212 *Is pyschologically impossible.* It does not take seriously the catastrophe that the crucifixion was for the disciples. After that event they were broken, doubtful, and fearful men— not bold perpetrators of some cleverly hatched and daringly executed conspiracy.

5.231213 *Cannot account for the disciples' evident sincerity.* The sudden change in their lives and their subsequent suffering for what they proclaimed show clearly that these men were not hypocritical hoaxers but sincerely believed what they preached.

I cannot emphasize enough that no modern scholar would defend such a theory today. The only place you read about such things is in the popular, sensationalist press or in propaganda from behind the Iron Curtain.

5.23122 *Apparent death theory.* A second theory was the apparent-death explanation. Critics around the beginning of the nineteenth century such as Heinrich Paulus or Friedrich Schleiermacher defended the view that Jesus was not completely dead when He was taken down from the cross. He revived in the tomb and escaped to convince His disciples He had risen from the dead. Once again, today this theory has been completely given up. Again one might mention three factors supporting this consensus:

5.231221 *Is physically impossible.* First, what the theory suggests is virtually physically impossible. The extent of Jesus' tortures was such that He could never have survived the crucifixion and entombment.

5.231222 *Is religiously inadequate.* Even if Jesus had survived, His appearing to the disciples half-dead and desperately in need of medical attention would not have evoked their worship of Him as Lord. The conviction of the earliest disciples was that Jesus rose gloriously and triumphantly from the grave, not as one who had managed to barely escape death.

5.231223 *Makes Jesus a charlatan.* The theory says that Jesus tricked the disciples into believing in His resurrection. But this is a tawdry caricature of all that we know of the real Jesus, whose life and teachings belie such an interpretation of His character.

Again, I want to emphasize that no modern historian or biblical critic would hold to such a theory. You may say to yourselves at this point, "Well, then, what explanation of the empty tomb do modern critics offer who deny the resurrection?" The fact is, there simply is no plausible natural explanation available today to account for how Jesus' tomb became empty. If we deny the resurrection of Jesus, we are left with an inexplicable mystery.

      5.23123 *Conclusion.* We have seen that multiple lines of historical evidence prove that Jesus' tomb was found empty on Sunday morning by a group of His women followers. Furthermore, no natural explanation is available to account for this fact. That alone might cause us to believe in the resurrection of Jesus. But there is even more evidence to come. And that we shall consider below.

      5.232 THE RESURRECTION APPEARANCES
In 1 Corinthians 15:3-8, Paul writes:

> For I delivered to you as of first importance what I also received, that Christ died for our sins according to the Scriptures, and that He was buried, and that He was raised on the third day according to the Scriptures, and that he appeared to Cephas, then to the twelve. After that He appeared to more than five hundred brethren at one time, most of whom remain until now, but some have fallen asleep; then He appeared to James, then to all the apostles; and last of all, as it were to one untimely born, He appeared to me also.

That is a truly remarkable claim. We have here the testimony of a man personally acquainted with the first disciples, and he reports that they actually saw Jesus alive from the dead. More than that, he says that he himself also saw an appearance of Jesus alive after His death. What are we to make of this claim? Did Jesus really appear to people alive after His death?

      To answer this question, we need to consider two major points: first, the fact of the resurrection appearances of Jesus; and second, explaining the resurrection appearances.

      5.2321 *The fact of the resurrection appearances.* Let us consider together the first point: the fact of the appearances of Jesus. Once again, time will not allow us to examine in detail all the evidences for Jesus' post-resurrection appearances. But I would like to examine three main lines of evidence.

      5.23211 *Paul's testimony proves that the disciples saw appearances of Jesus.* We saw that in 1 Corinthians 15 Paul gives a list of witnesses to Jesus' resurrection appearances. Let us look briefly at each appearance to see whether it is plausible that such events actually took place.

      5.232111 *Appearance to Peter.* We have no story in the gospels telling of Jesus' appearance to Peter. But the appearance is mentioned here in the Old Christian saying, and it is vouched for by the apostle Paul himself. As we know from Galatians 1:18, Paul spent about two weeks with Peter in Jerusalem three years after his Damascus road experience. So Paul would know personally whether Peter claimed to have had such an experience or not. In addition to this, the appearance to Peter is mentioned in another old Christian saying found in Luke 24:34: "The Lord has really risen, and has appeared to Simon!" So although we have no detailed story of this appearance, it is quite well attested. As a result, even the most skeptical New Testament critics agree that Peter saw something that He called an appearance of Jesus alive from the dead.

5.232112 *Appearance to the twelve.* This is the best-attested resurrection appearance of Jesus. We have stories of this apparently had personal contact with these people, since he knew that most notable feature of this appearance is the physical demonstrations of Jesus' showing His wounds and eating before the disciples. The purpose of the physical demonstrations is to show two things: first, that Jesus was raised *physically;* and second, that He was the *same Jesus* who had been crucified. Thus, they served to demonstrate both *corporeality* and *continuity* of the resurrection body. There can be little doubt that such an appearance occurred, for it is attested in the old Christian saying, vouched for by Paul, who had personal contact with the twelve; and it is described by both Luke and John.

5.232113 *Appearance to the 500 brethren.* The third appearance comes as somewhat of a shock: then He appeared to more than 500 brethren at one time! This is surprising, since we have no mention whatsoever of this appearance elsewhere in the New Testament. This would make one rather skeptical about this appearance, but it comes from old information that Paul had received, and Paul himself apparently had personal contact with those people, since he knew that some had died. This is seen in Paul's parenthetical comment "most of whom remain until now, but some have fallen asleep." Why does Paul add this remark? The great New Testament scholar of Cambridge University, C. H. Dodd, replies, "There can hardly be any purpose in mentioning the fact that the most of the 500 are still alive, unless Paul is saying, in effect, 'The witnesses are there to be questioned.' "[10] Notice: Paul could never have said this if the event had not occurred. He could not have challenged people to ask the witnesses, if the event had never taken place and there were no witnesses. But evidently there were witnesses to this event, and Paul knew that some of them had died in the meantime. Therefore, the event must have taken place.

I think that the appearance is not related in the gospels because it

10. C. H. Dodd, "The Appearances of the Risen Christ: A study in the form criticism of the Gospels," p. 128.

probably took place in Galilee. As one puts together the various appearances in the gospels, it seems that they occurred first in Jerusalem, then in Galilee, and then in Jerusalem again. The appearance to the 500 would have to be out of doors, perhaps on a hillside outside a Galilean village. Since the gospels focus their attention on the appearances in Jerusalem, we do not have any story of this appearance to the 500 because it occurred in Galilee.

5.232114 *Appearance to James.* The next appearance is one of the most amazing of all: He appeared to James, Jesus' younger brother. What makes this amazing is that apparently neither James nor any of Jesus' younger brothers believed in Jesus during His lifetime. (See Mark 3:21, 31-5; John 7:1-10). They did not believe He was the Messiah, or a prophet, or even anybody special. But after the resurrection, all of a sudden Jesus' brothers pop up in the Christian fellowship in the upper room in Jerusalem (Acts 1:14). There is no further mention of them until Acts 12:17. This is the story of Peter's deliverance from prison by the angel. What are Peter's first words? "Report these things to *James.*" In Galatians 1:19 Paul tells of his two-week visit to Jerusalem about three years after his Damascus Road experience. He says that besides Peter, he saw none of the other apostles *except James* the Lord's brother. Paul at least implies that James was now being reckoned as an apostle. When Paul visited Jerusalem again fourteen years later, he says there were three "pillars" of the church in Jerusalem: Peter, John, and *James* (Gal. 2:9). Finally, in Acts 21:18 James is the sole head of the Jerusalem church and of the council of elders. We hear no more about James in the New Testament; but from Josephus, the Jewish historian, we learn that James was stoned to death illegally by the Sanhedrin sometime after A.D. 60 for his faith in Christ.[11] Not only James but also Jesus' other brothers became believers and were active in Christian preaching, as we see from 1 Corinthians 9:5: "Do we not have a right to take along a believing wife, even as the rest of the apostles, and the brothers of the Lord, and Cephas?"

Now, how is this to be explained? On the one hand, it seems certain that Jesus' brothers did not believe in Him during His lifetime. On the other hand, it is equally certain that they became ardent Christians, active in the church. Many of us have brothers. What would it take to make you believe that your brother is the Lord, so that you would die for this belief, as James did? Can there be any doubt that the reason for this remarkable transformation is to be found in the fact that "then He appeared to James"? Even the skeptical New Testament critic Hans Grass admits that the conversion of James is one of the surest proofs of the resurrection of Jesus Christ.[12]

---

11. Josephus *Antiquities of the Jews* 20.200.
12. Hans Grass, *Ostergeschehen und Osterberichte*, p. 80.

5.232115 *Appearance to "all the apostles."* This appearance was probably to a limited circle somewhat wider than the twelve. For such a group, see Acts 1:21-2. Once again, the facticity of this appearance is guaranteed by Paul's personal contact with the apostles themselves.

5.232116 *Appearance to Paul.* The final appearance is just as amazing as the appearance to James: "last of all," says Paul, "He appeared to me also." The story of Jesus' appearance to Paul just outside Damascus is related in Acts 9:1-9 and is later told again twice. That this event actually occurred is established beyond doubt by Paul's references to it in his own letters.

This event changed Paul's whole life. He was a rabbi, a Pharisee, a respected Jewish leader. He hated the Christian heresy and did everything in his power to stamp it out. He was even responsible for the execution of Christian believers. Then suddenly he gave up everything. He left his position as a respected Jewish leader and became a Christian missionary. He entered a life of poverty, labor, and suffering. He was whipped, beaten, stoned and left for dead, shipwrecked three times, in constant danger, deprivation, and anxiety. Finally, he made the ultimate sacrifice and was martyred for his faith at Rome. And it was all because on that day outside Damascus, he saw "Jesus our Lord" (1 Cor. 9:1).

5.232117 *Conclusion.* We can call these appearances hallucinations if we want to, but we cannot deny that they occurred. The late New Testament critic of the University of Chicago, Norman Perrin, states, "The more we study the tradition with regard to the appearances, the firmer the rock begins to appear upon which they are based."[13] Paul's testimony makes certain that on separate occasions different groups and individuals saw Jesus alive from the dead. This conclusion is virtually indisputable.

5.23212 *The gospel accounts of the resurrection appearances are historically reliable.* Time does not permit me to go into all the reasons supporting this conclusion. So let me mention just one:

5.232121 *There was insufficient time for legend to accumulate.* Perhaps the greatest difficulty for those who say that the resurrection accounts are legendary is that the time period between the events and the writing of the gospels was too short to allow legend to substantially accrue. Julius Müller's critique has never been answered:

> Most decidedly must a considerable interval of time be required for such a complete transformation of a whole history by popular tradition, when the series of legends are formed in the same territory where the heroes actually lived and wrought. Here one cannot imagine how such a series of legends

13. Norman Perrin, *The Resurrection According to Matthew, Mark, and Luke,* p. 80.

could arise in an historical age, obtain universal respect, and supplant the historical recollection of the true character and connexion of their heroes' lives in the minds of the community, if eyewitnesses were still at hand, who could be questioned respecting the truth of the recorded marvels. Hence, legendary fiction, as it likes not the clear present time, but prefers the mysterious gloom of grey antiquity, is wont to seek a remoteness of age, along with that of space, and to remove its boldest and most rare and wonderful creations into a very remote and unknown land.[14]

Müller's critique is still valid today and is confirmed by A. N. Sherwin-White, a historian of Greek and Roman times.[15] Professor Sherwin-White is not a theologian; he is a professional historian of times prior to and contemporaneous with Jesus. According to Sherwin-White, the sources for Roman and Greek history are usually biased and removed one or two generations or even centuries from the events they record. Yet, he says, historians reconstruct with confidence the course of Roman and Greek history. When Sherwin-White turns to the gospels, he states that for the gospels to be legends, the rate of legendary accumulation would have to be "unbelievable." More generations would be needed. The writings of Herodotus enable us to determine the rate at which legend accumulates, and the tests show that even two generations is too short a time span to allow legendary tendencies to wipe out the hard core of historical facts. Julius Müller challenged scholars of the mid-nineteenth century to show anywhere in history where within thirty years a great series of legends had accumulated around a historical individual and had become firmly fixed in general belief. Müller's challenge has never been met.

Because there was not sufficient time for legend to accumulate, the gospel accounts of the resurrection appearances must be substantially accurate historically. That brings us to our third point:

    5.23213 *The resurrection appearances were physical, bodily appearances.* In support of this point, I want to examine two supporting sub-points.

    5.232131 *Paul implies that the appearances were physical.* He does this in two ways.

    5.2321311 *First Corinthians 15:34-44.* First, he conceives of the resurrection body as physical. In 1 Corinthians 15:42-44 Paul describes the differences between the present, earthly body and the future, resurrection body, which will be like Christ's. He draws four essential contrasts between the earthly body and the resurrection body:

14. Julius Müller, *The Theory of Myths, in Its Application to the Gospel History Examined and Confuted*, p. 26.
15. A. N. Sherwin-White, *Roman Society and Roman Law in the New Testament*, pp. 188-91.

The earthly body is:	But the resurrection body is:
mortal	immortal
dishonorable	glorious
weak	powerful
physical	spiritual

Now only the last contrast would make us think that Paul did not believe in a physical resurrection body. But what does he mean by the words that I have translated here as "phyiscal/spiritual"? The word translated "physical" (NASB, "natural") literally means "soul-ish." Now obviously, Paul does not mean that our present body is made out of soul. Rather by this word he means "dominated by or pertaining to human nature." Similarly when he says the resurrection body will be "spiritual," he does not mean "made out of spirit." Rather he means "dominated by or oriented toward the Spirit." It is the same sense of the word "spiritual" as when we say someone is a spiritual person. In fact, look at the way Paul uses exactly those same words in 1 Corinthians 2:14-15:

A natural man does not accept the things of the Spirit of God; for they are foolishness to him, and he cannot understand them, because they are spiritually appraised. But he who is spiritual appraises all things yet he himself is appraised by no man.

Natural man does not mean "physical man," but "man oriented toward human nature." And *he who is spiritual* does not mean "intangible, invisible man" but "man oriented toward the Spirit." The contrast is the same in 1 Corinthians 15. The present, earthly body will be freed from its slavery to sinful human nature and become instead fully empowered and directed by God's Spirit. Thus, Paul's doctrine of the resurrection body teaches a physical resurrection.

5.2321312 *Distinction between a vision and an appearance.* Second, Paul, and indeed all the New Testament, makes a distinction between an appearance of Jesus and a vision of Jesus. The appearances of Jesus soon ceased, but visions continued in the early church. Now the question is: what is the difference between an appearance and a vision? The answer of the New Testament would seem to be clear: a vision, even if caused by God, was purely in the mind, while an appearance took place "out there" in the real world. It is instructive to compare here Stephen's vision of Jesus in Acts 7 with the resurrection appearances. What Stephen saw was a vision, for no one else present experienced anything at all. By contrast the resurrection appearances took place in the world "out there" and could be experienced by anybody. Paul could rightly call his experience on the Damascus Road an appearance, even though it took place after the ascension, because it involved real manifestations in the world, which Paul's companions also experienced. Thus, the distinction between a vision and an appearance of Jesus also implies that the resurrection appearances were physical.

5.232132 *The gospel accounts prove the appearances were physical and bodily.* Again, I want to make two points.

5.2321321 *Every appearance is physical and bodily.* First, every resurrection appearance related in the gospels is a physical, bodily appearance. The unanimous testimony of the gospels in this regard is quite impressive. If *none* of the appearances were originally bodily appearances, then it is very strange that we have a completely unanimous testimony in the gospels that *all* of them were physical, with no trace of the supposed original, nonphysical appearances. The gospels are unanimous in their presentation of the appearances as physical and bodily.

5.2321322 *The gospel accounts have been shown to be historically reliable.* As we have seen (5.232121), there was insufficient time for legend to accumulate. If all the appearances were originally non-physical visions, then one is at a complete loss to explain the rise of the gospel accounts. Since there was insufficient time for legend to accumulate, the gospel accounts must be basically reliable; and therefore, the appearances were physical and bodily.

5.23214 *Conclusion.* Thus, on the basis of these three lines of evidence, we can conclude that the fact of Jesus' physical, bodily resurrection appearances is firmly established historically. But how do we explain these appearances? That leads me to my second major point:

5.2322 *Explaining the resurrection appearances.* If one denies that Jesus actually rose from the dead, then he must try to explain away the resurrection appearances psychologically.

5.23221 *Hallucination theory.* It is said that the appearances were merely hallucinations on the part of the disciples. But the hallucination theory faces formidable difficulties.

5.232211 *Shatters on points 5.23212 and 5.23213 above.* We saw in point 5.23212 that the gospel accounts of the resurrection appearances are fundamentally reliable, and in point 5.23213 that the appearances were physical, bodily appearances. Therefore, the hallucination theory is completely ruled out of court from the beginning.

5.232212 *Cannot plausibly account for the number and various circumstances of the appearances.* Jesus did not appear to just one person but to many persons. He did not appear just one time but many times. He did not appear in just one place and circumstance but in many places under varying circumstances. He did not appear just to individuals but to groups. And he did not appear just to believers but to unbelievers (James, Paul). Hallucinations simply cannot account for these facts.

5.232213 *Fails to provide psychological disposition in the disciples for hallucinations.* Third, the disciples were not psychologically disposed toward hallucinations. Hallucinations require a special emotional mood before they can occur. Hence, they are usually associated with drugs or mental illness. But in the disciples' case any predisposition toward hallucinations was lacking. The crucifixion was a catastrophe for the disciples; it shattered any hopes they might have had that Jesus was the Messiah. As far as they were concerned, the final act had been played and the show was all over. They were in no way disposed to see hallucinations of Jesus alive. Probably one of the greatest weaknesses of the hallucination theory is that it cannot really take seriously what a disaster the death of Jesus must have been for the disciples. For if we understand the seriousness of that event, we can see that the disciples would have had no inclination to hallucinate that Jesus was alive.

5.232214 *Cannot account for the disciples' belief in Jesus' resurrection.* Fourth, hallucinations would never have led to the conclusion that Jesus had been raised from the dead. I am going to develop this point in 5.233223, but in passing let me explain that since a hallucination is just a projection of the mind, it cannot contain anything that is not already in the mind. But the resurrection of Jesus was radically foreign to the disciples' minds in at least two respects, as we shall see.

5.232215 *Fails to explain the full scope of the evidence.* Fifth, hallucinations fail to account for the full scope of the evidence. The hallucination theory only seeks to explain the appearances, but it says nothing about the empty tomb. To explain the empty tomb one would have to conjoin another theory to the hallucination theory. But the resurrection of Jesus is a simpler explanation, since it accounts for all the facts, and therefore is to be preferred. Thus, for these five reasons, the hallucination theory fails to plausibly explain the resurrection appearances.

5.23222 *Conclusion.* It is sure that in multiple and varied circumstances, different individuals and groups saw Jesus physically and bodily alive from the dead. Furthermore, there is no way to explain this away psychologically. So once again, if we reject the resurrection of Jesus as the only reasonable explanation of the resurrection appearances, we are left with an inexplicable mystery.

5.233 THE ORIGIN OF THE CHRISTIAN FAITH

The third fact from which the resurrection of Jesus may be inferred is the very origin of the Christian faith.

5.2331 *The fact of the origin of the Christian faith.* Even the most skeptical New Testament scholars admit that the earliest disciples at least *believed* that Jesus had been raised from the dead. In fact, they pinned nearly everything on it. To take just one example: the belief that Jesus was the Messiah. The Jews had no conception of a dying, much less a rising, Messiah. According to Jewish belief, when the Messiah came he would establish his throne in Jerusalem and reign forever. The idea that the Messiah would die was utterly foreign to them. We find this attitude expressed in John 12:34: "The multitude therefore answered Him, 'We have heard out of the Law that the Christ is to remain forever; and how can You say, "The Son of man must be lifted up?" Who is this Son of man?' " Here Jesus predicts His crucifixion, and the people are utterly mystified. The Messiah would live forever—so how could He be "lifted up"? It is difficult to overemphasize what a disaster the crucifixion was, therefore, for the disciples' faith. Jesus' death on the cross spelled the humiliating end for any hopes they had entertained that He was the Messiah.

But the belief in the resurrection of Jesus reversed the catastrophe of the crucifixion. Because God had raised Jesus from the dead, He was seen to be Messiah after all. Thus, Peter proclaims in Acts 2:23, 36: "This Jesus God raised up again, to which we all are witnesses. . . . Let all the house of Israel know for certain that God has made Him both Lord and Christ—this Jesus whom you crucified." It was on the basis of belief in the resurrection that the disciples could believe that Jesus was the Messiah.

Thus, without this belief in the resurrection, early Christianity could not have come into being. The origin of Christianity hinges on the belief of the early disciples that God had raised Jesus from the dead. But the question is: How does one explain the origin of that belief? As R. H. Fuller says, even the most skeptical critic must posit some mysterious x to get the movement going.[16] But what was that x?

5.2332 *Explaining the origin of the disciples' belief in Jesus' resurrection.* If one denies that the resurrection itself was that x, then one must explain the disciples' belief in the resurrection as the result of either Christian influences or Jewish influences. That is to say, one must hold that the disciples came up with the idea of Jesus' resurrection either because of the influence of early Christianity or because of the influence of Jewish beliefs.

5.23321 *Not from Christian influences.* Now clearly

16. R. H. Fuller, *The Formation of the Resurrection Narratives*, p. 2.

their belief in Jesus' resurrection cannot be explained as a result of Christian influences, simply because there was no Christianity yet. Since the belief in the resurrection was itself the foundation for Christianity, it cannot be explained as the later product of Christianity.

5.23322 *Not from Jewish influences.* The question therefore is: would the disciples have come up with the idea that Jesus had been raised from the dead because of Jewish influences? Again, the answer would seem to be no.

5.233221 *O.T. belief in resurrection.* To understand this, we need to look at what the Jewish conception of the resurrection was. The belief in the resurrection of the dead is mentioned three times in the Old Testament: Isaiah 26:19, Ezekiel 37, and Daniel 12:2. During the intertestamental period, the belief in the resurrection of the dead became a widespread hope. In Jesus' day, this belief was held to by the party of the Pharisees, although it was denied by the party of the Sadducees. So the belief in resurrection was itself nothing new but rather was a prominent Jewish belief.

5.233222 *Difference between O.T. concept of resurrection and Jesus' resurrection.* But the Jewish conception of the resurrection differed in two fundamental respects from the resurrection of Jesus.

5.2332221 *O.T. resurrection always occurred after the end of the world.* First, in Jewish thought the resurrection always occurred after the end of the world. The renowned New Testament scholar Joachim Jeremias explains:

> Ancient Judaism did not know of an anticipated resurrection as an event of history. Nowhere does one find in the literature anything comparable to the resurrection of Jesus. Certainly resurrections of the dead were known, but these always concerned resuscitations, the return to the earthly life. In no place in the late Judaic literature does it concern a resurrection to *Doxa* [glory] as an event of history.[17]

For a Jew the resurrection always occurred after the end of history. He had no conception of a resurrection within history. We find this typical Jewish frame of mind in the gospels themselves. Jesus' disciples had no conception of a resurrection occurring within history. Look at John 11:23-24, for example. Here Jesus is about to raise Lazarus from the dead. He tells Martha, "Your brother shall rise again." What is her response? "Martha said to Him, 'I know that he will rise again in the resurrection on the last day.'" She had no inkling of a resurrection within history; she thought Jesus was talking about the resurrection at

---

17. Joachim Jeremias, "Die älteste Schicht der Osterüberlieferung," p. 194.

the end of the world. I think that it is for this same reason that the disciples had so much trouble understanding Jesus' predictions of His own resurrection. They thought He was talking about the resurrection at the end of the world. Look at Mark 9:9-11, for example.

> And as they were coming down from the mountain, He gave them orders not to relate to anyone what they had seen, until the Son of Man should rise from the dead. And they seized upon that statement, discussing with one another what rising from the dead might mean. And they asked Him, saying, "Why is it that the scribes say Elijah must come first?"

Here Jesus predicts His resurrection, and what do the disciples ask? "Why is it that the scribes say Elijah must come first?" In the Old Testament, it was predicted that the prophet Elijah would come again before the great and terrible Day of the Lord, the judgment day when the dead would be raised. The disciples could not understand the idea of a resurrection occurring within history, prior to the end of the world. Hence, Jesus' predictions only confused them. Thus, given the Jewish conception of the resurrection, the disciples after Jesus' crucifixion would not have come up with the idea that He had been raised. They would have only looked forward to the resurrection at the last day and, in keeping with Jewish custom, perhaps preserved His tomb as a shrine where His bones could rest until the resurrection.

    5.2332222 *O.T. resurrection was always a general resurrection, never that of an individual.* Second, in Jewish thought, the resurrection was always the resurrection of all the righteous or all the people. They had no conception of the resurrection of an isolated individual. Ulrich Wilckens, another prominent New Testament critic, explains:

> For nowhere do the Jewish texts speak of the resurrection of an individual which already occurs before the resurrection of the righteous in the end time and is differentiated and separate from it; nowhere does the participation of the righteous in the salvation at the end time depend on their belonging to the Messiah, who was raised in advance as 'First of those raised by God' (1 Cor. 15:20).[18]

So once again we find that the resurrection of Jesus differed fundamentally from Jewish belief. The disciples had no idea of the resurrection of an isolated individual. Therefore, after Jesus' crucifixion, all they could do was wait with longing for the general resurrection of the dead to see their master again.

For these two reasons, then, we cannot explain the disciples' belief in

18. Ulrich Wilckens, *Auferstehung*, p. 131.

Jesus' resurrection as a result of Jewish influences. Left to themselves, the disciples would never have come up with the idea of Jesus' resurrection after His crucifixion. C. F. D. Moule of Cambridge University concludes:

> If the coming into existence of the Nazarenes, a phenomenon undeniably attested by the New Testament, rips a great hole in history, a hole the size and shape of the Resurrection, what does the secular historian purpose to stop it up with? . . . the birth and rapid rise of the Christian Church . . . *remain an unsolved enigma for any historian who refuses to take seriously the only explanation offered by the Church itself.*[19]

    5.233223 Translation versus resurrection. But let us push the argument one step further. Suppose the disciples were not simply "left to themselves" after the crucifixion. Suppose that somehow Jesus' tomb was found empty, and the shock of finding the empty tomb caused the disciples to see hallucinations of Jesus. The question is: Would they then have concluded that He had been raised from the dead?

    Now you are probably thinking: "But those theories have already been refuted and shown to be false." That is true. But let us be generous and suppose for the sake of argument that this is what happened. Would the disciples have concluded that Jesus had been raised from the dead?

    The answer would seem to be no. This brings us back to a point I mentioned earlier (5.232214). Hallucinations, as projections of the mind, can contain nothing new. Therefore, given the current Jewish beliefs about life after death, the disciples would have projected hallucinations of Jesus in heaven or in Abraham's bosom. And such visions would not have caused belief in Jesus' resurrection.

    At the most, it would have only led the disciples to say Jesus had been *translated*, not *raised*. You see, the Jews had another belief besides resurrection, called translation. In the Old Testament, figures such as Enoch and Elijah did not die but were translated directly into heaven. In a Jewish writing not in the Bible called The Testament of Job, the story is told of the translation of two children killed in the collapse of a house: The children are killed when the house collapses, but when the rescuers clear away the rubble their bodies are not to be found. Meanwhile, the mother sees a vision of the two children glorified in heaven, to where they have been translated by God. It cannot be emphasized enough that for the Jew a translation is not the same as a resurrection. They are distinct categories. Translation is the bodily assumption of

---

19. C. F. D. Moule, *The Phenomenon of the New Testament*, pp. 3, 13.

someone out of this world into heaven. Resurrection is the raising up of a dead man in the space-time universe.

Thus, given Jewish beliefs concerning translation and resurrection, the disciples would never have preached that Jesus had been raised from the dead. At the very most, the empty tomb and hallucinations of Jesus would have only caused them to believe in the translation of Jesus, for this fit in with their Jewish frame of thought. But they would not have come up with the idea that Jesus had been raised from the dead, for this contradicted the Jewish belief in at least two fundamental respects.

        5.2333 *Conclusion.* The origin of Christianity owes itself to the belief of the earliest disciples that God had raised Jesus from the dead. That belief cannot be accounted for in terms of either Christian or Jewish influences. Even if we grant, for the sake of argument, that the tomb was somehow emptied and the disciples saw hallucinations—which we have seen to be false anyway—the origin of the belief in Jesus' resurrection still cannot be explained. Such events would only have led the disciples to say that Jesus had been translated, not resurrected. The origin of the Christian faith is therefore inexplicable unless Jesus really rose from the dead.

5.234 CONCLUSION

Now we are ready to draw the conclusion to all three of our discussions: First, we saw that numerous lines of historical evidence prove that the tomb of Jesus was found empty by a group of His women followers. Furthermore, no natural explanation has been offered that can plausibly account for this fact. Second, we saw that several lines of historical evidence established that on numerous occasions and in different places Jesus appeared physically and bodily alive from the dead to various witnesses. Again, no natural explanation in terms of hallucinations can plausibly account for these appearances. And finally, we saw that the very origin of the Christian faith depends on belief in the resurrection. Moreover, this belief cannot be accounted for as the result of any natural influences.

These three great, independently established facts—the empty tomb, the resurrection appearances, and the origin of the Christian faith—all point to the same unavoidable conclusion: that Jesus rose from the dead.

5.24 PRACTICAL APPLICATION

The material I have presented on the resurrection can be nicely summarized into an evangelistic message that can be used effectively on university campuses. It can even be used in personal evangelism, if you can arrange with the person with whom you are sharing to set up a time when you can lay out the evidence. It is more effective to thus lay out the case as a whole rather than present and discuss it piecemeal, for the impact of the cumulative case is greater.

For example, I was once discussing the gospel with a student who seemed open but was hesitant. I challenged him to consider the evidence for the resurrection of Jesus, and he told me, "If you can prove that Jesus rose from the dead, I'll become a Christian." So I made an appointment to see him next week to lay out my case. When I met with him again, I submitted the evidence to him for an uninterrupted twenty minutes and then asked him what he thought. He was virtually speechless. I asked, "Are you now ready to become a Christian?" "Well, I don't know," he said indecisively. So I said that he should think about it some more and that I would come back again next week to see what he had decided. By the third week, he was ready, and together in his dorm room we prayed to invite Christ into his life. It was one of the most thrilling experiences I have had in seeing God use apologetics to draw someone to Himself.

Let me encourage you to work up a talk or a case of your own that you can use in evangelistic meetings or contacts. And then always be prepared to give this defense to anyone who calls you to account for the hope that is in you.

Conclusion
The Ultimate Apologetic

During this course we have examined many intellectual arguments in support of the Christian faith. I have argued that we can know Christianity is true because of the self-authenticating witness of God's Holy Spirit, and that we can show it to be true by means of rational argument and evidence. We have seen the human predicament without God and immortality, and how this leads to futility and despair. But we have also examined the evidence for a Christian solution to this predicament: evidence that a personal Creator of the Universe exists and that Jesus Christ's offer of eternal life to those who believe in Him is genuine, being confirmed by His resurrection from the dead. But now I want to share with you what I believe to be the most effective and practical apologetic for the Christian faith that I know of. This apologetic will help you to win more persons to Christ than all the other arguments in your apologetic arsenal put together.

This ultimate apologetic involves two relationships: your relationship with God and your relationship with others. These two relationships are distinguished by Jesus in His teaching on the duty of man: "And one of them, a lawyer, asked Him a question, testing Him, 'Teacher, which is the great commandment in the law?' And He said to him, ' "You shall love the Lord your God with all your heart, and with all your soul, and with all your mind." This is the great and foremost commandment. The second is like it, "You shall love your neighbor as yourself." On these two commandments depend the whole Law and the Prophets' " (Matt. 22:35-40). The first commandment governs our relationship to God; the second our relationship with our fellow man. Let us examine each of these relationships in turn.

First, our relationship with God. This is governed by the great commandment:

> Hear, O Israel! The Lord is our God, the Lord is one! And you shall love the Lord your God with all your heart and with all your soul and with all your might. And these words, which I am commanding you today, shall be on your heart; and you shall teach them diligently to your sons and shall talk of them when you sit in your house and when you walk by the way and when you lie down and when you rise up. And you shall bind them as a sign on your hand and they shall be as frontals on your forehead. And you shall write them on the doorposts of your house and on your gates. (Deut. 6:4-9)

Notice the importance given to this commandment—loving God is to be our preoccupation in life. Sometimes we get the idea that our main duty in life is to serve God, maybe by being a great apologist, and forget, as J. I. Packer reminds us, that our primary aim ought to be to learn to know God:

> We both can and must get our life's priorities straight. From current Christian publications you might think that the most vital issue for any . . . Christian in the world today is . . . social witness, or dialogue with other Christians and other faiths, or refuting this or that '-ism', or developing a Christian philosophy and culture, or what have you. But our line of study makes the present day concentration on these things look like a gigantic conspiracy of misdirection. Of course, it is not that; the issues themselves are real and must be dealt with in their place. But it is tragic that, in paying attention to them, so many in our day seem to have been distracted from what was, is, and always will be the true priority for every human being— that is, learning to know God in Christ.[1]

In our relationship with God we are to give Him His legal right— namely, all that we have and are. The Christian is to be as a matter of course totally dedicated to God (Rom. 12:1-2) and filled with the Holy Spirit (Eph. 5:18). For His part God gives to us positionally, as we are in Christ, forgiveness of sins (Eph. 1:7), eternal life (Rom. 6:23), adoption as sons (Gal. 4:5), and the availability of unlimited help and power (Eph. 1:18-19). Think of how much that means! Moreover, He gives to us experientially, as we are Spirit-filled, the fruit of the Spirit: love, joy, peace, patience, kindness, goodness, faithfulness, gentleness, and self-control (Gal. 5:22-3). When this relationship is intact, the product in

---

1. J. I. Packer, *Knowing God* (London: Hodder & Stoughton, 1973), p. 314.

our lives will be righteousness (Rom. 6:16), and the by-product of righteousness is happiness. Happiness is an elusive thing and will never be found when pursued directly; but it springs into being as one pursues the knowledge of God, and His righteousness is realized in us.

The other relationship is our relationship with our fellow men. This is governed by the second great commandment, as Paul explains: "The commandments, 'You shall not commit adultery, You shall not kill, You shall not steal, You shall not covet,' and any other commandment, are summed up in this sentence, 'You shall love your neighbor as yourself.' " (Rom. 13:9, RSV). Why is love the great commandment? Simply because all the other commandments are the outworking of love in practice (Rom. 13:10). When we love others, we simply show that we have understood God's love for us, and it is being worked out in our lives toward others. As John says, "If God so loved us, we also ought to love one another" (1 John 4:11). What does love involve? To begin with, it means possessing the characteristics of love described in 1 Corinthians 13. Can we say, "I am patient and kind, I am not jealous or boastful, arrogant or rude; I am not selfish or irritable or resentful; I am not happy about wrong, but I rejoice in the right; I bear all things, believe all things, hope all things, endure all things?" Moreover, love will involve having a servant's heart, a willingness to count others better than yourself and to serve and look out for their interests as well as your own (Gal. 5:13b-14; Phil. 2:3). Certainly Jesus Himself is our supreme model here: think of how He washed his disciples' dirty feet!

What will be the result when these two relationships are strong and close? There will be a unity and warmth among Christians. There will be a love that pervades the body of Christ; as Paul describes, "speaking the truth in love, we are to grow up in all aspects into Him, who is the head, even Christ, from whom the whole body, being fitted and held together by that which every joint supplies, according to the proper working of each individual part, causes the growth of the body for the building up of itself in love" (Eph. 4:15-16). And what will be the result of this unity through love? Jesus Himself gives us the answer in His prayer for the church: "that they may all be one; even as Thou, Father, art in Me, and I in Thee, that they also may be in Us, that the world may believe that Thou didst send Me. . . . I in them, and Thou in Me, that they may be perfected in unity, that the world may know that Thou didst send Me, and didst love them, even as Thou didst love Me" (John 17:21-23). According to Jesus our love is a sign to all men that we are His disciples (John 13:35); but even more than that, our love and unity are living proof to the world that God the Father has sent His Son Jesus Christ and that the Father loves men even as He loves Jesus. When the people see this—our love for one another and our unity through love—then they will in turn be drawn by this to Christ and will respond to the gospel's offer of salvation. More often than not, it is what you *are* rather than what you *say* that will bring an unbeliever to Christ.

This, then, is the ultimate apologetic. For the ultimate apologetic is: your life.

Index

The reader should also consult the Analytic Outline for specific subjects and persons.

Moody Press, a ministry of the Moody Bible Institute, is designed for education, evangelization, and edification. If we may assist you in knowing more about Christ and the Christian life, please write us without obligation to Moody Press, c/o MLM, Chicago, Illinois 60610